Criminal Justice
Recent Scholarship

Edited by
Marilyn McShane and Frank P. Williams III

A Series from LFB Scholarly

Increased Surveillance of Sex Offenders
Impacts on Recidivism

Lisa Williams-Taylor

LFB Scholarly Publishing LLC
El Paso 2012

Copyright © 2012 by LFB Scholarly Publishing LLC

Library of Congress Cataloging-in-Publication Data

Williams-Taylor, Lisa, 1972-
  Increased surveillance of sex offenders : impacts on recidivism / Lisa
Williams-Taylor.
    p. cm. -- (Criminal justice: recent scholarship)
  Includes bibliographical references and index.
  ISBN 978-1-59332-479-7 (hbk. : alk. paper)
  1. Sex offenders--United States. 2. Sex offenders--Rehabilitation--
United States. 3. Sex crimes--United States--Prevention. 4.
Recidivism--United States. I. Title.
  HV6592.W55 2012
  364.15'3--dc23
                                        2011026581

ISBN 978-1-59332-479-7

Printed on acid-free 250-year-life paper.

Manufactured in the United States of America.

Table of Contents

List of Tables vii

List of Figures ix

Preface xi

Acknowledgements xiii

CHAPTER 1: Sexual Offenses 1

CHAPTER 2: Sexual Behavior and Deviancy: A Historical
     Perspective 9

CHAPTER 3: Theory and Typologies of Sexual Offending 21

CHAPTER 4: Recidivism 53

CHAPTER 5: Sex Offender Risk Management Statutes 83

CHAPTER 6: An Intensive Supervision Program 117

CHAPTER 7: Impacts of Increased Surveillance 133

CHAPTER 8: Implications and Recommendations 167

Appendix 181

Bibliography 195

Index 215

List of Tables

Table 1: Definition of Sexual Abuse by Age of the Victim 2

Table 2: Rape in New York City by Year 7

Table 3: Theories of Sexual Violence 35

Table 4: Typologies of Rapists 42

Table 5: Typologies of Child Molesters 50

Table 6: Risk Factors Significantly Correlated with Recidivism 62

Table 7: Risk Assessment Tools 68

Table 8: Stages of Relapse: The Child Molester 78

Table 9: Coding Scheme 131

Table 10: Analyses and Sample Used 132

Table 11: Age 134

Table 12: Race/Ethnicity 134

Table 13: Offending Characteristics 136

Table 14: Inclusion Criteria 141

Table 15: Demographic and Risk Factors by Comparison Groups 142

Table 16: Chi-square and Independent Samples T-test Results for
Comparison Groups by Demographic and Risk Factors ... 144

Table 17: Recidivism Among Comparison Groups 145

Table 18: Risk Factors and General Recidivism 150

Table 19: Logistic Regression: Predictors of General Recidivism 152

Table 20: Risk Factors and Non-compliance Recidivism 154

Table 21: Logistic Regression: Predictors of Non-compliance
Recidivism 155

Table 22: Risk Factors and Violent Recidivism 156

Table 23: Logistic Regression: Predictors of Violent Recidivism 158

Table 24: Risk Factors and Sexual Recidivism 159

Table 25: Logistic Regression: Predictors of Sexual Recidivism 160

Table 26: Percent of Participating Offenders that Violently
          Recidivate by Typology 162

Table 27: Logistic Regression: Violent Recidivism and Sex
          Offender Typology 163

Table 28: Non-compliant Recidivism by Number of General
          Recidivism Arrests 164

List of Figures

Figure 1: Sample Breakdown..125

Figure 2: Recidivism: Arrests of Participants 147

Figure 3: Recidivism Type: Arrests of Participants..........................147

Figure 4: Percent of Participants Recidivating by Felony and
        Misdemeanor History 152

Preface

Few crimes have captured society's attention more than sexual offenses, partially because of horrific cases involving perpetrators targeting and killing children during a sexual assault. Sex offenders are often portrayed as incurable and unmanageable. In fact, many politicians and other public officials have said that these individuals should just be locked up indefinitely. However, due to current statutes, the release of most sex offenders from incarceration is inevitable, meaning they need to reintegrate into society. For this reason, it is critical to understand what motivates individuals to commit sexual offenses, what reduces the likelihood of recidivism, and the best method of managing and supervising sex offenders in the community.

This book examines recidivism rates of those monitored by an intensive supervision and management program for high-risk sex offenders. It will review risk factors and various types of recidivism, compliance with Megan's Law, and models for differentiating between high-risk or low-risk to reoffend or abscond from registration. This is important to the criminal justice community and vital to understanding these types of public safety initiatives.

Acknowledgements

I would like to thank Karen Terry for her assistance in obtaining the data needed to study sex offender statutes and their effectiveness and her careful review of this work. To Michael White, I thank you for reviewing the methodology and statistical analyses used for this study. Your guidance and feedback helped ensure this book would be sound from a methodological standpoint. Lastly, I also thank Susan Ramsey, David Strong, and Richard Brown, three researchers I worked with at the start of my career. Each encouraged my growth by giving me opportunities to learn and experiment with research. Their teachings were invaluable to the work I have done so far and will continue to be the standard by which I conduct all future research.

The Division of Criminal Justice Services (DCJS) and the New York Criminal Justice Coordinator's Office furnished the confidential data for this book. DCJS was not responsible for the methodology or statistical analyses chosen. The views and conclusions expressed herein are those of the author and do not represent or reflect the official position or policies of DCJS, the New York Criminal Justice Coordinator's Office, or the Children's Services Council of Palm Beach County.

CHAPTER 1

Sexual Offenses

The interest in and study of sexual violence has increased substantially over the past few decades. An increase in media and political attention has heightened society's awareness of the problem and exposure of the issue has stirred a renewed interest in the study of managing these offenders. One issue that continues to surface is that not all offenders are alike and the crimes they commit vary substantially. For example, two men[1] may both be convicted of a sexual crime; yet one is convicted of raping someone while the other has been convicted of unlawful surveillance (video recording someone without her knowledge or consent). Although both are convicted of a sex crime, the level of violence involved differs considerably. The risk of reoffense also varies depending on type of offense committed. For these reasons, there is no universal definition of a sexual offense.

Defining Sexual Offenses

Defining and categorizing sexual offenses is difficult given the various levels of severity and to whom they are targeted. Many sexual offenses, but not all, involve an offender forcing or coercing a victim against his or her will to engage in sexual activity. These crimes may or may not involve physical contact or force. The level of violence and force used at the time of the crime elevates the degree of the charge, so a person that uses greater force may be charged with a felony versus a misdemeanor.

---

[1] While females do sexually offend, the vast majority of offenders are male. Thus, all examples within this book will refer to males as the perpetrator.

1

Some crimes may involve forced sexual intercourse, including oral penetration, while others involve touching a person without their consent. This may include touching a child, either above or below the clothes, or rubbing against someone for sexual gratification. The age of the victim often impacts the offense class (misdemeanor/felony) and criminal charge because a minor is unable to give consent. For example, according to New York's Penal Law Code definition of sexual abuse, the charge of sexual abuse changes from a class B misdemeanor when the child is 14 years old or older to a class A misdemeanor when the victim is under 14 years old and to a class D felony when the victim is under 11 years old.

Table 1: Definition of Sexual Abuse by Age of the Victim

Section	Class	Charge	Definition
130.55	B Mis-demeanor	Sexual abuse in the 3rd degree	A person who subjects a person to sexual contact without consent; the **victim is less than 17 years, but more than 14 years old** and the defendant is less than five years older.
130.60	A Mis-demeanor	Sexual abuse in the 2nd degree	A person who subjects a person to sexual contact who is incapable of consent by some reason other being under 17 years or is **under 14 years.**
130.65	D Felony	Sexual abuse in the 1st degree	A person who subjects a person to sexual contact by forcible compulsion or who is incapable of consent due to being physically helpless or who is **under 11 years old.**

Source: Quoted in part from Looseleaf Law Publications (1996-97), Division of Criminal Justice Services (n.d.) and Findlaw (n.d.).

Other reasons for a person's inability to give consent are mental and physical incapacity. For example, the person may be intoxicated from alcohol or drugs, may be mentally handicapped, suffer from a mental illness, or be physically helpless and unable to consent to engage in sexual activities. In these cases, force may or may not be used.

On the other hand, some sexual crimes involve no physical contact. Child pornography (NY CLS Penal Law § 263.11 and 263.16), defined as the visual depiction of a child under age 18 engaged in sexual behavior, may include manipulation and exploitation only. Some child pornographers do not physically molest the children they take pictures of, instead engaging in these acts for commercial profit only. This is not to say that these children are not victimized or that they will not suffer many of the same ill affects as those that are physically abused.

Other examples of crimes involving no physical contact include public lewdness (NY CLS Penal § 245.00) and unlawful surveillance (NY CLS Penal § 250.45 and 250.50). The definition of public lewdness is the intentional exposure of ones private or intimate body parts. This act of exposing oneself to strangers or unsuspecting parties is commonly known as exhibitionism. Unlawful surveillance is defined as the use or installation of imaging devices to view, broadcast or record the intimate parts of a person (e.g. when a person is dressing or undressing) without that person's knowledge or consent. This behavior is commonly referred to as voyeurism. Both of these crimes, which do not involve direct contact with the victim, may also be diagnosable psychiatric disorders (i.e. paraphilias) if there is a compulsive need to commit the act and it causes problems for the individual. Notably, most sexual offenses are not diagnosable medical conditions.

The American Psychiatric Association's (1994) Diagnostic and Statistical Manual of Mental Disorders (Fourth Edition) (DSM-IV) defines these disorders in detail. Exhibitionism (diagnostic code 302.4) is defined as "recurrent, intense sexually arousing fantasies, sexual urges, or behaviors involving the exposure of one's genitals to an unsuspecting stranger," which lasts at least six months and causes clinically significant distress or impairment to the individual (p.525). Whereas, Voyeurism (diagnostic code 302.82) is defined as "recurrent, intense sexually arousing fantasies, sexual urges, or behaviors involving the act of observing an unsuspecting person who is naked, in the process of disrobing, or engaging in sexual activity" lasting over a period of at least six months and causing clinically significant distress or impairment to the individual (p.532). Neither of these offenses includes physically touching another human being and in the case of voyeurism, the victim may not even be aware that she is being victimized. For example, in New York, Stephanie Fullmer, a 29-year-old Long Island woman was filmed while in her bedroom for many months by her landlord without her knowledge. After finding out that she had been victimized and later discovering that she had no legal recourse, she lobbied for legislation that would make this type of behavior a felony. Before this incident, this behavior was not considered a serious crime. The bill, Stephanie's Law, was passed on June 12, 2003, making video voyeurism a felony and a sex crime requiring the offender to register under the Sex Offender Registration Act.

Sexual Offenses in New York

In New York, sexual offenses are specified in article 130 of the penal law codes. While each of these offenses is cause for the convicted offender to register as a sexual offender, other offenses also require registration. These include, unlawful imprisonment (135.05 and 135.10), kidnapping (135.20 and 135.25), patronizing a prostitute (230.04. 230.05, and 230.06), prostitution (230.30, 230.32, and 230.33), sex trafficking (230.34), disseminating indecent material to a minor (235.22), unlawful surveillance (250.45 and 250.50), incest (255.25, 255.26 and 255.27), and crimes involving child pornography (263.05, 263.10, 263.20, and 263.25). The Appendix shows the sexual offense statutes as well as the list of other offenses that require registration.

Prevalence of Sexual Crimes

Sexual crimes affect the lives of hundreds of thousands of people each year, often causing psychological and physical trauma to the immediate victim, as well as profoundly impacting his or her families and friends. Sexual crimes affect individuals of all races, ethnicities, gender, and ages. No one is safe from the risk of sexual victimization.

Though researchers estimate varying levels of the prevalence of victimization, all indicate that sexual victimization rates are high. For instance, Spitzberg (1999) estimates that 13% of women and 3% of males will be raped at some point during their lifetime. According to Rand and Catalano (2007), results of the National Crime Victimization Survey indicated that of those respondents 12 years old or older there were 272,350 incidents of rape or sexual assault in 2006. It is estimated that an individual is sexually assaulted every 2.4 minutes and rape occurs every 6.5 minutes in the U.S. (Catalano, 2004). In one survey exploring the prevalence of sex crimes on college campuses, results indicated that female college students have a high probability of being victims of sexual assault, with male college students being the most likely perpetrator. Approximately one in every four female college students reported being victimized (Bachman, Paternoster, & Ward, 1992, p.344). In a report released by the National Institute of Justice and the Bureau of Justice Statistics, researchers found that approximately three percent of college women experience a completed and/or attempted rape during a typical college year (Fisher, Cullen, & Turner, 2000). According to Rothman and Silverman (2007), "as many as 20–25% of women and 3% of men are sexually assaulted during their college careers" (p.283). Furthermore, in a telephone survey conducted between 2001 and 2003, one in 59 adults (2.7 million women and 978,000 men) reported that they had experienced a sexual assault at some point during the past year and that one in 15 or 7% (11.7 million women and 2.1 million men) had been raped during their lifetime. Of those that reported being raped, 60.4% of females and 69.2% of males said they were raped or sexually assaulted as a child (Basile, Chen, Black, & Saltzman, 2007).

In regards to the sexual victimization of children, in 2009, 65,964 (9.5%) victims (ages 0-17) of sexual abuse were reported to child protective services nationwide (U.S. Department of Health and Human Services, 2010). According to a review of studies by Holmes and Holmes (2002), 10-50% of all children experience some form of sexual assault before their eighteenth birthday. More specifically, one in three women and one in five men report that they were sexually abused before the age of eighteen (Briere, 1992). According to Snyder (2000), over two-thirds of all sexual assaults reported to law enforcement involve individuals under the age of 18. Even more disturbing is that 34% of these victims were ages 12 and under and 14% were younger than six. When Basile and colleagues (2007) conducted a nationally representative telephone survey, 25.5% of females who reported being raped indicated that they were first raped before age 12 and 34.9% were raped between the ages of 12 and 17. Of the males in the study who had been raped, 41.3% were first raped before age 12 and 27.9% were first raped between the ages of 12 and 17.

Data from the Bureau of Justice Statistics National Crime Victimization Survey indicates that the number of sexual assaults/rapes of those 12 years and older decreased by 9.5% between 2004 and 2005[2], from 209,880 to 191,670 respectively (Catalano, 2006). Although this trend, like the overall decrease in violent crimes, is notable, according to the 2006 National Crime Victimization Survey, only 41.4% of sexual assaults are reported to law enforcement (Rand & Catalano, 2007). Many sexual assaults never come to the attention of authorities, often because of the perpetrators' relationship with the victim. Reasons for underreporting these types of crimes vary, but some examples include fear of the victim, manipulation of the victim by the perpetrator, or decisions by other adults that it is a family affair or private matter that does not need to be brought to the attention of outsiders. It is worth noting that of adolescents who are sexually assaulted, 70% are assaulted in their home and the offender is a family member in approximately 34.2% of the incidents (Snyder, 2000). In addition, acquaintances commit 58.7% of sexual assaults, while strangers perpetrate only 7% of assaults (Snyder, 2000). According to Jacobs (2003), another example is what occurred in the Catholic Church when the hierarchy allegedly hid and ignored numerous cases of child sexual abuse for decades in an effort to handle the situation itself, as well as protect its reputation. For these reasons, many, if not most, abusers never become known to the criminal justice system and are therefore never subjected to legal consequences (e.g., registration and notification). Thus, the true rates of rape and sexual assault are believed to be significantly higher than reporting systems indicate.

Prevalence of Sexual Crimes in New York

According to the 2007 Uniform Crime Reports, 2,926 cases of forcible rape were reported in New York State - 15.2 per population of 100,000 (U.S. Department of Justice, 2008). That equates to one rape committed every three hours. However, the Uniform Crime Reports do not include carnal abuse, rape without force, statutory rape, and other sexual offenses. Thus, the rates are likely much higher. In New York City,

---

[2] 2006 data could not be used for comparisons or trend analysis because of methodological issues.

the New York Police Department CompStat Unit reported 1,296 rapes within all boroughs in 2008, three or four per day. This is a slight decrease from 2007 when 1,303 rapes were reported. Overall, there has been a steady and significant decrease within most boroughs between 1990 and 2008. Brooklyn had the highest percentage decrease (70.2%), followed by Manhattan (62%) and the Bronx (51.9%) (Table 2).

Table 2: Rape in New York City by Year

Boroughs	Year					
	1990	1995	2001	2005	2007	2008
Manhattan	689	600	319	363	259	262
Bronx	644	763	502	357	312	310
Brooklyn	1,154	1,078	718	465	357	344
Queens	559	503	353	402	330	314
Staten Island	80	74	38	54	45	66
Total	3,126	3,018	1,930	1,641	1,303	1,296

Note: Years correspond to available online data via NYPD CompStat Unit
Source: New York City CompStat Unit Report (n.d.): 2006, 2008 & 2009 data.

With respect to children, according to the U.S. Department of Health and Human Services (2010), there were 2,769 cases of child sexual abuse reported in 2009 in New York, meaning that more than seven children are sexually victimized each day in New York State. These statistics substantiate the claims of current researchers that the problem of sexually motivated crimes is monumentally significant (Holmes & Holmes, 2002).

Generally, while the prevalence rate of sexual crimes has decreased nationally, it remains a common occurrence. Given the significant impact on the lives of the victims, their family and friends, and the community, understanding who is most likely to commit these crimes is critically important.

CHAPTER 2

Sexual Behavior and Deviancy: A Historical Perspective

American society has decided that there is no greater villain than the sex offender. Terrorists, drug dealers, murderers, kidnappers, mobsters, gangsters, drunk drivers, and white collar criminals do not elicit the emotions and evoke the political response that sex offenders do (Wright, 2008, p.17).

Definitions of sexual crimes and views of perpetrators have changed throughout history. Society and the court system have defined sex offenders and their crimes differently depending on the mind-set and attitudes of the time. As values and norms change, so does society's tolerance of sexual behavior. Behavior that at some points in time was considered criminal may no longer be thought of in the same way. Also changing has been the amount of attention these crimes receive. This evolution in focus and level of interest has become known as moral or sex crime panics. Crimes involving women and children have had a long history of causing moral panics. These cases often involve violence against our most vulnerable, which outrages society and causes people to advocate for stricter regulation of sex offenders and continued research to aid in understanding why people offend and how to prevent future offenses.

Changing Views of Sexual Behavior

The late ninetieth and early twentieth centuries have become known as the Progressive Era, a time of reform after a long period of societal unrest, disorganization, unemployment, poverty, and crime due to the vast growth within industrialized cities. It was during this period that the social hygiene movement began, "a campaign to change American attitudes toward sex" (Burnham, 1973, p.885). During the Progressive Era, women and children were given additional rights – women entered the workforce in jobs other than servant work and the justice system explored the abuse and neglect of children (e.g., labor laws were passed). Stricter crime prevention and control tactics were also major efforts of the Progressive Era and "the courts began to regularly monitor sexual behavior," including prostitution and child sexual abuse (Terry, 2006, p.23). According to Terry (2006), "It was this change in social structure that instigated the modification of "age of consent" laws for sexual behavior…" (p.23). Age of consent has changed dramatically throughout history. At one point, there was no specific legal age of consent for sexual conduct. Then, throughout the eighteenth century, the consenting age was only ten-years-old and now in most jurisdictions it is between 16 and 18 years of age.

Another example of how views of behavior have changed throughout history is incest. In the late 19th century, incest began to be discussed more openly and agencies started taking an active stance against it. For example, in 1878, the Massachusetts Society for the Prevention of Cruelty to Children, an interest group who focused on intrafamilial sexual abuse, heightened the interest on this topic through advocacy and by educating the public (Gordon, 1988). However, at other points in time, the focus was more on "stranger danger" (i.e. the pervert who jumps out from behind a bush to attack his victim), resulting in a decrease in interest and willingness to discuss incest. In fact, during the mid-1900s, incest was rarely discussed because it was believed to be an uncommon event. According to Gordon (1988), academic experts reported that incest was an "extremely rare, one-in-a million occurrence" (p.60). Thus, as can be surmised from these examples, interest levels fluctuated greatly depending on social influences at the time.

Along with changing views are cycles of legislation regarding the criminalization of sexual behaviors. Classified at one point in time as criminal, now some acts are considered "normal" or tolerated types of behavior. At various points in history, homosexuality, excessive masturbation, and adultery were classified as criminal acts requiring fines, imprisonment, and even death (Jenkins, 1998, p.22). Although each at different times was highly prosecuted, today, many of the laws regarding these types of crimes are currently not enforced or have been taken completely off the books.

How the legal system defines severity of sexual crimes has also varied by era and by region. For example, during the mid-twentieth century, New York reduced its punishment for homosexual relations from a felony offense with a 12-year sentence to a misdemeanor with a maximum penalty of 90 days in jail. At the same time, California was increasing the sentence for this same crime from ten to 20 years (Guttmacher & Weihofen, 1952, p.155). These changes in sentencing within states were occurring during a heightened time of unrest. The 1960s and 1970s marked both social and sexual revolutions. There were significant changes in people's perceptions and attitudes towards social injustice and sexual behavior. Traditional roles and beliefs were tested, civil rights were at the forefront, and sex became an open topic. The 1960s also marked the start of the homophile or gay liberation movement, which fought for anti-discrimination in the workforce and in the criminal justice system. As time went on, homosexuality became increasingly tolerated and accepted among mainstream society and in 1973, the American Psychiatric Association no longer categorized homosexuality as a mental disorder (Freedman, 1987, p.103).

In addition, there were important advances in science and medicine, including the development of oral contraceptives – first introduced in the 1960s. These allowed for a more reliable form of birth control. Pornography was also viewed more openly and the Presidential Commission on Obscenity rejected the assertion that pornography caused harm to those that possessed it (Jenkins, 1998, p.109). The civil rights movement was also at the forefront during this time and the women's revolution of the 1960s, also known as the second wave of feminism, stressed women's rights and empowerment. It was during this movement that women fought against sexual violence and their revictimization in the court system. While the feminist movement had impacts on many fronts, advocacy for what is now termed rape shield laws was one of the major accomplishments in relation to the criminal justice system and sexual crimes. Until this point, it was common practice in rape trials to blame the victim and question the truthfulness of her accusations. These laws, first enacted in 1970, minimized the type of victim information allowed into trial – prohibiting the defendant's attorney from unwarranted intrusions into the private life of the alleged victim (Call, Nice, & Talarico, 1991; Flowe, Ebbesen, & Putcha-Bhagavatula, 2007). The attorney could no longer attack the victim's morality in an attempt to portray her as unchaste or otherwise 'having asked for it' (Byrnes, 1998; Klein, 2008). All states now have rape shield laws in effect (Flowe et al., 2007). This advancement, among the others discussed, are prime examples of how society has changed its views of sexuality and deviancy throughout time.

Sexual Deviancy and Waves of Panic

Definitions of sexual deviancy have evolved in response to educational influences and social morality (Jenkins, 1998). According to researchers, the definition of sex offenders, sexual crimes, and sexual deviancy are socially constructed realities, based on research, case law, and the church (Jenkins 1998; Sutherland, 1950; Terry, 2006). Thus, the concept of sexual deviancy changed significantly between the late nineteenth century and the early twenty-first century with the emergence of the sexual psychopath, sexual murderer, and various periods of sexual panic.

The Sexual Psychopath

Throughout the 1880s into the 1900s, there was a heightened interest in sex offenders, sexual deviancy, and in particular the sexual psychopath. In 1801, Phillip Pinel, recognized as defining the term psychopathy, found that some of his patients engaged in uncontrollable violence towards others. He found that while they knew that what they were doing was irrational, they were unable to stop themselves (Arrigo & Shipley, 2001, p.327). By the early 1900s, "most discussions of the psychopath included at least a section on sexual types, such as overt homosexuals, exhibitionists, sadists, masochists, and voyeurs. Some authors explicitly linked such deviants to the commission of sexual crimes" (Freedman, 1987, p.91). Freedman (1987) reports that the concept of a sexual psychopath derived from a combination of factors and people including psychiatrists, social change, sexuality, and the public's perception of "uncontrolled desires" and deviancy (p.87).

This interest in the sexual psychopath was greatly influenced by the work of Richard von Krafft-Ebing, a German physician and neurologist who in 1886 wrote *Psychopathia Sexualis*, a novel on deviant sexual behavior using a series of case studies. Krafft-Ebing is credited with coining the terms sadism and masochism and asserted that all humans have an "innate desire to humiliate or hurt" and that "sexual emotion, if hyperesthetic, might degenerate into a craving to inflict pain" (quoted in Arrigo & Shipley, 2001, p.333). Although Krafft-Ebing did note that some individuals might engage in sexual violence, his primary focus was on various sexual disorders and paraphilias. When he used the term *psychopathia sexualis,* he "implied no more than mental disease or disturbance" (Jenkins, 1998, p.38-39), such as those suffering from pedophilia or homosexuality.

In this work, Krafft-Ebing described the act of pedophilia as the result of a mental weakness due to "senile dementia, chronic alcoholism, paralysis, mental disability due to epilepsy, injuries to the head, apoplexy and syphilis" (Jenkins, 1998, p.100). In other words, he believed that people "were not wicked, immoral creatures, but merely sick" (Kennedy, 2001, p.167). He discussed homosexuality in much the same way (Terry, 2006, p.24). He noted that homosexuality, a perversion, might be inborn (Money, 2003), and that it, like many other sexual acts and perversions, is the result of uncontrollable sexual desires. He believed that perversions occur because of psychological abnormalities and degeneracy. Moreover, according to Bauer (2003), Krafft-Ebing emphasized that perversions were not criminal in nature and he later participated in a petition to abolish paragraph 175 of German law, which criminalized homosexuality (p.24).

As emphasized by Kraff-Ebing, psychopathic behavior is not necessarily criminal behavior. The diagnosis of psychopathy has changed throughout history, referring to insanity at some points and more currently to describe a person having a personality disorder and displaying antisocial behavior (Andrade, 2008). However, during the 1930s, sexual psychopathy became a legal construct describing individuals that could not control their sexual desires leading to criminal behavior. Sexual psychopath statutes were passed as a means of treating these individuals and allowing for their indefinite incapacitation deeming them at risk to harm themselves or others.

The Sexual Murderer

Another highly discussed topic during the late 1880s and early 1900s was sexual murder. While there have always been incidents of sexual killings, it was not until the late 1800s that these murders became commonly recorded and discussed among the public (Jenkins, 1998). Although research has led to an increase in knowledge regarding deviant sexual interests and behaviors and has shown that violent sexual crimes are rare events in history, the perception that they are pervasive has continued - most speculate this is a direct result of media coverage of high profile cases (Jenkins, 1998). For example, although there were violent sexually motivated crimes occurring in America, none appears to have received as much media attention as the case of Jack the Ripper, a classic example of a sexual predator, psychopath, and murderer. Cases like this one in the 1880s incited the public's interest in understanding this type of behavior - the actions of a mentally unstable sexual murderer. Researchers strived to gain knowledge regarding individuals that were unable to control their sexual desires and behavior and were therefore, driven to kill.

The First Sex Crime Panic: The Early 1900s

Although the case of Jack the Ripper caused a great deal of panic in England, it was not until the early 1900s that the first documented panic occurred in America. This phenomenon of panic was first formulated in the 1970s by British sociologists Stanley Cohen and Stuart Hall. They coined the term, *moral panic,* and described how the media and single cases can promote intense and irrational fear. Their definition is as follows:

> Societies appear to be subject, every now and then, to periods of moral panic. A condition, episode, person or group of persons emerges to become defined as a threat to societal values and interests; its nature is presented in a stylized and stereotypical fashion by the mass media ... Sometimes the object of the panic is quite novel and at other times it is something which has been in existence long enough, but suddenly appears in the limelight. Sometimes the panic passes over and is forgotten, except in folklore and collective memory; at other times it has more serious and long-lasting

repercussions and might produce such changes as those in legal and social policy or even in the way society conceives itself (Cohen, 1972, p.9).

These panics can be targeted towards any group believed to be deviant and threatening to society – in regards to the discussion here, the panic is focused on sexual offenders. The crux of the first sex crime panic resulted from, like other panics later, an increase in reported sexual murders of women and children, many of which were covered in the media. For example, the *New York Times* reported 17 serial murder cases between 1911 and 1915 and in Atlanta, between 1910 and 1912, 40 women were found murdered (Jenkins, 1998). In 1912, Frank Hickey was accused of sexually killing boys in New York City. This case was sensationalized in the newspapers. Then in 1913, Leo Frank was accused of the sexual killing of 13-year-old Mary Phagan in Atlanta. Frank was sentenced to death, but before his sentence could be carried out, there was a lynching in 1915 and he was hung by the citizens of the city. This same year marked the sexual murder of two other small children in New York City. According to Jenkins (1998), this heightened media attention caused people to walk the streets looking for sexual perverts. People who were thought to be sexual criminals were attacked in the streets during this time of panic.

The Second Wave of Panic: 1930s through the 1950s

Much like the first sex crime panic, the attention during the 1930s through the 1950s focused on stranger crimes. In fact, this focused attention has been referred to as "stranger danger" or the belief that "dirty old men," sexual perverts or sex fiends were the primary victimizers of children (Gordon, 1988). This period marked a time of heightened fear that sexual deviants were lurking around waiting for just the right time to attack the most vulnerable. This was also a time of fear regarding the sexually motivated murder of children. As Sutherland (1950) claimed, the murder of children is very effective in creating hysteria. He quotes author Austin MacCormick, who published an article in *Mental Hygiene* titled "New York's Present Problem," as stating,

For a while it was utterly unsafe to speak to a child on the street unless one was well-dressed and well-known in the neighborhood. To try to help a lost child, with tears streaming down its face, to find its way home would in some neighborhoods cause a mob to form and violence to be threatened (p.143).

Also instigating this fear was the infamous case of Albert Fish, a 65-year-old sexual predator and child murderer. In New York on June 23, 1928, Fish arrived at the Budd household as a potential employer for 18-year-old Paul Budd who had placed an ad in the Sunday edition of a newspaper asking for work. After offering farm work to Paul, he asked whether he could take Paul's younger sister to a party at his own sister's house. Grace was allowed to go and never returned home. Many years later Fish wrote a letter to the Budd's describing the killing. Police were able to trace the letter and Fish was arrested and sentenced to death. Executed in January 1936, Fish is believed to have assaulted many other young people and to have murdered at least three others.

By the mid 1930s, there were many more examples that a sex crime panic was in effect. For example, editors of the *New York Times* created a new column in their newspaper titled "Sex Crimes" due to the vast number of articles that were being published that year (Freedman, 1987, p.83). Furthermore, J. Edgar Hoover declared a "war on the sex criminal," stating that "the sex fiend, most loathsome of all the vast army of crime, has become a sinister threat to the safety of American childhood and womanhood" and that "should wild beasts break out of circus cages, a whole city would be mobilized instantly. But depraved human beings more savage than beasts, are permitted to rove America almost at will" (quoted in Freedman, 1987).

Because of this war against the sexual predator and highly publicized cases of sexual murderers like Albert Fish, anti-crime legislation dedicated specifically to sexual offenders was drafted. These laws mimicked the "social security" laws found in Europe which aimed to protect the public (Sutherland, 1950). The first "sexual psychopath" statute was passed in 1937 in Michigan and although this groundbreaking act was held unconstitutional, the following year Illinois enacted its first law without incident. These sexual psychopath laws allowed for the civil commitment of a person indefinitely or until he could prove that he was no longer a danger to himself or others.

Interestingly, in 1938, a year after the first psychopath law was enacted, at a national conference on "The Challenge of Sex Offenders," numerous psychiatrists pleaded for the halt of any additional castration or long-term sentencing legislation because there was no evidence of an increase in sexual crimes – just an increase in media coverage (Freedman, 1987, p.95). This plea from psychiatrists did little to prevent further legislation. Rather, California, Massachusetts, Minnesota, Ohio, and Wisconsin implemented sexual psychopathy legislation shortly thereafter.

Interestingly, in the early 1940s, there was a short break in the sex crime panic, as seen by the halt in states passing sex offender legislation (Vermont was the only state to pass a law during this time) and marked decrease in newspaper and magazine articles covering sexual violence (Freedman, 1987, p.96). One researcher asserts that this was primarily due to World War II and the legitimization of male violence focusing on the external enemy (Freedman, 1987, p.96). This decline in attention eventually stopped post-war and the pendulum began swinging the other way once again. Between 1947 and 1949, eight states passed sexual psychopath laws (Jenkins, 1998, p.82) and by the mid-1950s, 13 additional states, as well as the District of Columbia had sexual psychopath statutes in effect (Freedman, 1987, p.97). In 1950, New York passed its version of a sexual psychopath law, but was innovative in that it required that there was a criminal proceeding for all cases and once found guilty of the sexual crime, then and only then would the offenders' mental capacity be examined to determine psychopathy. In addition, according to Guttmacher and Weihofen (1952), New York was the first state to allow for indeterminate sentencing of criminals, including sexual offenders.

Through the late 1950s, medicalizing crime (meaning focusing on medical causes and interventions) continued, but there was also a focus on social issues at this time. More specifically, most psychiatrists believed that statutory rape, sexual abuse, and incest were the result of social circumstances and mental abnormality. Many believed that these sexual crimes primarily occurred among "groups with low cultural standards" and in overcrowded neighborhoods (Guttmacher & Weihofen, 1952, p.159). These criminals continued to be labeled degenerates, perverts or psychopaths and the use of civil commitment continuously increased during this time. According to Terry (2006), some psychopathy statutes included peeping, lewdness, and impaired morals as acts that could result in being designated as a psychopath. Terry (2006) also notes that the severity and level of violence used during the commission of the sexual crime was less of an issue than it is now because both misdemeanors and felonies could result in commitment (p.30). Besides the increase in number of commitments, there was also a distinct racial difference in the type of sentencing. According to Freedman (1987), while white men were mostly found guilty of minor offenses and those involving children, black men were overrepresented in the number found guilty of rape. Whites were more likely to be hospitalized and blacks were more often executed or imprisoned for their crimes (p.97).

The Third Wave of Panic: 1980s and 1990s
Over time there has been a marked change in how society has labeled sexual offenders – starting with "feebleminded" or as being inflicted with a biological abnormality, to then calling them "perverts" and "psychopathic sex fiends" and finally during the 1980s, the media portrayed most offenders as probable members of pedophile rings or satanic cults (Gordon, 1988; Jenkins, 1998). Much like the previous panics, child sexual abuse was seen as occurring outside of the home. During this period, the perpetrators were believed to be those that cared for children, such as teachers and child care providers. For example, in 1983 the media covered the McMartin preschool case. The McMartins, who owned and operated a child care center in California, were accused and charged with numerous acts of child sexual abuse. The trial proceeded for over six years and resulted in no convictions. However, this case caused a substantial increase in attention regarding child sexual abuse, as well as increased fear. Newspapers and television channels covered stories about the suspected sexual abuse by caretakers creating public panic causing many families to question the safety of their children while in the care of others (Jenkins, 1998).

Also during this time, the misperception that kidnappers were lurking around every corner expanded. While the media focused attention on kidnappers as strangers taking children, the truth was that non-custodial parents were the most likely offenders. While research has shown that family and other trusted adults, such as acquaintances and friends, commit the vast majority of sex offenses, media coverage has distorted the public's perception. For example, Jenkins (1998) reported that the coverage of pedophilia in the Catholic Church had greatly impacted mainstream society's belief that this crime was quite prevalent, which was a distortion of reality. Another influencer on this panic was the media attention on children murdered during the commission of sexual crimes. In fact, most of the laws passed during this time can be directly linked to a child's death. One example was Megan's Law, which was passed after a young child was kidnapped, sexually assaulted and murdered by a neighbor. Cases like this caused people to question whether their children were safe in their own communities. This anxiety over the safety of the most vulnerable members of our society has caused panic resulting in hurried legislation with various shortcomings (i.e. they are poorly conceptualized, poorly drafted, overly broad in scope, and promote unfortunate consequences).

CHAPTER 3

Theory and Typologies of Sexual Offending

Directly related to the range of sexual offenses is the diversity of offenders. There are various underlying etiologies and motivations for sexual offending. While some people may be biologically predisposed to pedophilia making it difficult for them to control their desires for children, others may have experienced an early childhood trauma (e.g. a victim of rape or abuse) resulting in a disturbed personality prompting the victim to become a perpetrator. Researchers are continuously studying how best to categorize offenders in an effort to develop classification systems that are more comprehensive. While taxonomies are not foolproof, they do have a "potential role of enhancing the efficacy of clinical decision making about treatment, management, and disposition" of offenders (Knight et al., 1989, p.4). In additional, according to Knight and colleagues (1989), "...understanding the taxonomy of child molesters can provide indispensable guidance in studying the etiology of sexual abuse" (p.4). Motivations also vary greatly depending on the type of offender. For example, some rapists are motivated by rage and humiliation while others are motivated by the need for power. These differences in motive manifest in differing types of offenses, levels of violence used, and risk of reoffense.

Key Theoretical Perspectives of Offending

The etiology of sexual deviancy and offending is complex and as researchers have pointed out, no single theoretical perspective can fully explain why an individual engages in certain types of behavior or commits sexual crimes (Fishbein, 2001; Terry, 2006). What may deter one offender may actually excite another (Groth, 1979). According to Binkley and Beech (2001), no theories to date "adequately explain either the etiology and maintenance of sexually abusive behavior or provide a comprehensive description of the offense process itself" (p.51). Sex offenders are a heterogeneous group and thus a multidisciplinary approach to explaining the causes of sexual deviancy is required. Fishbein (1994) asserts that criminal behavior in general requires social, environmental, psychological, and biological scientists and researchers to work together to explain and manage antisocial behavior.

Throughout the last century, the prominent theoretical perspective of sexual crime has changed. Various schools of thought emerged at different points in time. These include, but are not limited to, the medical model which viewed offender's behavior as directly related to physiology, the psychoanalytic perspective which viewed sexual deviancy as resulting from unresolved issues from ones childhood, and feeblemindedness or emotional instability (Sutherland, 1950). Today, while some would continue to argue in favor of emotional instability, most would subscribe to an eclectic perspective, which includes a cognitive behavioral approach to understanding sexual deviancy.

Some of the most common explanations of sexual violence today are biological, psychological, including psychoanalytic, social learning, cognitive behavioral, and feminist theories. And, although each has its own independent explanation, many modern theorists often use a more integrated approach, which takes into consideration the heterogeneity of this type of perpetrator – the sex offender.

Biological Theory

Before the emergence of biological theory, most theorists subscribed to "classical thinking," or the belief that criminals, like everyone else, have free will to choose whether to engage in unlawful acts. Rational decision-making and contemplation of pleasure versus pain influenced decision-making. The premise was that individuals weigh potential outcomes based on whether they will result in positive or negative consequences (Akers, 2000).

Biological positivism, on the other hand, viewed human behavior as being governed by the laws of nature, not free will (Gottfredson & Hirschi, 1990, p.47). This new way of thinking, which embraced the use of empirical evidence, was first used to explain deviancy and criminal behavior during the 1870s (Akers, 2000). At this time, theorists began focusing on the human body to explain why people do the things they do. Researchers believed that criminals engaged in unlawful behavior because of their physiological and psychological make-up (Akers, 2000, p.42). Deviancy was seen as a factor of evolution or in other words, that over time, specific traits biologically pass from one generation to another and eventually lead to the development of new deviant species. This was an important shift in thinking because people began to not only view criminal behavior from a medical or biological perspective, but view people's deviant behavior was the direct result of an illness or inherited factors. Thus, these individuals were in need of treatment to overcome the illness (Traub & Little, 1994). As Conrad and Schneider (1994) noted, a person designated as 'sick' should be absolved from blame and culpability because he is not in control of his actions. There is no purposeful malfeasance or wrongdoing on the part of the offender.

Biological positivists believed that although there were other influential factors that contributed to crime, such as environmental and situational factors, a person's inborn abnormalities explained the causes of criminal behavior (Akers, 2000, p.42). According to biological theorists, it was because of these inherited or innate traits, also termed biological markers, that a person would exhibit criminal characteristics early in life and would commit criminal acts in adolescence and continue to engage in such behavior well into adulthood.

During the early 1880s, sexual perversion or the concept of a person feeling compelled to commit sexual deviant acts also came to the forefront of psychiatric medicine (Jenkins, 1998). In 1883, Francis Galton, a renowned anthropologist and researcher, coined the word *eugenics*, the science of controlling human breeding. The concept was to control reproduction to improve the human species so that only those individuals with exceptional genes would reproduce. During this time professionals claimed that castration or sterilization were appropriate treatment for sexual offenders given the need to prevent them from having offspring that would inherit their deviant compulsive sexual behavior. Eugenics became a powerful movement with many individuals subjected to involuntary sterilization.

In the early twentieth century, Cesare Lombroso, scientific criminologist and father of biological positivism, began researching the causes of psychopathy. He believed that criminals had a specific physiognomy, specifically evident in facial features. Lombroso focused on physical traits, such as cranial structure, pigmentation, ear size, and even left-handedness to explain psychopathy in criminals. Two specific types of criminals were identified, the born criminal or what we call today, the psychopath, and those considered mentally insane. The born criminal was defined as a person who is absent of shame, empathy, self-control and is impulsive (Lombroso, 1911, p.366). The mentally insane were defined as suffering from a mental illness and were often considered more dangerous than the born criminal because not only did they have the same evil motives, but their behavior was often sporadic and indeterminable, making them highly dangerous. In 1913, Charles Goring disputed Lombroso's specific claims, reporting that stature and body-weight were the biological traits that differentiated criminals from law-abiding citizens. He also reported biological differences in those suffering from alcoholism, epilepsy, risky sexual behavior, insanity, and lower intelligence levels (Gottfredson & Hirschi, 1990, p.51). While these theorists differed in specifics, the fundamental notion that biological differences existed and significantly influenced criminal behavior was the same (Gottfredson & Hirschi, 1990). The belief that biology affected behavior also influenced how these criminals were punished. According to biologists, these offenders were mostly in need of medical, chemical, or surgical treatment, not legal. Laws and punishment would have no effect on these criminals. They needed to have their impulses and behaviors altered through biological treatments or to be completely isolated from the rest of the world, mainly in hospitals.

Before this time, the primary deterrent for sexual deviants was punishment through imprisonment. In 1911, the same year Lombroso wrote his book, *Crime: Its Causes and Remedies,* Massachusetts passed the Massachusetts Briggs Act. The Briggs Act provided an allowance to the court to commit habitual offenders found to be mentally defective in mental health facilities. In addition, if the defendant exhibited tendencies toward becoming a recidivist and was likely to harm the public, the law permitted the court to commit these defendants as well, without ever being convicted of the sexual crime (Guttmacher & Weihofen, 1952). According to Jenkins (1998), this statute was one of the most aggressive positivist statutes of this period with its focus on habitual offending. Fully implemented by 1921, this statute became the basis for all later sexual psychopath laws or laws aimed at preventing further crime through detention in a mental facility (Jenkins, 1998, p.40).

"Biological criminology," as originally presented by Lombroso and other early positivists, was largely discredited because of the lack of research to support it (Fishbein, 1994). In addition, people have noted that medicalizing criminality encourages and permits antisocial behavior by removing individual responsibility (Conrad & Schneider, 1994). Currently, biological theorists are more apt to subscribe to the principle of conditional free will, which asserts that while individuals have the ability to rationally decide their actions, there is often preset or inborn traits that promote or lay the foundation for later behavior. Predetermined characteristics, such as low IQ, mental and physical disabilities, or biological disorders, make it more difficult for the person to abstain from unlawful or sexually deviant behavior, but not impossible or out of ones control completely.

There are diagnosable disorders that may lead to prosecutable sexual crimes such as pedophilia, exhibitionism and voyeurism. These psychiatric disorders, listed in the American Psychiatric Association's (1994) DSM-IV, are called paraphilias. Paraphilias involve intense sexual fantasies/urges lasting at least six months and causing significant distress or impairment in the person's life. They may lead to sexual offending if the person cannot control his urges. For example, pedophilia (i.e. interest in children) may result in committing child sexual abuse. The focus of paraphilias is as follows:

- Exhibitionism (302.4) – exposing one's genitals to an unsuspecting stranger
- Fetishism (302.81) – nonliving objects
- Frotteurism (302.89) – touching and rubbing against a nonconsenting person
- Pedophilia (302.2) – prepubescent children
- Sexual Masochism (302.83) – the act of being humiliated, beaten, bound, or otherwise made to suffer
- Sexual Sadism (302.84) – the act of causing or viewing someone being humiliated, or psychologically or physically made to suffer

- Transvestic Fetishism (302.3) – cross-dressing
- Voyeurism – observing an unsuspecting stranger who is naked, disrobing, or engaging in sexual activity
- Other Paraphilia (302.9) – examples include telephone scatologia (obscene phone calls), necrophilia (corpses), partialism (focus on a single part of the body), zoophilia (animals), coprophilia (feces), among others

It is important to note that most sexual offenders do not suffer from a psychiatric disorder and even for those that do, their diagnosis may or may not be related to committing the sexual offense. For example, fetishes, sadism and masochism are not criminal acts in and of themselves unless they involve an unwanted assault on another individual. However, a clear understanding of psychiatric or medical disorders and their potential impact on actions is important. For example, while substance use disorders, mental illness or neurological disorders (e.g. psychosis, senility, and mental retardation) do not cause someone to commit an offense, it may play a significant part in criminal propensity due to its inhibiting effects (Knight, Carter, & Prentky, 1989, p.11; McGrath, 1991). Furthermore, these types of biological disorders are important to understand given their impact on sexual recidivism (Prentky, Knight, & Lee, 1997). In fact, those that suffer with multiple paraphilias are at higher risk to reoffend (McGrath, 1991).

In addition to psychiatric medical conditions, research has shown that other biological factors, such as focal brain lesions, bitofrontal tumors, traumatic brain injuries, and endocrinological abnormalities (e.g. increased testosterone levels) have all been linked to changes in sexual behavior (Saleh & Guidry, 2003). Research on testosterone indicates that the level of testosterone in males has shown to vary at different stages of the life-cycle, especially increasing during puberty and adult life, but decreasing with age. This may help explain why the rate of sexual violence decreases with age. However, while research has shown that testosterone levels are highest in the morning and during the fall or early winter months (Brooks & Reddon, 1996), it has also shown that the prevalence of sexual assault, specifically rape, is most common during the summer and at night (McGrath, 1991). This raises a question about the impact testosterone levels has on sexual crime.

Although mixed, many research studies support a positive relationship between plasma testosterone levels and aggression and impulsivity. For instance, in one study, prisoners with violent histories in adolescence and chronic violent offenders had higher levels than non-violent offenders (Hill, Briken, Kraus, Strohm, & Berner, 2003, p.411). In another study, researchers found that rapists who were categorized as most violent based on previous history had significantly higher plasma testosterone levels than did other non-violent sex offenders (Rada, Laws, & Kellner, 1976). However, in other studies testosterone did not appear to be associated with sexual deviancy (Tedeschi & Felson, 1994). Thus, because results remain inconclusive, the true impact of testosterone on sexually violent behavior remains in question and the use of medications in treating sexual offending behavior is still being researched.

In summary, biological theorists are still researching how physiology is related to criminal behavior, including sexual crimes. Thus far, literature supports findings that many psychophysiological factors affect sexual deviancy. More specifically, according to Fishbein (2001), there can be dysfunctions in the neurotransmitters, specifically within the serotonin and dopamine systems, which can cause individuals to engage in stimulation-seeking behaviors, to act violently, aggressively or impulsively, and to lack the ability to empathize (p.45). Many studies have shown a specific relationship between aggression, criminal behavior and androgens, or in other words, increased testosterone levels (Hill et al., 2003; Rada et al., 1976; Tedeschi & Felson, 1994). Although there is good reason to believe that biological factors are related to sexual offending, much more work needs to be done to show any conclusive causal links between heredity, biological traits and sexual crime (See Chapter Four for more detail).

Psychological Theories

The psychological theories commonly used to describe the etiology of criminal sexual behavior are psychoanalytic theory, social learning theory and cognitive behavioral theory.

Psychoanalytic Theory. Psychoanalysts believe that criminal behavior stems from experiences early in a person's life that negatively affect his personality, behavior, and way of thinking and processing information. Harmful experiences, especially those during early development, can significantly increase a person's chance of having personality disorders, cognitive disorders, and emotional and behavioral problems, such as aggressive and violent tendencies and psychopathology. Theorists believe that these types of disorders make people less likely to control behavior and moderate reactions to stressors. Some have hypothesized that personality disorders also make isolation more likely. This ultimately affects the person's ability to cope due to decreased support, making relapse more likely (Chesire, 2004). In fact, it has been argued by some researchers that psychopathy may be the determining factor for aggression in some sexual offenders, which may mean that type of sex offender is secondary to the psychopathic personality disorder (Chesire, 2004, p.634). For example, you may have two child molesters, but only one with an inability to feel remorse (i.e. antisocial personality). Groth also believed that sexual offenses, specifically rape, were a result of a "personality dysfunction" (Groth, 1979, p.84).

Personality disorders are critical in understanding motivations and behavioral control, which influences management. Offenders that have diagnosable personality disorders, such as antisocial personality disorder, may have extreme difficulty feeling empathy and remorse and most likely have extreme problems with impulsivity and deceitfulness – each of these factors affects their ability to be rehabilitated. Rather, while most people feel anxious or experience other emotional reactions when they are about to engage in behavior that is not socially accepted (i.e. increased heart rate, sweating, palpitations, dry mouth, and/or faintness), antisocial offenders do not experience these symptoms because of a hypoaroused autonomic nervous system, decreasing the likelihood that offending behavior will be deterred (Fishbein, 1994, p.446). In fact, some research suggests that psychopaths actually seek risk-taking and sensation-seeking behavior (Tedeschi & Felson, 1994). Sexual sadists often fit this profile.

Psychoanalysts, much like biological theorists, examine individual's propensities to commit crime. Sigmund Freud, a renowned Viennese psychiatrist and neurologist, founded the psychoanalytic perspective during the 1890s. One of its primary principles was psychic determinism or in other terms, that behavior cannot be controlled freely and was the result of intrapsychic forces (Bootzin, Acocella, & Alloy, 1993, p.26). Psychoanalytic theory explained crime as an abnormality or disturbance in the emotional development of the child, which has long-term impacts later in adulthood. In the beginning, this theoretical perspective mainly explored cases where individuals were labeled sexually deviant, such as homosexuals and those with paraphilias. It was not until the 1970s that psychoanalysts began to examine more serious violent sexual offending (Terry, 2006).

According to psychoanalytic theory, the male child experiences fear of castration, which stems from incestuous desires for the mother and fear that the father will castrate him for these desires. More specifically, when a child is between approximately three and five years old, he enters the phallic stage of development and experience an oedipal crisis. During this stage of development, the child is preoccupied and begins to experiment with his genitalia. The child is curious and envious of the opposite sex and begins to develop romantic feelings towards the opposite sex parent, also called the Oedipus complex in boys and the Electra complex in girls. It is also during this stage that boys notice that their mothers do not have a penis and fear that their mother was castrated and they will be castrated too for their incestuous feelings. For this reason, these feelings are repressed and lead to a fixation in the phallic stage of development. A person that is fixated at this stage never learns to control his sexual desires and manage instinctual sexual behavior because of a very strong id, the part of the psyche that strives for instant gratification of sexual and aggressive desires. Holmes and Holmes (2002) describe these urges as hedonistic drives. Fixation at the phallic stage coupled with psychic trauma is what can lead to sexual deviancy and crime.

Groth (1979) also provides a description of how psychoanalytic theory explains sexual assault. In most cases, rape is not a crime of passion, sexual desire or attraction. The motivation is anger and the need to exert power over the victim. Psychoanalysts believe that rapists often experience these needs and desires due to unconscious anger towards women, especially their mother. Theorists speculate that rapists and other sexual offenders have experienced some sort of painful, unresolved sexual conflict or other type of trauma during early development, such as maltreatment or rejection (Craissati, McClurg, & Browne, 2002; Groth, 1979, p.108; Marshall, 1989). In most cases, the mother has caused some sort of psychic trauma through psychological abuse or incestual acts. This trauma triggers a fissure in the person's personality and psychosocial development (Holmes & Holmes, 2002), causing the male to feel like he lacks control of his life, to feel inferior and insecure in his masculinity, to lack a sense of self-identity, to fear rejection and humiliation, and to have an uncontrollable need for power. In turn, this perpetrator has an unmanageable need to demonstrate his anger, domination, and superiority over his victims. Because the motivations and what the person receives in terms of emotional fulfillment from the sexual assault can vary greatly among offenders, typologies of rapists have been developed. For example, Groth (1979) explains that there are anger rapists, power rapists, and sadistic rapists – each motivated by different factors (e.g. aggression, the need for power, and the need for power gained through torment and suffering, respectively) (See rapists typologies, Table 4).

Social Learning and Cognitive Behavioral Theories. Towards the mid-twentieth century, the theoretical perspectives of human behavior began to change. Social learning and cognitive behavioral explanations of behavior became the popular approach. Albert Bandura, a psychologist that believed that the environment influences a person's actions, began to expand the theory of personality development to include psychological and cognitive processes (Bandura, 1974).

Social learning theory, originally founded by Bandura, is one of the most popular theories used to explain behavior. Ronald Akers and others have expanded this theory to explain criminal behavior, including describing the sources of sexual deviancy. Although this theoretical perspective, like psychoanalytic theory, suggests that sexual offending behavior is shaped from early experiences in one's life, the actions of offenders are seen as chosen, not innate. People have free will even if they are prone to certain behavior due to these early influences. Although some may have mental disorders that influence their actions, most individuals know right from wrong and are able to make rational choices based on their perception of the consequences.

The main components of social learning theory are observational learning, modeling, imitation, reinforcement, and conditioning. This theory has also been expanded over time to incorporate cognitive and environmental aspects of learning. The foundation being that not only modeling, but also interpretation or our mental processes and the current situation or environmental factors that surround us, effect learned behavior. Thus, this perspective is based on the principle that behavior results from an interaction of behavioral, cognitive, and environmental factors (Akers, 2000). Criminal behavior is learned from exposure to law-violating behaviors, attitudes, and motivations of those we are close to, especially family members and friends. The type of role models the child has growing up impacts the development of his personality, values and behaviors (Groth, 1979). Also, the extent that one's observations influence later behavior is impacted by the duration, frequency and intensity of exposure (Akers, 2000, p.73).

Disruptions in the family's composition, abuse and neglect, substance use, criminal behavior and inappropriate sexual behavior influence the child's development (Groth, 1979, p.195). For example, family violence may impact the child's views of how women should be treated. A child that experiences or views inappropriate sexual contact or such behavior on a recurrent basis will internalize this abuse and act out on these internalizations. According to Groth (1979), the actions of an adult child molester may be a repetition or duplication of the sexual abuse he was exposed to in early life (p.102). The individual has learned to imitate earlier experiences. This person may also seek out children for sexual gratification because he feels more comfortable with them and believes he is showing the child love. The pleasurable feelings he gets when he victimize others, otherwise known as positive reinforcement, reinforces his actions. He may also have the irrational belief that the child wants the sexual relationship, a cognitive distortion that is the direct result of misinterpreting the child's behavior as sexual in nature. This is particularly evident in cognitive behavioral theories of deviancy, which expanded this original social learning theory.

Cognitive behavioral perspectives to understanding sexual violence suggest that cognitive distortions promote deviant sexual behavior. Sykes and Matza (1957) refer to these distortions as justifications and propose that distortions precede criminal behavior and make violence possible. They believe that any disapproval the criminal experiences from their social network is neutralized or deflected, thus allowing the individual to act out. Distortions are psychic tools used by individuals to deal with anxiety and discomfort ultimately permitting the individual to feel at ease with his behavior – they are defense mechanisms, a concept originally conceptualized by Sigmund Freud. Sex offenders typically use the following types of defense mechanisms:

- Rationalization/Justification – accepts responsibility, but denies the act is wrong (e.g. the woman was intoxicated, the woman really meant "yes");
- Excuses – admits the act is wrong, but denies full responsibility (e.g. an accident, psychiatric condition);
- Denial – rejects reality in regards to the severity of the act, its impact on the victim, and potential consequences (e.g. it wasn't rape – they were friends);
- Projection – blames others for the act (e.g. woman or child seduced him, she was promiscuous);
- Minimalization – diminishes damage caused, violence, and effects of the act (e.g. child was not hurt)

These defenses enable the individual to cope with behavior and urges he is unable to explain and manage. For example, an offender may blame the child for his crime, reporting that the child wanted the sexual act to take place because he/she showed sexual interest (justification/projection); thus, the child was not harmed in the act (denial/minimalization).   According to English, Pullen and Jones (1997), "sex offenders typically have developed complicated and persistent psychological and social systems constructed to assist them in denying and minimizing the harm they inflict on others, and often they are very accomplished at presenting to others a facade designed to hide the truth about themselves" (p.2).

According to a study by Barbaree (1991), over half of all rapists and child molesters denied their crimes and many minimized its effects. In one study, Abel et al. (1989) found that child molesters have many distortions including their beliefs that what they are doing does not harm children and that children are interested in the offenders sexually. In another study conducted with rapists, researchers found that some of the most common reasons reported to justify or excuse rape were that the woman seduced the offender, the woman said "no," but she meant "yes," and that the woman asked for it by the way she acted or dressed (Scully & Marolla,1984).   Each of these justifications helps the offender rationalize his actions and encourages continued deviancy. This perspective, that sexual deviancy results from social learning experiences and that a person's cognitive interpretation and distortions of reality promote deviancy is one of the most accepted to date.

Feminist Theory

During the 1960s, the second-wave of feminism began, also called the "women's liberation movement." The women and men involved in this movement strived to promote greater political and economic equality. This theory and its focus on sexual crimes, particularly rape, expanded during the 1970s. Rape was not explored from an individual or psychological viewpoint, but from a sociological and cultural perspective. Specifically, theorists believed that there were sociological and cultural forces that directly caused sexual violent behavior (Lisak, 1991). Lisak (1991) believed that these cultural forces shape individuals attitudes and affect their propensity to act out aggressively. For instance, while women are culturally and socially parented to be submissive, men are raised to have hypermasculine qualities and misogynistic views. This is evident in our socializing girls to "act like a lady" and that boys should not "act like a little girl."

In 1975, Susan Brownmiller, a feminist researcher wrote a historical, groundbreaking work on rape. Brownmiller (1975) explored rape as a phenomenon that has existed since biblical times resulting from issues such as patriarchy, subordination of women, and the socialization of women to become victims. Supporting her views, researchers have described what has become known as the backlash hypothesis – that women's equality threatens men and may actually perpetuate rape (Russell, 1975; Martin, Vieraitis, & Britto, 2006). Radical and liberal feminist's each theorize that when women's status and equality is high, rates of rape decrease because of the appreciation and respect that the women receive (Martin et al., 2006). Females that are not devalued are consequently less likely to be victimized. A historical example of this concept would be Brownmiller's (1975) discussion of viewing women as property to be bought, sold, and raped, especially during war times. Raping women was a part of the victory and punishment to the enemy. Brownmiller (1975) also believed that pornography fosters rape-supportive attitudes in that the pro-violent attitudes and depictions within pornographic material often lead people to be desensitized to sexual violence. These pornographic materials often depict women as subordinate to men and through objectification, promote women's inferiority and secondary status in society. And, as noted by other theorists, attitudes towards women have a significant relationship with sexual aggression (Feller, 1992).

While there is no single feminist theory on child sexual abuse, according to the radical feminist perspective, "all men are socialized to hold attitudes and exhibit behaviors that are directly associated with sexual offending: the beliefs of sex offenders are not held because they are sex offenders, but because they are men" (Purvis & Ward, 2006, p.301). The motivating factor of sexual assault is gender and more specifically, that men need to exert power over females.

As shown in Table 3, the theories of sexual offending have changed considerably over time. What is also clear is that there is not one perspective that fully explains why people commit sexual offenses and trying to find a single factor or cause for this type of behavior results in flawed thinking (Finkelhor, 1984; Marshall & Barbaree, 1990). That is not to say that the perspectives discussed are uninformative to understanding sexual offending, but that a more integrated and multifactor approach may be more useful (Finkelhor, 1984). For example, Ward and Siegert (2002) created what is known as the Pathways Model for child sexual abuse, which uses this integrated approach. This model incorporates the best components from three separate integrated theories – Finkelhor's Precondition Model, Hall and Hirschman's Quadripartite Model and Marshall and Barbaree's Integrated Theory (Ward & Siegert, 2002, p.319). The Pathways Model shows that there are various routes leading to offending behavior, but each pathway includes a developmental component, a dysfunctional psychological component (e.g. insecure attachment, abuse/neglect, distortions), and the opportunity to offend (Ward & Siegert, 2002). Each pathway involves risk and protective factors and takes into consideration "learning events, biological, cultural and environmental factors" (Ward & Beech, 2006, p.60). Appreciating that various factors impact why people offend and understanding the possible key risk factors for offending is vitally important given their impact on motivation, victim target, type of treatment, and recidivism.

Typologies of Sexual Offenders

Researchers have developed a variety of typologies for sexual offenders, particularly rapists and child molesters. These typologies are often seen as key determinants when examining risk of recidivism and

Table 3: Theories of Sexual Violence

Theory	Time Period	Key Characteristics
Biological		
	Late 1800s – Early 1900s	Inborn traits, deviancy passed from one generation to another, illness, eugenics
	Early 1900s – Mid-1900s	Physiognomy (e.g., cranial structure, left-handedness, body-weight), psychopath vs. mental insanity
	Mid-1900s – Current	Conditional free will, biological disorders, low-IQ, low self-esteem, poor social skills, dysfunctions in the neurotransmitters (serotonin and dopamine), testosterone and aggression
Psychological		
Psychoanalytic	Late 1800s – Early 1900s	Psychic determinism (i.e. no free will), fixation in the phallic stage of development, repression
	Early 1900s – Mid-1900s	Need for instant gratification (i.e. the id)
	Mid-1900s – Current	Need for power, aggression caused by unconscious anger towards mother, unresolved conflict/trauma
Social Learning/ Cognitive Behavioral	Mid-1900s – Current	Free will (i.e. not innate), rational decision-making, observational learning, modeling and imitating aggression, environmental exposure (e.g., family violence, abuse/neglect), cognitive distortions
Feminist		
	Mid-1900s – Current	Sociological view, cultural forces shaping attitudes towards women and children, views of women as submissive and subordinate influencing victimization (e.g., pornography)
Integrated		
	Current	Utilizes biological, developmental, social learning, psychological, cultural, and environmental components

when exploring what type of punishment and/or intervention/treatment modality would be most effective in curtailing the risk of reoffending (Broadhurst & Loh, 2003). First, typologies assist intervention staff in developing effective treatment plans that are dependent upon offender characteristics and behaviors. The treatment modality chosen often depends on what motivates the offender to commit his crime(s). Second, typologies assist with theory-building and understanding why certain people commit sexual offenses, which helps practitioners and researchers understand and detect symptoms and triggers so that future offenses may be prevented (Richards, Washburn, Craig, Taheri, & Yanisch, 2004, p.97). Lastly, because there is evidence that suggests that offenders have differing modus operandi, typologies have been used to assist law enforcement. Being able to differentiate between various motivations can assist investigators with profiling and thus narrowing the number of suspects (Knight, 1999, p.305). For example, by definition, a power rapist displays very different patterns and has different motivations for offending than a sadistic rapist.

Rapists

According to Richards et al. (2004), "Rape offenders display a wide range of heterogeneity in regard to the versatility of their criminal histories, pre-offense lifestyle, age and gender preference in victims, criminally deviant attitudes and beliefs, and the degree of force, brutality, and physical harm caused during their offenses" (p.97). Thus, being able to classify types of rapists based on specific factors and commonalities can be very helpful.

Groth's Typology. While there are different rapist typologies and no universally accepted classification system, Nicholas Groth, a researcher who studied the psychodynamics of rape through clinical practice with offenders and victims of sexual crime, developed the typology that is most commonly used today. Most other rapist typologies are based on his classification system. According to Groth (1979), there are three types of rapists, (1) the anger rapist, (2) the power rapist, and (3) the sadistic rapist (Table 4). Research has supported Groth's typology of the anger and sadistic rapist, but not his power rapist. However, the researchers admit that this may be the result of methodological shortcomings (Richards et al., 2004).

Anger Rapist. For the anger rapist, sex and hostility are merged. There is a need to release anger and rage in the form of brutality and physical attack towards the victim. The weapon used is sex and the motive is revenge for some real or imagined insult (Groth, 1979, p.17). In these offenses, the victim is always visibly injured. The anger rapist uses sex to degrade and humiliate his victim(s). Researchers have found that this rapist usually acts impulsively and his acts are not premeditated. This perpetrator is often responding to some type of stressor that has made him resentful or angry towards those that have wronged him, especially women (Groth, 1979, p.16).

Power Rapist. Unlike the anger rapist, the power rapist does not wish to inflict physical harm on the victim, but instead he feels a need to own him/her (Groth, 1979, p.25). According to Groth (1979), "the intent of the offender usually is to achieve sexual intercourse with his victim as evidence of conquest, and to accomplish this, he resorts to whatever force he finds necessary to overcome his victim's resistance and to render her helpless" (p.26). Offenses occur as a way for the offender to validate himself as a man and show his virility. Often victimization occurs after the perpetrator experiences a blow to his self-esteem. This type of offender fantasizes about the attack, but of course, the assault never lives up to his fantasy. He believes the victim wanted the encounter and in fact was looking for it or asking for it. In fact, some offenders will ask their victim if they enjoyed it because they really do not believe that they have harmed the victim in any way.

Sadistic Rapist. Opposite of the power rapist is the sadistic rapist, who needs to punish, harm, destroy, and intentionally brutalize the victim in order to feel gratified during the assault. It is actually the tormenting and suffering of the victim that excites him. This rapist has no remorse. As Groth (1979) reports, the more brutal the attack, the more suffering the victim endures, the more powerful and excited the offender becomes (p.46). This offender will often keep souvenirs of the attack so that he can relive the crime repeatedly, becoming sexually excited each time. Although rare, this rapist is usually guilty of those crimes involving sexual homicide or physical mutilation.

Hazelwood and Burgess' Typology. In 1987, Hazelwood and Burgess developed an expansion of Groth's typology in their work entitled,

"Practical Aspect of Rape Investigation: A multidisciplinary Approach." Their typology included four kinds of rapists – two of which have power as their motivation and two for which anger is the motivating force. These are (1) the power assertive rapist, (2) the power reassurance rapist, (3) the anger retaliatory rapist, and (4) the anger excitation rapist (Table 4).

Power Assertive Rapist. This offender is entitled, arrogant and narcissistic. He has an extreme sense of superiority and feels that rape is acceptable because he is entitled to offend against anyone he chooses. This offender is often seen as a "mans-man." He is very good at conning people, which helps him in attracting his unsuspecting victims. This individual will usually use his fists as his weapon and may assault the victim repeatedly. Although his attack is brutal, his intention is not to kill his victim.

Power Reassurance Rapist. This type of rapist feels completely inadequate as a person. Thus, he feels the need to gain power and therefore forces his victims to have sex. However, interestingly, the power-reassurance rapist is sometimes referred to as a "gentleman rapist" or an "unselfish rapist" because of how different he appears in relation to other types of more violent rapists (Douglas & Olshaker, 1998). This is not to say that this rapist does not harm his victim(s) or that the rape is less traumatic, but that there is often less physical violence associated with this attack. There is also evidence that sometimes this offender actually inquires whether the victim is feeling any discomfort during the attack as if he cares about the victim. He may apologize, and/or may even ask the victim out on a "second" date (Douglas & Olshaker, 1998). This rapist often fantasizes that a relationship has been established and when his feelings are not reciprocated, he is devastated and must try to relive the fantasy over again with a new victim.

Anger Retaliatory Rapist. This rapist displaces his anger onto his victim. He gains gratification from the release of hostile emotions and anger by degrading his victim. When profilers find that the victims remind them of the offender's mother or wife, the anger-retaliatory rapist is the most likely perpetrator. Frequently a precipitating event has taken place that angers the offender. He in turn takes out his aggression on someone else. The degree of violence varies dramatically depending on how the person exhibits anger. For example, the rape may entail mostly verbal abuse or may involve numerous serious physical assaults, such as beatings.

Anger Excitation Rapist. Although the anger-excitation (sadistic) rapist is the least common, he is the most dangerous. The sadistic action itself causes the offender to become extremely excited and wanting to increase the level of violence towards the victim. The aggression is not associated with anger, but with excitement. For this reason, this rapist does not act on impulse and is not looking to hurt someone because he is angry and frustrated, but because he sees it as enjoyable. This offender is often very social and charming. He enjoys the entire process of finding a victim and seducing him or her before engaging in torture, both physically and mentally. The sadistic rapist is also more likely to use a knife or other weapon to cause physical harm and is the most likely of all rapists to kill the victim, feeling no remorse. He will also often keep souvenirs as a way to relive the incident.

Douglas and Olshaker's Typology. Douglas and Olshaker discuss a classification system with four typologies in their book *"Obsession."* This system is quite similar to that of Hazelwood and Burgess in that it also includes the (1) power reassurance rapist, (2) the anger or the anger retaliatory rapist, and (3) the sadistic rapist. However, while Hazelwood and Burgess describe the power assertive offender, Douglas and Olshaker label their fourth type of rapist as the (4) exploitative rapist. Researching both this model and that created by Hazelwood and Burgess, McCabe and Wauchope (2005) found evidence to support both of these typologies (Table 4).

Power Reassurance Rapist. See Hazelwood and Burgess' Power reassurance rapist
Anger Retaliatory Rapist. See Hazelwood and Burgess' Anger retaliatory rapist
Sadistic Rapist. See Hazelwood and Burgess' anger excitation typology

Exploitative Rapist. A rapist considered exploitative often acts on impulse. This individual is less likely to have planned his attack. He is likely to take advantage of situations where there is an unsuspecting victim. Although unplanned, sometimes this perpetrator will search out victims of choice, but he does not fantasize about whom and how he will attack the victim as is often done by other types of offenders. This offender is also more likely to be selfish and not concerned with harming the victim. His gratification comes from dominating the victim and often involves multiple assaults during a single encounter.

Knight and Prentky's Typology. Lastly, a fourth model has been developed also building on the expanded typology of Hazelwood and Burgess. This system, the Massachusetts Treatment Center: Rapist Typology, version one (MTC:R1) was originally developed by Knight, Prentky and colleagues in 1983. Knight and Prentky have since refined their classification system with the most recent being version three (MTC:R3) (McCabe & Wauchope, 2005, p.241). This model has also been supported by research (McCabe & Wauchope, 2005; Richards et al., 2004). This taxonomy of offenders includes nine categories of rapists based on degree of fixation, social competence, and physical contact. The categories are (1) opportunistic high social competency, (2) opportunistic low social competency, (3) pervasively angry, (4) sexual sadistic-overt, (5) sexual sadistic-muted, (6) sexual non-sadistic high social competency, (7) sexual non-sadistic low social competency, (8) vindictive low social competency, and (9) vindictive moderate social competency (Table 4).

Opportunistic Rapist (Types 1 and 2). This rapist acts in an impulsive and predatory manner. Assaults appear to be highly impacted by situational and environmental factors. For example, a man witnessing a woman walking alone down a dark alley may take advantage of the opportunity to offend. Engagement in general criminality is common for this type of offender and this is yet another opportunity to offend. His motivation is not primarily anger or sexual gratification. There are two types within the opportunistically motivated rapist taxonomy, including the offender that is higher in social competence and one that is lower (Knight, 1999, p.311).

- Type 1 (High competent) – Higher social competency and first exhibited impulsivity in adulthood
- Type 2 (Low competent) – Lower social competency and first manifested impulsivity during adolescence.

Pervasively Angry Rapist (Type 3). For the pervasively angry rapist, antisocial behavior and general criminality is his way of life. Rape is yet another crime he engages in where there is an opportunity to harm another person. While his behavior of taking advantage of the opportunity to offend is similar to the opportunistic offender, his motivation is different. The pervasively angry offender's motivation is anger and needing to hurt someone in order to feel gratified. The assaults by this criminal are likely to cause serious bodily injury (Knight, 1999, p.312).

Sexual Rapist (Types 4, 5, 6 and 7). The sexual rapist has some form of sexual preoccupation (Knight, 1999, p.312). In this category there are four types of offenders, including the sadistic overt offender, the sadistic muted offender, the non-sadistic offender with high social competency and the non-sadistic offender with low social competency. For offenders within the sadistic typologies, there is a merging of aggression and sexual preoccupation. Within the non-sadistic typologies, aggression and sexual preoccupation are not merged. For this offender, there is evidence that the offender has overwhelming feelings of inadequacy.

- Type 4 (Sadistic overt) – Overtly acts upon his aggression in the violent attack
- Type 5 (Sadistic muted) – Aggression remains a fantasy. He does not overtly act out his aggression.
- Type 6 (Non-sadistic/ high competent) – Sexually preoccupied with higher social competency
- Type 7 (Non-sadistic/ low competent) – Sexually preoccupied with lower social competency

Table 4: Typologies of Rapists

Theorist/ Typology	Key Characteristics
Groth	
Anger	▪ Acts are impulsive and not premeditated ▪ Victim is visibly injured ▪ Acts involve degrading and humiliating the victim ▪ Victim often does not experience physical harm
Power	▪ Acts are a conquest and a way for the offender to validate himself
Sadistic	▪ Acts are brutal, sometimes resulting in sexual homicide or physical mutilation ▪ Victim suffering excites him, feels no remorse
Hazelwood and Burgess	
Power-Assertive	▪ Entitled, arrogant and narcissistic ▪ Acts are brutal, but he does not intend to kill his victim
Power-Reassurance	▪ Feels inadequate; acts are a method to gaining power ▪ Acts are less likely to result in physical violence ▪ Sometimes referred to as a "gentleman rapist"
Anger-Retaliatory	▪ Frequently a precipitating event angers the offender, resulting in displaced anger onto the victim ▪ Gains gratification by degrading his victim
Anger-Excitation (i.e. sadistic rapist)	▪ Increasing violence excites the offender ▪ Not impulsive, enjoys the entire process of finding a victim, seducing her and then torturing her, both physically and mentally ▪ Most likely of all rapists to kill the victim, feels no remorse
Douglas and Olshaker	
Power-Reassurance Anger-Retaliatory	▪ See Hazelwood and Burgess' typology
Sadistic Exploitative	▪ Impulsive ▪ Selfish and not concerned with harming the victim ▪ Gains gratification by dominating the victim

Table 4: Typologies of Rapists (continued)

Theorist/ Typology	Key Characteristics
Knight and Prentky	
Opportunistic	▪ Impulsive and predatory ▪ Assaults are highly impacted by situational and environmental factors ▪ Engages in general criminality ▪ Motivation is not primarily anger or sexual gratification
Pervasively Angry	▪ Exhibits anger in all areas of his life ▪ Antisocial behavior and general criminality is his way of life ▪ Motivation is anger and hurting someone
Sexual	▪ Merging of aggression and sexual preoccupation for the sexually sadistic offender ▪ Overwhelming feelings of inadequacy for the sexually non-sadistic offender
Vindictive	▪ Exhibits misogynistic anger ▪ Needs to humiliate and degrade women

Vindictive (Types 8 and 9). The vindictive rapist exhibits misogynistic anger, meaning non-sexualized anger specifically directed at women (Knight, 1999). This targeted anger and need to humiliate and degrade women is what distinguishes him from other types of rapists. There are two subtypes distinguished by level of social competency.

- Type 8 (High competent) – Higher social competency and first exhibited impulsivity in adulthood
- Type 9 (Low competent) – Lower social competency

There are many similarities among rapist classifications. For example, each of the researchers has discussed the offender who is motivated by anger. Typically, this person is seeking revenge or retaliation for some perceived wrongdoing. This person uses rape as a means of degrading the victim, which in turn is a release of pent-up aggression. Groth labeled this offender the *anger rapist*, Hazelwood,

Burgess, Douglas, and Olshaker, labeled this offender as the *anger-retaliatory rapist*, and Knight and Prentky labeled this rapist as the *vindictive rapist* or *pervasively angry rapist*.

Another similarity is the offender that is motivated by the harm he causes to the victim. For this offender, sex and aggression are merged. The act of brutalizing a person causes sexual excitement. This offender is the most likely to kill his victim. While Groth, Douglas, and Olshaker have termed this offender the *sadistic rapist*, Hazelwood and Burgess call this offender the *anger-excitation rapist*. Knight and Prentky have identified the sadistic rapist as Type 4 (*sadistic overt*) and Type 5 (*sadistic muted*); however, Type 4 is most similar to what has been described by the other researchers.

Each of the researchers also discusses the rapist who is motivated by the need for power. This offender feels inadequate and uses rape as a means of validating himself and rarely sees himself as hurting the victim. This rapist is known as the *power rapist* by Groth, *power-reassurance rapist* by Hazelwood, Burgess, Douglas, and Olshaker, and is similar to the *sexual non-sadistic rapist* discussed by Knight and Prentky. The last similarity is Douglas and Olshaker's *exploitative rapist* and Knight and Prentky's *opportunistic rapist.* In both taxonomies, the rapist acts in an impulsive manner, taking advantage of a situation where there is an unsuspecting victim. The motivating factor for these offenders is not anger or sexual gratification, but domination.

Differences among these typologies are primarily seen in the level of detail. For example, Hazelwood and Burgess expanded Groth's model by adding the *power-assertive rapist*. This offender is not using rape in order to feel powerful, but instead, rapes because he believes he is powerful. This offender is narcissistic and entitled. Knight and Prentky have taken the models and expanded them even more by not only considering motivating factors, but also other offender characteristics, including age when impulsivity began and level of social competency. They believe these offender characteristics are critical to categorizing offenders and may help in profiling rapists (Knight, 1999). Other researchers have also emphasized the importance of understanding offender characteristics in order to identify those predisposed to offending and for the purposes of treatment and management (Terry, 2006, p.71).

Child Molesters

"Adults are not the only victims of sexual assaults. Infants, preadolescent children, and teenage girls and boys are also frequent targets of sexual assault" (Groth, 1979, p.141). Understanding the etiology of sexual offending and differentiating between types of offenders (e.g. rapists versus child molesters), as well as specific categories within type of offender (i.e. specific types of child molesters) is critical to establishing effective treatment, understanding prognosis, as well as managing these sex offenders. For example, treatment for a molester who is primarily attracted to children is going to be different than treatment for someone who is attracted to adults, but victimizes a child because of some stressful event. According to Holmes and Holmes (2002), this second type of offender is least likely to reoffend if the situational factor(s) that prompted the offense is alleviated. Thus, as has been done for rapists, sex crime researchers have also developed various typologies for child molesters. Some of the most well-known and cited typologies are by Groth and Knight, Carter, and Prentky.

Groth's Typology. Groth first developed his taxonomy of child molesters in the late 1970s. He asserted that "only through negotiation and consent can sexual relations properly be achieved" (Groth, 1979, p.141). Therefore, because a child is unable to give consent to such an encounter, he or she cannot willingly engage in sexual relations with an adult. Although this is understood by general society, there are some individuals that feel otherwise. Primary sexual interest – adults versus children – is one of the most commonly used means of classifying child molesters (Terry, 2006, p.77). For example, Groth's well-known taxonomy includes two specific types, (1) the fixated child molester who is primarily attracted to children and (2) the regressed offender who is primarily attracted to adults (Table 5).

Fixated Child Molester. The fixated offender is primary sexually attracted towards children and is not usually attracted to adults – thus, he rarely marries. This individual has not fully completed his psychosexual development and is often childlike in his interests. He has few friends that are his age and definitely prefers to be around children. Researchers have also termed these offenders as "preferential" because of their preference for child companionship (Groth, Hobson, &

Gary, 1982; Howells, 1981; Quinsey, 1986). This child molester also usually begins to have these pedophiliac attractions early in life, usually during adolescence. Thus, there is often a history of reoccurring child molestation given the compulsive preoccupation with children. The fixated molester rarely hurts his victim and is likely to walk away if there is much resistance (Groth, Longo, & McFadin, 1982). He believes that he is in a loving relationship with the child. This relationship starts like a normal adult-adult relationship with a period of courting, which can take time. He often begins by establishing a friendship and buying gifts – this is often referred to as "grooming" the victim (Robertiello & Terry, 2007). He will only begin to introduce physical intimacy after a trusting relationship has been established. His primary target is male children (Holmes & Holmes, 2002).

Regressed Child Molester. The regressed molester has had adult relationships throughout his life and is very likely to have had sustained relationships, including marriage. This person is primarily attracted to and sexually involved with individuals his own age. With the regressed offender, the incident of molestation usually results due to a stressful event in his life, such as a divorce, loss of employment, and/or substance abuse. He has feelings of inadequacy, coupled with poor coping skills. This results in regressing to childhood when faced with difficult situations. This offender is more likely to be a one-time offender as long as the situational factor that triggered the offender to act out is resolved. This offender prefers females, but may victimize males if they are more available to him (Holmes & Holmes, 2002). Because this offender chooses his victim based on opportunity, he may victimize his own children (Robertiello & Terry, 2007).

Knight, Carter, and Prentky's Typology. In 1989, Knight, Carter, and Prentky created a classification system that was a variation of Groth's model. Their model, known as the Massachusetts Treatment Center: Child Molester Typology, version three (MTC:CM3) includes 10 types of offenders. The types are differentiated according to degree of fixation (Axis I) and amount of contact with the victim (Axis II). The first four groups of offenders (Axis I) are typed according to two constructs, fixation and social competence. Social competence is measured by looking at social and sexual relationships, such as employment history, adult roles and responsibilities, and relationships with other adults. A person rated as having high social competence has at least two of the following: employment at a single job for three or more years; has been involved in parenting responsibilities for at least three years; has been involved in an adult organization for at least one year; has had a sexual relationship with an adult for at least one year; and/or has engaged in other adult relationships and friendships lasting at least one year. These first four types include the (1) high fixation/low social competence, (2) high fixation/high social competence, (3) low fixation/low social competence, and the (4) low fixation/high social competence. The next six types of offenders (Axis II) are typed according to amount of contact the offender has had with the child, the meaning of that contact, the level of physical injury, and the presence or absence of sadism (Knight et al., 1989) (Table 5).

Axis I – High Fixation (Types 0 and 1). An offender considered highly fixated has had three or more sexual encounters with children and the time period between the first and third encounter is greater than six-months duration. This offender has long-lasting relationships with children and must have regular contact with them. A person under age 20 may be considered "high fixation" even if his encounters with children were within a six-month period if he meets criteria for enduring relationships and regular contact. The high fixation offender is then examined according to level of social competence. There are two types of high fixation offenders – the high fixation/low social competence and the high fixation/high social competence.

- Type 0 (High fixation/low social competence) – Meets criteria for high fixation offender and exhibits no more than one of the criteria for social competence
- Type 1 (High fixation/high social competence) – Meets criteria for high fixation offender and exhibits two or more of the criteria for social competence

Axis I – Low Fixation (Types 2 and 3). An offender that is considered low fixation must be over 20-years-old and have had all his sexual encounters with children within a six-month period. The low fixation offender is then typed according to level of social competence.

- Type 2 (Low fixation/low social competence) – Meets criteria for low fixation offender and exhibits no more than one of the criteria for social competence
- Type 3 (Low fixation/high social competence) – Meets criteria for low fixation offender and exhibits two or more of the criteria for social competence

Axis II – High Contact (Types 1 and 2). There are two types of molesters who are differentiated by the amount of contact they have had with their victims prior to the offense and why they began the relationship with the victims. Rather, there is the high contact/interpersonal offender and the high contact/narcissistic offender. The offender that rates as high contact is one that is involved in recreational activities or has an occupation that requires a great deal of contact with children. For example, a school-bus driver, a sports coach, or a boy scout leader. This individual usually puts himself in situations where children surround him. He may also visit children in the neighborhood or invite children to his home to "hang out" and play.

Once a victimizer is rated as having high contact, he is rated according to the meaning of his contact with children - as either interpersonal or narcissistic.

- Type 1 (High contact/ interpersonal) – Meets criteria for high contact offender and wants to establish relationships with children because he enjoys their company
- Type 2 (High contact/narcissistic) – Meets criteria for high contact offender and establishes relationships with children for the primary purpose of sexual victimization. The narcissistic offender has little or no concern for children

Axis II – Low Contact (Type 3 – Type 6). There are four types of low contact offenders. The low contact offender has just that, very little contact or no contact with children and the only contact he has with the victim is at the time he wishes to engage in sexual molestation. Within the low contact group, there is the offender whose offense results in low injury and one that results in high injury. Injury is measured by examining physical abuse delivered at the time of the crime. The offender that is considered low physical injury engages solely in slapping, shoving, and verbal abuse. There is no long-lasting physical injury to the victim. Conversely, the subgroups of high injury offenders engage in punching, choking, and other types of physically aggressive acts.

The final step in differentiating low contact subtypes is exploring whether the offender engages in non-sadistic or sadistic behavior. Of those that are low contact/low physical injury and low contact/ high physical injury, some offenders are considered non-sadistic, meaning that they only use as much force as necessary to control the victim and do not become excited by the victims fear or by the force itself. Other offenders labeled sadistic use more force than necessary and the act of forcing the victim is sexualized. The thought of the victim's pain and fear causes the offender to become sexually excited.

- Type 3 (Low contact/low physical injury/non-sadistic) – Does not meet criteria for high contact offender, uses minimally physically aggressive acts and does not become sexually excited by the victims fear, pain or act of aggression
- Type 4 (Low contact/low physical injury/sadistic) – Does not meet criteria for high contact offender, uses minimally physically aggressive acts, but has engaged in one of the following: non-damaging insertion of foreign objects, sadistic fantasies or behavior (See Knight et al., 1989, p.19), or sodomy
- Type 5 (Low contact/high physical injury/non-sadistic offender) – Does not meet criteria for high contact offender, uses physically aggressive acts either due to anger or due to an accident, but does not become sexually excited by the victims fear, pain or act of aggression
- Type 6 (Low contact/high physical injury/sadistic) – Does not meet criteria for high contact offender, uses physically aggressive acts and does become sexually aroused or derives pleasure from the victims fear or pain

All classification systems for child molesters include Groth's fixated and regressed offender. In Knight et al, (1989) Axis I taxonomies, they use the high fixation/low social competence and the low fixation/high social competence type of offender respectively. Also, under their Axis

Table 5: Typologies of Child Molesters

Theorist/ Typology	Key Characteristics
Groth	
Fixated	▪ Primary sexual attraction towards children, especially males ▪ Has few friends his age and prefers to be around children ▪ Pedophiliac attractions begin early in life, usually during adolescence ▪ Rarely hurts his victim ▪ Relationship starts like a normal adult-adult relationship with a period of courting and "grooming" the victim
Regressed	▪ Primarily attracted to and sexually involved with adults ▪ Acts of molestation usually result due to some stressful event Feelings of inadequacy, coupled with poor coping skills ▪ Prefers females
Knight, Carter, and Prentky	
Axis I – High Fixation (Types 0 & 1)	▪ Has had three or more sexual encounters with children ▪ The time period between the first and third encounter is greater than six-months duration ▪ Has long-lasting relationships with children and must have regular contact with them
Axis I – Low Fixation (Types 2 & 3)	▪ Must be over 20-years-old ▪ Has had all his sexual encounters with children within a six-month period
Axis II – High Contact (Types 1 & 2)	▪ Involved in recreational activities or has an occupation that requires a great deal of contact with children ▪ Usually puts himself in situations where children surround him
Axis II – Low Contact (Types 3 – 6)	▪ Very little or no contact with children

II typologies, the high contact/interpersonal is most like Groth's fixated offender and the low contact/low physical injury/non-sadistic is most like Groth's regressed offender. Rather, the regressed offender is one that offends because of some situational factor and views the child as a pseudo-adult (Danni & Hampe, 2000). For this reason, the offender is less likely to use physical aggression and will not become sexually excited by his act of aggression.

While both models describe similar typologies, Knight and colleagues (1989) have significantly expanded Groth's taxonomy to consider other offender/offense characteristics. For example, while Groth's fixated offender generally has high levels of contact with his victim as does Knight, Carter, and Prentky's interpersonal and narcissistic offenders, they differentiate between those that enjoy children (interpersonal) versus those that have very little concern for children's welfare (narcissistic). Knight et al. (1989) also include many other types based on aggression and sadism. Both are important additions given their link with recidivism and treatment outcomes.

Other Considerations

Interestingly, McCabe and Wauchope (2005) found that there are other important considerations and characteristics to consider along side typologies. These include the offenders' environment and situational factors. This finding supports other research indicating that variables such as stress, substance use, loss of employment, ending of a relationship, and other factors may influence an offender's propensity to offend, as well as their type of offense. Also important, many offenders do not fit into only one category. For example, what about the fixated offender who primarily seeks and desires children but marries a women because it provides access to her children? For this reason, categorizing offenders may not always be useful to clinicians and those working directly with offenders because of their heterogeneity and complexity (Bickley & Beech, 2001).

CHAPTER 4

Recidivism

Recidivism, or relapsing into criminal behavior or committing a subsequent offense, is of great concern to the public, especially given the numerous high-profile, violent sexual assault cases by repeat offenders. There are specific risk factors related to recidivism, as well as differences in rates depending on type of offender, criminal history, and participation in treatment. Research indicates that some assessments using known risk factors are able to help predict risk of recidivism, including the SONAR, SORAG, RRASOR and the Static-99. In addition, research suggests that some treatments have been moderately successful in decreasing recidivism, namely the use of biochemical agents and cognitive behavioral therapy. The extent of their success remains in debate given the methodological shortcomings associated with recidivism research.

Shortcomings in Recidivism Research

Recidivism research is plagued with difficulties, including true prevalence rates, categorizing offenders, varying ways in which recidivism is operationalized, and differing follow-up rates. As such, outcome studies differ vastly in their results.

Prevalence Rates
Although some offenders do reoffend and are apprehended, the true prevalence rate of recidivism is unknown because many crimes go undetected (Abel et al., 1987; Hanson & Morton-Bourgon, 2005; Marshall & Barbaree, 1988). For example, in one study, the ratio of

arrests to sexual crimes (rape or child molestation) was only one to 30 according to self-reports (Abel et al., 1987). Marshall and Barbaree (1988) conducted a study using "unofficial records" and found that for every official offense, there were 2.4 other crimes committed and 2.7 victims. Sample and Bray (2003) note that the 1995 National Crime Victimization Survey indicated that only 32% of sexual assault victims reported the crime to authorities, which was much lower than victims of robbery (60.6%) and burglary (50.3%).

However, these findings do not indicate that every offender recidivates. In fact, researchers believe that few offenders commit most of the crimes and the worst crimes (Soothill & Fransis, 1998). Hanson and Morton-Bourgon (2005) conducted a meta-analysis consisting of 82 recidivism studies and found that while 36.2% of the sexual offenders generally recidivated, only 13.7% sexually recidivated and 14.3% violently recidivated. However, they also report that these percentages are probably underestimates given that many crimes go undetected.

Also clear from a review of studies is that sex offenders do not necessarily have higher recidivism rates than other offenders (e.g. burglars, drug offenders). Sample and Bray (2003) conducted a study examining arrests in Illinois between 1990 and 1995 and found general recidivism (within five years) was highest for those who committed robbery (74.9%) and burglary (66%) compared to 45.1% of sexual offenders. In another study, researchers found that of 9,691 sex offenders, rapists were rearrested for general recidivism (within three years) at a much lower rate (46%) than those convicted of burglary (76%), robbery (70.2%), and drug offenses (66.7%) (Langan & Levin, 2002).

Categorizing Offenders
Another difficulty in assessing recidivism rates relates to the categorization of sexual offenders. Too often sex offenders are dichotomously categorized into either a sex offender (yes/no) or predator (i.e. a person who has a history of violent sexual offending and who has a mental abnormality or personality disorder that makes him likely to commit sexually violent offenses) (yes/no) (Simon, 2000), without exploring the fundamental differences among subtypes of offenders. This is a problem because not all sex offenders are predators

and different subtypes of offenders have different levels of risk for future offending, treatment outcomes, triggers for reoffense, as well as varying background and demographic characteristics (Hanson & Bussière, 1996) – all of which may suggest the need for different types of management to prevent recidivism.

Despite the issues discussed previously, defining the type of sex offender is critical to calculating and comparing recidivism rates. To start with, there is the differentiation between the *generalist* and the *specialist*. Generalists engage in a variety of criminal behaviors. For these offenders, "sexual offending is just another type of behavior they are displaying within a broad criminal repertoire" (Soothill, Francis, Sanderson, & Ackerley, 2000, p.56). According to Lussier (2005), several studies support the idea of the generalist offender. For example, in two separate studies, one of which was a meta-analysis, Hanson and colleagues found that sex offenders as a group had a much higher general recidivism rate than sexual recidivism rate (Hanson & Bussière, 1996; Hanson & Morton-Bourgon, 2004). Knight and Prentky's *opportunistic rapist* is another example. This offender may commit a rape because it is convenient; he may just as well have committed burglary if that opportunity had arisen instead. In other words – the *opportunistic rapist* is a generalist. In a study conducted in 1985, researchers found that those that were most violent were also more likely to have other arrests for crime in general than either exhibitionists or pedophiles (Bedarf, 1995). According to Bedarf (1995), "this finding supported a previously asserted contention that sexual assault demonstrates a tendency toward violent behavior which is not always expressed sexually" (p.895).

On the other hand, the specialist is believed to have a high probability to recommit another sexual crime. Many people believe that sex offenders are specialists and that once someone commits a sexual crime, they are sure to do it again (Miethe, Olson, & Mitchell, 2006; Sample & Bray, 2003). In fact, sex offender legislation is based on this belief (Soothill et al., 2000). However, research does not support this assumption. Reviews of various studies indicate that most offenders do not specialize (Lussier, 2005; Parkinson, Shrimpton, Oates, Swanston, &. O'Toole, 2004; Simon & Zgoba, 2006). Even among those that are more likely to commit subsequent sexual offenses, such as the child molester, most have histories of other non-sexual crimes (Simon &

Zgoba, 2006). Nonetheless, there is some evidence supporting both categories of offenders, lending credence to the assertion that sex offenders are heterogeneous and no single type exists. This may mean that most offenders have a propensity for crime in general, some specialize, and victim choice and type of offense will not always be obvious. The distinction between these two categories of offenders, generalist versus specialist, is important because there is a presumption that most offenders specialize and target certain types of victims. However, because not all offenders are alike, profiling, treatment and management of offenders are negatively impacted if all offenders are treated as specialists (Lussier, 2005). This creates, as Lussier (2005) describes it, a taxonomic trap (p.287).

In addition to differentiating between a generalist and a specialist, understanding recidivism rates and how they vary by sex offender typology (e.g., child molester) and subtype (e.g., incest or extrafamilial) is important. For example, of offenders that target children, research shows that incest offenders have lower sexual recidivism rates than other types of offenders (Hanson & Bussière, 1998; Quinsey, 1977). More specifically, Frisbie and Dondis found that 10.2% of incest offenders recidivated compared to 21.5% of extrafamilial offenders who assaulted non-related females and 34.5% who offended against males (Quinsey, 1977). In a study conducted by Firestone et al. (2000), 15% of extrafamilial child molesters followed for 12 years, sexually recidivated. Although results are mixed, it has also been found that extrafamilial child molesters have higher long-term recidivism rates than do rapists (Doren, 2002). Conversely, in a meta-analytic study, Hanson and Bussière (1998) examined 61 studies with a total of 23,393 offenders. The researchers found that the rearrest rates, defined as those rearrested or reconvicted for a sex offense over a four-five year period, was 18.9% for rapists and 12.7% for child molesters. When the researchers examined rates for those who committed non-sexual violent crimes, the rates were 22.1% for rapists and 9.9% for child molesters.

In another study that looked at 107 offenders consisting of both low (n=75) and high (n=32) risk offenders, the authors tracked the criminals for a mean follow-up period of 3.7 years. Overall, there was a 21% reoffense rate, including 10.3% for violent offenses and 3.7% for repeat sexual offending (Wilson, Stewart, Stirpe, Barrett, & Cripps, 2000, p.183). Researchers also found that those considered lower risk were significantly more likely to offend within a family context than those rated as high-risk (Wilson et al., 2000). This lower rate may be the result of a true lower reoffense rate, a decrease in reporting, and/or lack of access to victims (Doren, 2002, p.149).

In a 1985 study of sexual recidivism, researchers found that on average, within ten years of release, rearrest rates were 11.3% (Bedarf, 1995). When examining this data in more depth, it became clear that rates varied greatly depending on typology. Exhibitionists had the highest rate at 20.5%, followed by sexual assaulters at 10.4%, and pedophiles at a percentage rate of 6.2%. Typology and risk associations were also supported by a study done in 1988 for the California Department of Justice. Rapists had the highest sexual recidivism rate (25.2%) when compared to sex offenders who were convicted of such crimes as indecent exposure or molestation (16.8%) (Bedarf, 1995). Conversely, according to Quinsey (1977), Frisbie and Dondis conducted a study of 1,760 sexual psychopaths and found that exhibitionists had the highest reoffense rate at 40.7%, followed by individuals that had histories of sexual violence (35.6%). Differences between these studies may be the result of variations in operationalizing recidivism, follow-up time, or other differences and therefore should not be compared.

Operationalizing Recidivism

Operationalization of recidivism is also a concern when comparing rates between studies. For example, recidivism may be measured as any of the following: new arrest for a sex crime, any new non-sex crime arrest, new conviction, commitment to custody, or other term defined by the researcher(s). This is important because rates may differ substantially depending on the definition employed. In addition, sex offenses are defined differently across the states and thus make comparing recidivism rates problematic. Other questions to consider are whether the researchers are defining the offender's recidivism rate by examining general criminal recidivism, violent recidivism or only sexual recidivism. Recidivism may be measured differently according to whether or not the crime involved a victim. If a researcher is measuring child molestation recidivism, he/she may only look at new child molestation charges. For these reasons, it is difficult to compare studies and it is equally important that when discussing recidivism rates, definitions and calculations be consistent (Fry-Bowers, 2004). It was for this reason that the above discussion of recidivism rates by typology and subtype was a review of findings and not a comparison between studies.

Follow-up Issues

Other concerns when comparing studies of recidivism are the follow-up time-frames used. Many studies have insufficient follow-up periods. There is evidence that the longer you follow sex offender behavior, the higher the rates of recidivism (Barbaree & Marshall, 1988; Furby et al., 1989; Langevin et al., 2004; Soothill & Bibbens, 1978). Another research concern is making sure that each offender has the same time at risk to reoffend (Prentky & Burgess, 2000). A sample of offenders where some have had periods of incarceration or institutionalization and others have not may have different recidivism rates simply based on opportunities to reoffend. This factor may lead to problems with sampling and generalization when comparing study findings.

It is important to keep in mind each of these issues and shortcomings (i.e. prevalence rates, categorizing offenders, operationalizing recidivism, and follow-up issues) when reviewing and comparing studies examining recidivism. Each will have an impact on outcomes.

Risk Factors and Recidivism

Many risk factors have been repeatedly linked with recidivism (Table 6). These factors are separated into two types, static and dynamic. Static variables are those that do not change (fixed), such as gender, race, and historical data, while dynamic variables do change over time. Examples of dynamic factors include unemployment status, current substance abuse, antisocial lifestyles, noncompliance with supervision, victim access, sexual preoccupations and attitudes, and acute changes in mood (Hanson & Harris, 2001a). Dynamic variables are divided into two other subtypes, stable and acute variables. Stable variables are those that continue for months or years and acute variables are those that may only remain for days or minutes (Craissati & Beech, 2003, p.42).

Many studies have examined the relationship between these factors and recidivism. For example, prior criminal history is often correlated with antisocial behavior and often predicts continued engagement in sexual deviancy (Scalora & Garbin, 2003; Hanson and Harris, 2001a; McGrath, 1991). The number of prior criminal offenses and the types of crimes committed (Hanson & Bussière, 1998; Freeman & Sandler, 2008; Gendreau, Little, & Goggin, 1996; Prentky et al., 1997), as well as the number of victims involved in criminal incidents often predicts recidivism (Barbaree and Marshall, 1988; Proulx, Paradis, McKibben, Aubut, & Quimet, 1997). While findings are mixed (Sturgeon & Taylor, 1980), levels of force, use of weapons, or injury to the victim have been found to be significantly correlated to recidivism (Barbaree & Marshall, 1988; Dempster & Hart, 2002; Långström & Grann, 2000; Proulx et al. 1997).

Hostility and sexual recidivism have also been examined. Marshall and Barbaree (1990) believe that hostility exhibited by sex offenders is due to early problems in childhood, causing these individuals to have poor social skills and resulting in issues with controlling inappropriate sexual and aggressive thoughts and feelings. Hostility has been found to be significantly related to prior violent offenses, the use of violence during sexual offenses, and recidivism, including both sexual and violent recidivism (Firestone, Nunes, Moulden, Broom, & Bradford, 2005, p.277). In fact, even after the researchers controlled for level of risk using a risk assessment tool (i.e. the RRASORmod), the relationship between hostility and recidivism remained significant. When hostility was evaluated by offender type, findings indicated that it was significantly associated with intrafamilial and extrafamilial child molesters and particularly their pre-offense affective state (Proulx, Perrault, & Ouimet, 1999). There was no significant relationship with rapists, diverse offenders, or those with no specific victim type. In another study, researchers found that sexual offenders who used excessive force during the commission of their offense were significantly more likely to have higher rates of hostility than those who did not use excessive force (Rada, Laws, Kellner, Stivastava, & Peake, 1983). Hanson and Morton (2003) completed a meta-analysis and found evidence that hostility and recidivism among sexual offenders were related.

Researchers have also found that having a sexual interest in children (Escarela, Francis, & Soothill, 2000; Grubin, 1997; Prentky & Burgess, 2000), especially boys (Hanson & Bussière, 1998; Hanson & Harris, 2001a; Roberts et al., 2002, Wilson et al., 2000) increases chances of reoffending. For example, according to Quinsey (1977), Frisbie and Dondis conducted a study of 1,760 sexual psychopaths and found that among child molesters, those that committed crimes against males had the highest recidivism rate (34.5%). In support of this finding, Knight and colleagues (1989) report that victim sex "appears to be an important discriminating characteristic among child molesters" (p.10).

Hanson and Bussière (1998), among others, have found that prior history of sexual crimes is significantly related to later sexual recidivism (Prentky & Burgess, 2000; Prentky et al., 1997). In addition, according to Abel, Mittleman, Becker, Rathner and Rouleau (1988), the diversity of sex offenses committed by the offender is also related to recidivism. Hanson and Bussière (1996) found that those with a varied background in sexual offending are more likely to recidivate than those with a single offense type.

Another factor associated with committing additional crimes is the offender's relationship to the victim, particularly if there is no prior relationship. Sex offenders that victimize strangers are more likely to reoffend (Hanson & Bussière, 1998; Hanson, Steffy, & Gauthier, 1993; Lang, Pugh, & Langevin, 1988; Proulx et al., 1997; Scalora & Garbin, 2003).

Researchers have also questioned whether sentence length received for past crimes has an impact on recidivism. There has been some support for targeting and incarcerating chronic offenders for longer periods of time (i.e. selective incapacitation) to promote public safety (Wolfgang, Figlio, & Sellin, 1972). However, there has been limited research examining sentence length and its deterrent effect on reoffending among sex offenders. In one study, Proulx et al. (1997) found that child molesters that recidivate (sexually, violently, and generally) had significantly longer sentences than those that did not recidivate. In a more recent study, Kunselman and Vito (2002) found that longer sentencing did little to moderate future acts of violence, and thus only served a retributive function. Rather, they found that when rapists served at least 20% of their sentence, they were less likely to recidivate compared to those that served less than 20%, but also found that recidivism rates did not decrease for those that served more than 20% (Kunselman & Vito, 2002). Given these limited studies, more research examining the impact of sentence length on sex offender recidivism is needed, especially concerning different types of offenders.

There is also a lack of research on compliance with probation and parole requirements and its relationship to recidivism. Specifically, by virtue of being non-compliant, researchers are unable to follow offenders longitudinally (Williams, McShane, & Dolny, 2000). However, there has been some research suggesting that certain demographic variables may relate to non-compliance with community supervision strategies. For example, according to Farrell (2002), recent research conducted in England indicates that younger offenders (those under age 30) and those with longer probationary periods (more than one year) were more likely to abscond. Nonetheless, given the scarcity of research in this area, much more research is needed.

Various demographic variables have also been linked to reoffending, such as marital status and age of the offender. Marital status, specifically never being married has been linked to sexual recidivism by many researchers (Abel et al., 1988; Hanson & Bussière, 1998; Rice, Quinsey, & Harris, 1991; Roberts, Doren, & Thorton, 2002; Scalora & Garbin, 2003). Reasons for the increase in recidivism risk include issues with social competence and problems with establishing adult relationships, among others. Researchers have also repeatedly found that being young when the sexual crime was committed, as well as when the individual first commits any criminal act are both associated with and predictive of recidivism (Furby et al., 1989; Hanson & Bussière, 1998; Scalora & Garbin, 2003). More specifically, Roberts et al. (2002) found that perpetrators ages 18 to 35 were most at risk for sexual recidivism. Another study found evidence that while age over 40 may diminish the prevalence of sexual offense recidivism for rapists, it does not do the same for pedophiles or sexual sadists (Dickey, Nussbaum, Chevolleau, & Davidson, 2002, p.211). Researchers Dickey et al. (2002) believe the probable reason for this distinction is that rapists primarily use physical force during the commission of their crimes and after age 40 there is a distinct decline in physical ability, as well as a decrease in libido (p.213). On the other

Table 6: Risk Factors Significantly Correlated with Recidivism

Variable	Study(s)
Prior criminal history	
Number of prior offenses	Prentky et al., (1997)
Type of crime(s) (including violent crimes, diversity of crimes, history of sexual crimes)	Prentky et al., (1997); Hanson & Bussière (1998); Hanson & Bussière (1996); Gendreau et al. (1996); Prentky & Burgess (2000); Abel et al. (1988);
Number of victims	Barbaree & Marshall (1988); Proulx et al. (1997)
Level of force, weapons, or injury to the victim	Barbaree & Marshall (1988); Dempster & Hart (2002); Långström & Grann (2000); Proulx et al. (1997)
Sexual interest in children	Escarela et al., (2000); Prentky & Burgess (2000); Grubin (1997)
Sexual interest in boys	Hanson & Bussière (1998); Hanson & Harris (2001a); Knight et al., (1989); Roberts et al., (2002); Quinsey (1977); Wilson et al. (2000)
Relationship to victim	Hanson & Bussière (1998); Hanson et al., (1993); Lang et al., (1988); Proulx et al., (1997); Scalora & Garbin (2003)
Sentence length	Kunselman & Vito (2002)
Demographic Factors	
Age (including current age and age at first offense)	Farrall (2002); Furby et al., (1989); Hanson & Bussière (1998); Scalora & Garbin (2003); Roberts et al. (2002)
Marital status (Single)	Abel et al., (1988); Hanson & Bussière (1998); Rice et al., (1991); Roberts et al. (2002); Scalora & Garbin (2003)
Treatment	Hall (1995); McGrath (1991); Gallagher, Wilson, Hirschfield, Coggeshall, & MacKenzie (1999); Fry-Bowers (2004); Hanson & Bussière (1998); Hanson & Harris (2001a); Schweitzer & Dwyer (2003)

hand, pedophiles do not primarily use force, but use manipulation to coerce their targets - something that does not change as the offender gets older. Thus, while Gottfredson and Hirschi (1990) have theorized that targeting offenders is unnecessary given that most general offender's age-out of crime, this would not apply to pedophiles. Is this true for other types of sexual perpetrators? Additional research is needed in this area.

Lastly, although sex offender treatment efficacy continues to be debated, many researchers believe that treatment does decrease recidivism, especially if you explore recidivism over time (Hall, 1995). The U.S. Department of Justice estimated that when sex offender recidivism is examined after three years, treated offenders recidivate less than those that received no treatment, 15-20% compared to 60% respectively (McGrath, 1991). Cognitive-behavioral treatment seems to have the greatest effect (Gallagher, Wilson, Hirschfield, Coggeshall, & MacKenzie, 1999, Ward & Gannon, 2006). Failure to complete treatment (Fry-Bowers 2004; Hanson & Bussière, 1998), as well as failure to comply with supervisory responsibilities have been associated with a higher risk of reoffending (Hanson & Harris, 2001a). According to Schweitzer and Dwyer (2003), there is enough evidence to support the use of treatment programs to target repeat sexual offenders and violent offenders to aid in decreasing recidivism long-term.

This research on risk factors has aided in the development of risk assessment tools (Table 7). These tools use static and dynamic factors to help determine the level of dangerousness an offender poses to the public, including whether an offender will be subjected to community notification – a type of sex offender management policy (see Chapter 5). These tools vary by state. In New York, the offender has a risk assessment hearing to determine level of dangerousness. The static risk factors assessed are historical, such as use of violence, level of sexual contact with the victim, number of victims, duration of offending behavior, age of victim, if the victim suffered from a mental illness or was physically helpless, relationship with the victim, and general criminal history variables, such as age of first sex crime, number and nature of prior offenses, recent commission of a sex crime, and past substance use. The dynamic variables used to make an assessment are acceptance of responsibility, supervision level, living arrangements, and employment status. These factors are then given a point value that determines the level of dangerousness and risk for reoffending. According to Bickley and Beech (2001), "...offenders who are perceived as being of high risk will often receive greater restrictions on their liberty, such as indeterminate sentences, post-sentence detention, and long-term community supervision" (p.58). Thus, a number of risk assessment tools have been developed that help distinguish between sex offenders who are of higher or of lower risk of being reconvicted. Some of these tools are universal and help predict general criminal recidivism, while others are specifically designed to be used with sexual offenders and to predict sexual recidivism. For example, the Minnesota Multiphasic Personality Inventory (MMPI), the Psychopathy Checklist-Revised (PCL-R), the Violence Risk Appraisal Guide (VRAG), and the polygraph are all used to measure risk of general criminal recidivism. A few examples of assessment tools that measure risk of sexual recidivism are: the Minnesota Sex Offender Screening Tool-Revised (MnSOST-R), the Sex Offenders Need Assessment Rating (SONAR), the Sex Offender Risk Appraisal Guide (SORAG), the Rapid Risk Assessment for Sex Offender Recidivism (RRASOR), the Static-99, and the Structured Anchored Clinical Judgment-Minimum Version (SACJ-MIN). The following information provides a brief introduction to these assessments.

General Assessments:
Minnesota Multiphasic Personality Inventory (MMPI). A verbal personality assessment tool designed to determine psychopathology. Of particular relevance to studying sexual offenders are the scales measuring sexual behavior and deviance, substance abuse, personality, and violence. While this test is routinely used with sexual offenders, according to Marshall (1996) the results of the MMPI have been confusing and often do not distinguish between offenders and non-offenders and therefore, he does not recommend using this tool with sex offenders. In support of Marshall's assertion, other researchers have also found considerable overlap among sex offenders and control groups on mean MMPI scales (Curnoe & Langevin, 2002, p.803). Nonetheless, despite these research findings, this test continues to be used and researchers are continuing to examine whether it may assist in determining risk for recidivism when used with specific types of sex offenders (e.g. child rapists) (Lev-Wiesel & Witztum, 2006).

Psychopathy Checklist-Revised (PCL-R). Measures psychopathy in offenders, which has been linked with recidivism, including how quickly someone recidivates and the level of violence used (Harris, Rice, & Cormier, 1991). Specifically, this tool explores impulsivity, irresponsibility, selfishness, remorse and callousness, among other characteristics and risk factors (Barbaree, Seto, Langton, & Peacock, 2001, p.497). This tool has been used to measure psychopathy in sex offenders. However, the problem is that not many sex offenders have been found to be psychopathic (Serin, Malcolm, Khanna, & Barbaree, 1994). Nonetheless, because psychopathy is associated with recidivism, items from this tool and scores from this checklist have been used in conjunction with other risk assessment instruments (e.g. VRAG and SORAG). According to researchers, the PCL-R does seem to predict recidivism in sexual offenders (Hanson & Harris, 2001a; Quinsey, Rice, & Harris, 1990.)

Violence Risk Appraisal Guide (VRAG). Assesses risk for violence using the following factors: whether the offender lived with both biological parents until at least 16 years of age, elementary school adjustment, history of alcohol abuse, marital status, non-violent offense history, failure of prior conditional release, age at offense, victim gender and level of injury, score on the Psychopathy Checklist-Revised, and psychiatric disorders (Barbaree et al., 2001, p. 498; Quinsey, Harris, Rice, & Cormier, 1998). This tool has been found to predict recidivism, including general, violent, and sexual recidivism (Barbaree et al., 2001; Langton et al., 2007).

Polygraph. An assessment tool measuring "truth telling," since offenders often deny their involvement in criminal behavior. Researchers have found this tool to be effective in eliciting disclosures of sex offending behavior (Ahlmeyer, Heil, McKee, & English, 2000), which has been shown to have a direct impact on recidivism (Abel et al., 1988; Hanson & Bussière, 1998; Hanson & Bussière, 1996; Prentky & Burgess, 2000; Prentky et al., 1997). While research has begun to provide some evidence as to the validity and reliability of the polygraph, there continues to be a need for additional research on its use with sexual offenders (Ahlmeyer et al., 2000).

Sex Offender Assessments:
Minnesota Sex Offender Screening Tool-Revised (MnSOST-R).
Examines sex-related convictions and sex offending history. It also
assesses whether or not the offender was under supervision when he
reoffended, whether the sexual offense occurred in a public place, the
amount of force or threat of force used, whether there were multiple
assaults on a single victim, the number of age groups assaulted, the age
and relationship to the victim, the age of the offender, juvenile
delinquency, substance use, employment history, discipline history
while incarcerated, treatment history, and the age at time of release
(Barbaree et al., 2001, p.500-501). Past research found that while this
tool predicted general recidivism, it did not significantly predict violent
or sexual recidivism (Barbaree et al., 2001). Current research
contradicts this finding and found that it does accurately predict sexual
recidivism. However, it still appears to fall short when compared to
other tools (i.e. the SORAG) given the training time required for
interpreting results and that it is not intended to be used with all sex
offenders (i.e. incest offenders) (Langton et al., 2007).

Sex Offenders Need Assessment Rating (SONAR). Helps to measure
changes in risk over time using various stable and acute factors
believed to influence risk. The stable factors include problems with
intimacy, having negative social influences and/or tolerant attitudes
towards sex offending, problems with regulating sexual impulses and
with general self-regulation. The acute factors include use of
substances, negative mood, anger issues, and having increased access
to victims. Researchers report that there is evidence of internal
consistency and ability to differentiate between recidivists and non-
recidivists using this tool (Hanson & Harris, 2001b, p.1).

Sex Offender Risk Appraisal Guide (SORAG). A modification of the
VRAG (Barbaree et al., 2001). While it also measures recidivism risk,
it was "developed specifically to predict violent recidivism among male
sex offenders" (Barbaree et al., 2001, p.492). This tool incorporates
most of the components of the VRAG, except victim injury and violent
and sex offense histories, age of the victim, and deviant sexual arousal
patterns (measured using plethysmography). This tool has been found
to predict general, violent, and sexual recidivism (Barbaree et al., 2001;

Langton et al., 2007).

Rapid Risk Assessment for Sex Offender Recidivism (RRASOR). Measures risk using various risk factors, including offending against a male or unrelated victim, prior sex offenses and being released from prison before age 25 (this specifically aids in examining opportunity to reoffend) (Barbaree, et al, 2001, 500; Hanson, 1997). According to Stalans (2004), one of the main shortcomings is that the tool only looks at documented official criminal history (p.586). However, it has been shown to be a reliable and valid instrument for assessing sex offenders' risk to recidivate (Austin, Peyton, & Johnson, 2003).

Static-99. Includes all four RRASOR items. In addition, it examines four or more prior sentencing dates, convictions for non-contact sex offenses, current index non-sexual violent offenses, prior non-sexual violent arrests, any offense against a stranger, not living with a partner or significant other for at least two years, and prior sexual history (Barbaree et al., 2001, p.500). Researchers have found that the Static-99 is predictive of various types of recidivism, namely general, violent, and sexual recidivism (Barbaree et al., 2001; Langton et al., 2007) and has become the most common type of risk assessment tool used with sexual offenders.

Structured Anchored Clinical Judgment-Minimum Version (SACJ-Min). Looks at prior and current offenses, stranger victims, male victims, never being married, convictions for hands-off sex offenses, substance abuse, residential care as a child, deviant sexual arousal, and psychopathy. According to Hanson and Thornton (2000), the SACJ-Min is nearly as equivalent in its ability to accurately predict recidivism as the RRASOR and combining the two tools is more accurate than either test independently (p.119).

Penile Plethysmography. A physiological assessment tool that measures penile tumescence (Bourke & Donohue, 1996, p.56). In other words, this device measures penile responses to stimuli presented in a laboratory setting (Grossman, Martis, & Fichtner, 1999). There are two types of assessments that measure deviant sexual preferences and urges, the volumetric phallometry and circumferential plethysmography. The first measures blood volume and the later measures circumference or erection.

Although used by many researchers, results are mixed as to their validity and reliability. For example, in one study, the phallometric assessment did accurately diagnose paraphilias and in another it positively predicted recidivism in 75% of the cases (Wilson et al., 2000; McGrath, 1991). However, in other studies, the tools did not differentiate between non-offenders and offenders (Marshall, 1996). Because of this issue, it has been suggested that these tools should not be used to measure sexual deviancy at a single point in time, but should measure persistent erotic interests over time (Craissati & Beech, 2003, p.49). Furthermore, according to Craissati and Beech (2003), "it has generally been found that only a relatively small proportion of offenders demonstrated deviant sexual arousal. These were generally child molesters with male victims" (p.50). Thus, because there have been discrepant findings in regards to the validity and reliability of these tools in determining recidivism risk, further research is warranted.

Table 7: Risk Assessment Tools

Assessments	Key Characteristics
General Assessments	
MMPI	▪ Measures psychopathology ▪ Generally, not recommended for use with sex offenders ▪ Does not distinguish between offenders and non-offenders
PCL-R	▪ Measures psychopathology in sex offenders - however, not many sex offenders are psychopathic ▪ Used with other risk assessment instruments ▪ Accurately predicts recidivism in sexual offenders
VRAG	▪ Measures risk for violence ▪ Uses score on the PCL-R ▪ Accurately predicts general, violent, and sexual recidivism
Polygraph	▪ Measures "truth telling" ▪ Effective in eliciting disclosures of sex offending behavior

Table 7: Risk Assessment Tools (continued)
Key Characteristics
Sex Offender Assessments

MnSOST-R	■ Measures risk of recidivism ■ Accurately predicts general recidivism ■ Mixed findings – violent or sexual recidivism
SONAR	■ Measure changes in risk over time ■ Accurately differentiates between recidivists and non-recidivists
SORAG	■ A modification of the VRAG – incorporates most components ■ Measures risk of recidivism ■ Predicts violent recidivism - male offenders ■ Accurately predicts general, violent, and sexual recidivism
RRASOR	■ Measures risk of recidivism ■ Main shortcoming - uses only official criminal history ■ Accurately predicts recidivism
Static-99	■ Measures risk of recidivism ■ Includes RRASOR items ■ Accurately predicts general, violent, and sexual recidivism ■ Most common type of sexual offender risk assessment
SACJ-MIN	■ Measures risk of recidivism ■ Nearly as equivalent in predicting recidivism as the RRASOR ■ Combining the two tools is more accurate than either test independently
Penile Plethysmography	■ Measures penile tumescence - deviant sexual preferences/urges ■ Volumetric phallometry and circumferential plethysmography ■ Mixed findings – predicting risk of recidivism

In summary, when examining tools specifically used with sexual offenders, some appear to be better able to accurately and consistently measure and predict recidivism. These tools include the SONAR, SORAG, RRASOR and the Static-99. While many others appear promising, more research is needed, especially given their use for community management decisions and in measuring treatment progress.

Treatment of Sexual Offenders

There are many myths regarding sexual offenders, namely that all sexual offenders are extremely dangerous, always recidivate, and that there is no rehabilitation that works with these offenders (Jenkins, 1998). Interestingly, while treatment research has shown positive or promising results for some types of offenders, some researchers have controversially argued that "nothing works" for sex offender treatment and believe that incarceration is the only method of controlling their behavior. In fact, according to Furby et al. (1989), "we can at least say with confidence that there is no evidence that treatment effectively reduces sex offense recidivism" (p.25). On the other hand, other authors have disputed this general dismissal of treatment. For example, in a study by Marshall and Pithers (1994), they argue that the programs that Furby and colleagues reviewed for effectiveness are no longer in use and that many past reviews did not incorporate one of the most new and promising treatments – cognitive behavioral therapy. In a similar response to other researchers' reports that nothing works for offenders in general, Smith, Gendreau, and Swartz (2009) reviewed meta-analyses completed to date regarding treatment programs that reduce recidivism and report that cognitive-behavioral treatment has been effective for sex offenders. Thus, because there are in fact studies indicating that treatment does have a beneficial effect and considering that the majority of offenders will, at some point, be released from prison, it is imperative to continue exploring what works in the realm of deterring and treating sexual offending.

There are currently two core treatment perspectives: biological treatment and cognitive behavioral treatment. While those treating offenders based on the biological model discuss management or cures in relation to a medical intervention, psychologists treat offenders by helping them alter the way they think and behave.

Biological Treatment
Based on the medical model, biological treatment views sex offending

as a result of a diagnosable medical disorder or condition. Much of the biologically-based treatment today is focused on procedures and medications that lower testosterone levels. Researchers have found promising results in reducing sexual drive and decreasing recidivism and/or aberrant behaviors and desires when testosterone levels are reduced (Hill et al., 2003; Saleh & Guidry, 2003; Grossman et al., 1999). Somatic therapies to reduce testosterone levels include both surgical and biochemical treatments.

Surgical treatment. Two examples include castration or sterilization and neurosurgery. Although sterilization began in the late 1880s, the enactment of medical statutes did not begin until almost 30 years later with Indiana enacting the first statute in 1907. Eleven other states trailed shortly thereafter between 1909 and 1913 (Guttmacher & Weihofen, 1952; Jenkins, 1998). Ultimately, at least 30 states passed sterilization laws (Guttmacher & Weihofen, 1952).

Surgical treatment has shown some positive effects. Grossman and colleagues (1999) cite a study conducted by Cornu in the early 1970s that demonstrated that castrated offenders followed from five to 30 years had a recidivism rates of 5.8% compared to 52% for those not castrated (p.351). However, because it is not 100% effective and is permanent, many believe castration should not be an option for treating offenders. Surgical treatment is not widely used today due to ethical issues, specifically its irreversibility.

Another controversial treatment is called neurosurgery or stereotaxic hypothalamotomy, a type of brain surgery, which entails removal of part of the hypothalamus. This surgery decreases sexual arousal and impulsivity due to disrupting the production of male hormones. Decreasing levels of impulsivity are important given its relationship with recidivism. According to McGrath (1991), in one study, rapists assessed as highly impulsive were almost three times as likely to be reconvicted for a new sexual offense. However, Grossman et al. (1999) report that the failure rate for this type of treatment is significant; thus, making this procedure highly risky and unethical.

Biochemical treatment. Biochemical treatment, otherwise known as "chemical castration," was first used because of its effect on reducing sexual interests and causing impotence. Two examples included estrogen treatment and neuroleptics. Estrogen treatment was the first type of "chemical castration" used by professionals. However, because of adverse side effects, there was limited use of this treatment. Neuroleptics or antipsychotics were also used early on, but again there was limited evidence as to their effectiveness and their side effects, specifically tardive dyskinesia (involuntary movements of the face or extremities), were irreversible. Nonetheless, Grossman et al. (1999) still believe that with the many new atypical antipsychotics developed, reassessment of biochemical treatment is warranted in the future.

Although there have been concerns with medical treatments in the past, current research involving the use of medication have shown positive results in terms of reducing sexual drive and may have an effect on reducing deviant sexuality. Currently, because some theorists believe that testosterone increases sexual misconduct and that testosterone antagonists may help reduce sexual deviancy, biochemical treatment is more focused on decreasing testosterone levels. In general, currently prescribed medications are either testosterone-lowering antiandrogen medications (synthetic progesterone derivatives and gonadotropin-releasing hormones) or serotonergic antidepressants, also known as selective serotonin reuptake inhibitors (SSRIs) (Saleh & Guidry, 2003, p.489). In a review of studies, Hill and associates (2003) report that low levels of serotonin metabolite have been linked with impulsive aggression (p.409). Some antiandrogen medications, including Medroxyprogesterone Acetate (MPA) (e.g. Depo-Provera) and Cyproterone Acetate (CPA), are in use and show promising results for those most at risk of reoffense (Tedeschi & Felson, 1994, p.28). Both have shown effects in decreasing paraphilic symptoms, ejaculation, libido, erections, orgasms, and deviant fantasies in offenders (Grossman et al., 1999; Hill et al., 2003; Saleh & Guidry, 2003), but results have been mixed. Other issues discussed are the high dropout rates for these treatments, as well as the fact that the medical management needed makes them quite costly (Grossman et al., 1999). More specifically, making sure that the offender is taking his medication regularly and has not altered its effect by taking synthetic testosterone or a libido-enhancing medication, such as Viagra, adds to estimated costs (Flack, 2005).

Although findings are not conclusive, this type of treatment is currently mandated by a few states, including California, Georgia,

Florida, and Louisiana for parolees with multiple sexual offense convictions. California was the first to begin its use with offenders that had been twice convicted of molesting a child under the age of 13 (Stalans, 2004, p.568).

Another example is gonadotropin-releasing hormones or Luteinizing Hormone-Releasing Hormone agonists (LHRH agonists), which are decapeptids that work within the hypothalamus. Examples include leuprolide acetate (leuprolide) and triptorelin. Both have indicated promising results in reducing and eliminating sexual behaviors. Leuprolide has reduced and for some individuals, completely eliminated erotic thoughts and imagery, as well as decreased frequency of ejaculation and erections. Triptorelin has demonstrated similar results, especially for those suffering from pedophilia.

Antidepressants, specifically SSRIs (e.g. Sertraline, Fluvoxamine, and Fluoxetine), have also shown promising results in decreasing libido, reducing sexual interest, impairing ejaculation, and decreasing inappropriate sexual behavior (Gerardin & Thibaut, 2004). However, they need to be explored more with controlled studies using larger samples (Hill et al., 2003; Saleh & Guidry, 2003, p.491). Possible reasons these medications seem to work is their effect on decreasing impulsiveness, depression, anxiety, and obsessive-compulsive behavior, as well as reducing testosterone serum levels and sexual appetite (Hill et al., 2003, p.409). Understanding how these SSRIs work is also important given their limited and minor side effects. Studying whether these medications work better with certain types of offenders or those that suffer from diagnosable disorders would also be beneficial. In a report by Hill and colleagues (2003), researchers suggest prescribing medications and treatment based on risk level of offender. Rather, they advocate for using SSRIs when the level is low or mild, CPA or MPA if there is no improvement with SSRIs or if the person is a moderate risk for a hands-on offense, and LHRH with or without CPA if the risk level is high.

Psychological Treatment

Over the years, treatment has evolved from the conception of curing an individual to one of helping him manage his behavior. In theory, the use of psychological treatments targeted at treating the root of the problem helps to eliminate inappropriate behavior and reactions to stimuli or triggers. This treatment decreases reinforcement of negative behavior, increases reinforcement of positive actions and aims to restructure impaired cognitive functioning related to acting out. Throughout history, sex offenders have been viewed as mentally ill or unable to control their behavior and therefore in need of psychiatric or psychological treatment. Theses individual treatments include psychodynamic therapy, behavioral therapy, cognitive therapy, and cognitive behavioral therapy, which has become the most commonly used sex offender treatment approach in the last 30 years.

Denial, minimization, relapse prevention, issues related to victim harm and victim empathy, supportive attitudes and beliefs and distortions and fantasies are all key aspects of cognitive behavioral treatment. The main goals of cognitive behavioral treatment are to increase the offender's ability to control actions and change his way of thinking – his belief system. In particular, Cognitive-behavioral therapy, which is considered the most effective form of therapy for sexual offenders (Winick, 1998), aims to help offenders learn to develop internal control. According to researchers, cognitive-behavioral treatment is used to correct distorted thinking by changing cognitive distortions, altering deviant sexual arousal patterns and preocccupations, decreasing the offender's use of denial, increasing victim empathy, and increasing social competence (Marshall & Barbaree, 1990; Stalans, 2004). For treatment to work, the offender must admit to wrongdoing, that he is engaging in problem behavior, and must willingly enter and participate in treatment (Winick, 1998). It has been estimated that 75% of sex offender treatment providers utilize cognitive-behavioral or relapse prevention as primary methods of treating sex offenders (Freeman-Longo, Bird, Stevenson, & Fiske, 1995). Some specific techniques are cognitive restructuring, aversion therapy, covert sensitization, imaginal desensitization, masturbatory reconditioning, social skills training, and relapse prevention (Grossman et al., 1999).

Cognitive Restructuring. A review of literature by Carich, Newbauer, and Stone (2001) shows that offenders' flawed thinking has been referred to as cognitive distortions, thinking errors, distorted private logic, disowning behaviors, irrational beliefs, and safeguarding strategies (p.5). Different types of offenders have different types of distortions. For example, depending on the type of rapist, one individual may believe that the victim wanted the sexual act to occur and another may feel that the victim deserved it because of the way she was acting (e.g., asking for it because of the clothes she was wearing). In an effort to alter the offenders' way of thinking (cognitive distortions) and break down defense mechanisms (Winick, 1998), the therapist engages the sex offender in cognitive-behavioral group therapy. Group treatment is beneficial to offenders because of the confrontation by other group members regarding defenses, which eventually leads to acknowledging responsibility for their actions (Stalans, 2004). Treatment also helps offenders understand and recognize the harm they have caused others with the hope that this will lead to victim empathy and reduce the risk for reoffense. Group treatment also helps the offender achieve personal control of deviant sexual impulses, fantasies, feelings, and behaviors (English et al., 1997, p.3). This is especially important given the effect deviant sexual interests and arousal can have on the amount of force used during the commission of a sexual crime, whether the criminal engages in sexual intercourse with the child and/or whether he offends against multiple victims (Barbaree & Marshall, 1988, p.278). One commonly used self-report assessment tool that measures distortions is the Multiphasic Sex Inventory (MSI). This tool can also help differentiate between types of offenders (i.e. child molesters, rapists, etc.) (Bourke & Donohue, 1996).

Aversion Therapy. Therapists employing aversion therapy link deviant sexual fantasies with physical punishment (e.g. noxious odors). A patient (i.e. the offender) is asked to contrive a series of fantasies regarding what excites him. These scripts are then presented to the therapist. The therapist utilizes these depictions along with visual aids of appropriate fantasies and alternates appropriate (visual) and inappropriate (verbal) depictions back to the patient. When presented with an inappropriate fantasy, the person is exposed to the aversive treatment (i.e. the noxious odor) and when presented with an appropriate fantasy he is not exposed to the aversive treatment. Thus, over time, through the process of experiencing positive and negative reinforcement, the offender changes his thinking and behavior in order to avoid punishment (the aversive treatment).

Covert Sensitization. Another technique used is covert sensitization where the individual envisions a deviant sexual image, stops his fantasy abruptly and begins to imagine and verbally describe a negative consequence to his sexual actions. For example, the offender may imagine and describe being caught in the act, his family's reaction, or being arrested or convicted. As the offender continues in therapy, he is encouraged to begin this aversive thinking at earlier stages of his fantasy, until he can visualize and verbalize negative consequences at the first glimpse of a negative fantasy. According to Grossman and colleagues (1999), this technique helps the patient begin to feel in control of his behavior, thought patterns, and teaches him that he can interrupt negative fantasies and thinking at any stage (p.354).

Imaginal Desensitization. Imaginal desensitization uses relaxation techniques, which have been found useful when treating sex offenders. Imaginal desensitization has been used to treat phobias and types of addictions, and is taught to sex offenders as another skill to help control their deviant behaviors. The offender, once having learned the relaxation techniques, visualizes his fantasy of choice. He is then instructed to think about his fantasy in stages and continue to remain relaxed throughout the process. At the last stage, right before he imagines committing the sexual offense, the scenario is modified and the offender never gets to complete the offense, but continues to remain calm and anxiety free (Bourke & Donohue, 1996). Through repeated practice and pairing relaxation techniques with requests for imagining the deviant fantasy, the offender is gradually taught that he can control his anxiety and the behavior that drives him to act on his fantasies and triggers. The offender learns to tolerate emotional discomfort. This method also incorporates cognitive restructuring, which helps to correct distorted thinking and affords the offender an opportunity to integrate and eventually internalize that he can in fact tolerate deviant urges and remain in control.

Masturbatory Reconditioning. One use of masturbatory reconditioning requires the patient to visualize his fantasy and at the point of ejaculation shift his thoughts to an appropriate, non-deviant desire. Two other forms are labeled verbal satiation and masturbatory satiation. These techniques create situations where the fantasy is no longer appealing to the person because the reinforcements are eliminated. The offender engaged in verbal satiation, verbalizes his deviant fantasy or urges repeatedly until these feelings are no longer appealing and the repetition becomes tedious. Masturbatory satiation requires the person to masturbate to ejaculation to a non-deviant fantasy and continue afterwards while visualizing deviant fantasies. Orgasm is paired with appropriate thinking, while pain and discomfort is linked with deviant fantasies.

Social Skills Training. Social skills training helps the offender learn, restructure, and/or improve social competence in relation to not only sexual relationships, but all intimate supports. Sex offenders and criminals in general often have issues with social anxiety and relationships. The reasoning is often low self-esteem, isolation, poor attachments, and poor social skills.

One primary technique utilized in social skills training is role-playing. This involves teaching a target skill and then having the individual model what he has learned (Bourke & Donohue, 1996). The therapist works with the offender by describing different circumstances that the offender may find himself in and working through the conversation and appropriate behaviors. Role-playing helps to alleviate fears and social anxiety. If the offender has particular problems with establishing relationships with women his own age, the treatment provider will focus the role-play on a similar situation. It may incorporate assertiveness training to help the person express himself and converse with others, as well as teaching the offender how to react in a socially acceptable way. It also helps in managing anger when the woman or person of interest does not reciprocate the same feelings.

Relapse Prevention. Relapse prevention techniques were originally designed to assist substance users in remaining abstinent. Pithers first initiated their use with sex offenders. Relapse prevention training helps heighten the awareness of the offender, his family and friends, as well as his therapists or other practitioners to triggers that may precede relapse. This helps the offender either completely avoid these high-risk situations or affords him the opportunity to learn how to deal with unforeseen situations and circumstances (Winick, 1998). Sex offenders must learn techniques to interrupt their offense cycles (Grossman et al.,

1999) and recognize lapses. A lapse precedes an actual relapse. It is defined as "voluntary risky sex-related behaviors that can lead to a relapse" (Stalans, 2004, p.566). Pinpointing what first triggers a lapse is critical to preventing a full-blown relapse (actual offending).

Table 8: Stages of Relapse: The Child Molester

Stages	Perceptions, Attitudes & Behavior
Stage 1 - proximal background factors	Current perception, such as the offenders' perceptions and attitudes towards sexual relationships between adults and children (Hudson et al., 1999, p.783)
Stage 2 - Distal planning	Seduction process, which includes covert planning or facilitating contact between himself and a child, chance contact, or explicit planning
Stage 3 - Contact	Establishing contact with the victim
Stage 4 - cognitive and arousal patterns	Explicit intention to offend arising from contact with the victim
Stage 5 - proximal planning	Establishing why they should offend. There are three styles, including self-gratification, victim focus, and a mutual focus on satisfying both the victim and offender
Stage 6 – the offense	The sexual offense occurs
Stages 7-9 – post-offense, evaluation, and resolving the situation	Evaluation of the offense, which can be either negative (feeling guilt and remorse) or positive (believing that the child liked it). From this evaluation, the offender decides how he will behave in the future (Hudson et al., 1999, p.785)

Researchers Hudson et al. (1999) have done extensive research in the area of relapse prevention. One example of what a relapse prevention model may look like is their child molestation model (See Table 8). They found that depending on specific choices within each stage of offending, the chance of relapse may be heightened. For example, if the person has a positive affect after offending, if his plan to offend was explicit versus implicit or if the post-evaluation was positive, he is more likely to relapse. Each of these factors also has major implications for treatment (Hudson et al., 1999, p.783-785).

Shortcomings and Treatment Efficacy Research

While biochemical and psychological treatments have shown positive results in their use with sexual offenders, there are some important critiques to note in regard to understanding and comparing treatment research. Examples include using non-experimental research designs, assessment problems, sampling issues, and problems regarding follow-up periods and with operationalizing recidivism.

First, while experimental research studies using random assignment of subjects to treatment and control groups is most advantageous in determining whether a modality is truly effective, these studies are for the most part impractical due to ethical concerns (Broadhurst & Loh, 2003). Some believe it would be unethical to treat some offenders and not others while waiting to see if the controls are more likely to commit further sexual or violent offenses. For this reason, most studies are not placebo-controlled or double-blind (Hill et al., 2003).

A second problem reported by researchers is in assessment. The most prevalent problem is in assessing dangerousness. Risk assessments have varying degrees of accuracy and none of them is 100% accurate. In addition, assessments often use self-report tools, which have inherent problems. These problems include diagnoses that are subjective and based on symptoms that are self-reported by individuals that are commonly known for having issues with denial. Critics have also argued that in many cases, it would behoove offenders to be honest because if they have a setback, it could negatively impact their upcoming or pending release from incarceration or prohibit their discharge if hospitalized or in a residential treatment facility. Assessments using diagnoses also require that the behavior causes significant distress in the offender's personal life, which will often not be the case because offenders are comfortable with their behaviors.

Third, sampling limitations have been discussed in depth, such as using populations or subjects that are incarcerated or hospitalized. These subjects may respond differently then those not incapacitated. In addition, research subjects are often invited to participate, which causes concern as to whether those that wish to participate are inherently different than those that do not. These offenders may be more motivated to do well. Another important issue to consider is that sex offenders, like all individuals have varying histories and other factors that can impact treatment outcomes. For example, comorbidity within samples has been found to impact results. Even if a sex offender has a diagnosis of Major Depression, which has been determined not to be related to why he committed his offense, the diagnosis may still have significant implications for treating him. The individual's ability to control and deal with emotional problems or mental illness can impact long-term outcomes and success in treatment. As reported by Hill and colleagues (2003), while sex offender and sex offenses are not diagnoses, thorough psychiatric, somatic, and criminological diagnostic assessments and histories are mandatory to assist in the identification of prognostic indicators (Hill et al., 2003, p.407).

Fourth, most treatment studies do not actually measure or evaluate recidivism (Maletzky & Field, 2003) because offenders are not given enough time to reoffend. Many research reports have very limited follow-up periods at the time they report success or failure of the treatment program (Grossman et al., 1999; Hill et al., 2003). Lastly, there are great discrepancies in operationalizing recidivism, resulting in inconsistent findings and inability to compare studies.

In summary, while treatment research has shown some positive findings in reducing recidivism, there are inherent problems with many of the studies. In addition, treatment may not work for everyone. For example, treatment is less successful for extrafamilial child molesters than incest offenders. Research also indicates that psychopathic offenders do not benefit from treatment (Stalans, 2004) and some insight-oriented programs can actually have a paradoxical effect of helping offenders deceive and manipulate individuals (Hare, 1996). According to Saleh and Guidry (2003), researchers have also begun to show that there are differences in response to treatment based on age, sex, and race/ethnicity. These findings suggest the need for diverse treatments. Thus, further research is needed, especially when studying treatment and its impact on recidivism because at this time it is not possible to predict precisely who will offend or know which offenders will benefit from treatment. When offenders are released from prison, some may be mandated to treatment, while others are not. Offenders are also subjected to varying degrees of monitoring – both legislatively and programmatically. Thus, understanding whether there are different outcomes dependent on level of supervision combined with level/type of treatment is important given the heightened attention and implementation of legislation for sexual offenders. In the meantime, legislative strategies, such as registration and community notifications laws have been employed to reduce recidivism. Like treatment, there is also a question as to whether legislation can help with impeding offending behavior.

CHAPTER 5

Sex Offender Risk Management Statutes

One of the most hotly debated issues in criminal law today
is how to manage the perceived risk of sex offenders loose
in the community (Durling, 2006, p.317).

Sex offender risk management policies are controversial. While
implemented across the nation as tools for protecting the community,
research on the effectiveness of these statutes on reducing recidivism is
limited. In fact, many opponents to this legislation believe that there
are collateral consequences that could actually lead to an increase in
offending over time.

The Evolution of Sex Offender Legislation

Over time, risk management statutes, including registration, community
notification, residency restrictions, global positioning system (GPS)
statutes, and civil commitment have been implemented. Sex offender
registries were the first attempt made by states to control recidivism
and have been in effect for over 50 years. California was the first to
implement such a law in 1944, followed by Arizona in 1951. Florida,
Ohio, Nevada, and Alabama enacted their version of these laws
between 1957 and 1967 (Matson & Lieb, 1996). The next crime
control strategy to follow was community notification in the 1990s.
Although sex offender legislation had been in effect for many years, it
began receiving the greatest attention during the 1990s when combined

with community notification. Since then, other topes of management strategies have been instituted, such as residency restrictions and global positioning systems.

Types of Sex Offender Legislation

Registration. State registries have been implemented to help monitor and track where offenders reside within the community. Originally designed as investigative tools, these registries assist law enforcement personnel in retrieving an offender list to aid in quick response when similar crimes are committed near where the offender resides. In addition, there is often DNA information that helps either identify or rule out possible suspects. While the concept of sex offender registration may be similar across states, there are distinct differences, such as who maintains the database, which offenses require registration, the information collected, and other specifications, such as timeframes for registration.

First, parties responsible for maintaining the registries vary by state and may include the police, departments of public safety or corrections, or the Attorney General (Tewksbury, 2006, p.2). Second, registerable offenses vary and are dependent on individual state statute. For example, according to Bedarf (1995), some states require registration for benign offenses, such as adultery in Arizona, bigamy in Louisiana and voyeurism in Ohio. Third, states differ in their data collection requirements. However, the typical information collected by law enforcement agencies includes the offender's name, address, date of birth, social security number, criminal history, employment information, vehicle registration and other identifying information such as fingerprints and photos. In addition, 22 states collect blood samples for DNA identification (Matson & Lieb, 1996; Adams, 2002). Fourth, specifications for registration vary by state. For example, states differ in their registration timeframes, risk assessment process, requirements about who registers, and registration conditions. In many states, risk levels influence how often and how long the offender is required to register, as well as who is privy to the offenders private information. Most offenders are initially required to register either prior to or immediately after release from confinement. Updating their information also varies from every 90 days to one time per year. Offenders have to register whenever they move to another location or state, but some states like New Jersey do not allow sex offenders to relocate to other states. How long a person is required to register depends upon risk level, state statute and crime, with timeframes ranging from 10 years to life. Lastly, the charge for non-compliance also varies by state - in New York it is a felony.

Community Notification. Community notification is the act of taking specific information about an offender and disseminating it to the public. Generally speaking, the method in which a state is to fulfill their community notification requirements was not specified by law (See Megan's Law). Thus, the method of dissemination varies greatly by state, but includes at least an internet website that is assessable by the public. Other methods include flyers, community meetings, and the police knocking on doors to notify community members. Some states have even required offenders to put signs up telling people of their sex offender status. In addition, because regulation has been rather loose, the information provided via community notification has also varied greatly by state. Although information is not consistent, a new federal statute will eventually lead to a national database created from the information provided by each individual state, including information on non-violent offenders (See Adam Walsh Act) (Farley, 2008).

Residency Restrictions. Residency restrictions are one of the most current methods used to control and manage the whereabouts of sexual offenders. These laws regulate where an offender can reside and are based on the assumption that offenders are more likely to offend if they are within the vicinity of children. This is based upon a routine activities framework, which states that when sex offenders and unsupervised or unguarded targets are at the same place at the same time then the risk for victimization is greater. In addition, it is believed that sex offenders purposefully choose their residence based on the opportunities to offend (Mustaine, Tewksbury, & Stengel, 2006a). Many jurisdictions have passed or at least introduced legislation to limit where offenders can live – usually excluding residences within 500 to 2,500 feet of schools, child care facilities, parks, bus stops, and any other places where children congregate (Durling, 2006; Wright, 2008). According to Berenson and Appelbaum (2010), there are at least 29 states with registry legislation on the books and in many areas where there is no statewide legislation, county and municipal governments have created their own residency restrictions.

Global Positioning System (GPS). The U.S. Department of Defense built the Global Positioning Satellite system during the 1970s (Johnson, 2002). In 1984, law enforcement agencies in New Mexico became the first to use GPS as a method to monitor criminal offenders (Levenson & D'Amora, 2007). Judges use this system as an alternative to incarceration and as a community supervision tool. For example, the court will give offenders bracelets to wear when released from prison or when placed on house arrest. When used as a form of surveillance, these electronic devices provide law enforcement with real-time geographic whereabouts of offenders at all times. If an offender travels to close to an area off limits, such as near a school or child care center, law enforcement is notified immediately. This will often result in a parole or probation violation and the offender will end up reincarcerated. The belief is that increasing the chance of apprehension may act as a deterrent and may decrease the likelihood of recidivism.

In the late 1990s, law enforcement agencies began targeting sex offenders with this type of surveillance. According to Johnson (2002), Florida was the first state to use GPS to track sex offenders under community supervision. In 2005 with the passing of the Jessica Lunsford Act, Florida required that any sex offender convicted of molesting a child be required to wear a satellite-tracking device for the rest of his life once no longer incarcerated (Padgett, Bales, & Blomberg, 2006). This concept has continued to gain momentum and by February 2006, 26 states reported that they were in the process of implementing electronic monitoring systems for sex offenders (Wright, 2008, p.36).

Civil Commitment. The sexual psychopath laws of the mid-twentieth century were the predecessors of today's civil commitment statutes (Wright, 2008, p.38). These laws allow for the indefinite commitment of offenders to a secure facility if they have a mental abnormality or personality disorder and are a danger to themselves or others. Civilly committed offenders typically have multiple child victims, psychiatric diagnoses, and high-levels of substance abuse (Wright, 2008, p.40). According to Levenson and D'Amora (2007), there are currently 18 states that have passed sex offender civil commitment statutes including Arizona, California, Florida, Illinois, Iowa, Kansas, Massachusetts, Minnesota, Missouri, Nebraska, New Jersey, North Dakota, Pennsylvania, South Carolina, Texas, Virginia, Washington, and Wisconsin (p.173-174). Most recently, the Adam Walsh Child Protection and Safety Act (2006) provided states with monetary incentives to expand civil commitment proceedings. How this incentive affects the number of states with civil commitment statutes remains to be seen.

High Profile Cases and Laws
Major influences on this renewed interest in sex offender legislation include high profile cases, the media, and government incentives. According to Wright (2008), there is a stage process impacting the evolution of sex offender legislation. These stages include: (1) a horrific sexual murder occurs – often involving a child; (2) the murderer (often a repeat offender) is identified and it becomes known that the offender was living in the presence of the family; (3) the local media learns about the murder and begins reporting, which eventually catches the attention of the national news media who do extensive coverage; (4) state or federal legislators learn about the murder and decide that a new law must be passed in order to prevent future crimes – this new law will amend past sex offender legislation; and (5) the new bill passes without controversy (Wright, 2008, p.19-20). This stage process, with minor variations, can be identified over and over again when examining high profile cases and their impact on the evolution of sex offender management policies.

In 1989, a repeat offender brutally raped and tortured a seven-year-old boy from Seattle (Jenkins, 2001). The perpetrator, Earl K. Shriner, had a history of violence against children dating back 24 years, including assault, kidnapping, and murder. While incarcerated, there was overwhelming evidence that he would reoffend once released. In fact, while in prison, "Shriner had designed a van that he reportedly proposed to use for abducting, torturing, and killing children" (Jenkins, 2001, p.191). Although correctional staff were aware of these warning signs, they released him because there was no legal means to continue his confinement. As a result, the state pushed for harsher sentencing and in 1990, Washington became the first state to enact a community notification statute, a provision of their Community Protection Act

(Steinbock, 1995). This act required registration, community notification, and prolonged and sometimes indefinite civil commitment for the most dangerous perpetrators in Washington (Jenkins, 2001).

Cases like this one have greatly impacted legislation. In fact, between 1990 and 2006, Congress passed various national sex offender bills as a result of cases involving specific individuals, also known as memorial laws. Some key examples include the Jacob Wetterling Crime against Children and Sexually Violent Offender Registration Act, Megan's Law, the Pam Lyncher Sexual Offender Tracking and Identification Act, the Adam Walsh Act, and Jessica's Law.

Jacob Wetterling Crime against Children and Sexually Violent Offender Registration Act. One of the first cases to draw national attention to predatory sexual offenders was that of Jacob Wetterling. Jacob was an 11-year-old boy, who while riding his bike with his brother and friend was violently abducted on October 22, 1989.   To date, he is still missing. Due to his disappearance, his parents began a crusade to require sex offenders to register with law enforcement. Appointed to the Minnesota Governor's task force, Jacob's parents campaigned to pass a state law demanding stricter sex offender registration requirements. In response to these efforts, in 1994, the U.S. Congress passed the Jacob Wetterling Crime against Children and Sexually Violent Offender Registration Act. This act became part of the Violent Crime Control and Law Enforcement Act of 1994 (Koenig, 1998). It required any individual convicted of a sex crime, kidnapping of a child, or any violent sexual offense against an adult, to notify proper authorities upon release from prison. This act laid the foundation for all later state and federal sex offender registration laws. Tewsbury (2006) reports that as of February 2001, statewide registries listed almost 400,000 sex offenders.

Megan's Law. In 1996, Congress amended the Jacob Wetterling Act making community notification mandatory based upon the case of Megan Kanka. In July 1994, a twice-convicted child sex offender and neighbor, abducted, violently raped, and murdered seven-year-old Megan. Megan Kanka lived in Hamilton Township, New Jersey with her parents. On July 29, 1994, she left home to go to a friend's house but her friend was unable to play. On her way back home, a neighbor,

Jesse Timmendequas, approached her. He asked her to come inside his home to see his puppy, at which point he accosted Megan and brutally raped and strangled her to death. The police found her body in a nearby park within 24 hours of the murder (Fodor, 2001). Timmendequas has been sentenced to death for this murder.

Megan's parents, Maureen and Richard Kanka fought for justice to ensure that Megan's death would result in something positive. The Kankas and their neighbors petitioned for the enactment of a law that would notify residents when sexual predators move to their community. Within three months of Megan's death, Governor Christine Todd Whitman signed Megan's Law into effect. This bill required that residents have access to information about sex offenders who may live in their neighborhood. President Clinton signed a federal version in May 1996, which required each state implement a sex offender registry and notify agencies and individuals of the whereabouts of dangerous sex offenders within the state.

Pam Lyncher Sexual Offender Tracking and Identification Act. Pam Lyncher was a real estate agent in Houston showing a house to who she thought was a prospective buyer. William David Kelley, a twice-convicted sex offender, proceeded to attack her, but her husband circumvented the assault. In 1993, Pam Lyncher established an organization known as Justice for All – an organization that gives victims a voice so that they are not forgotten. After her death, the Pam Lyncher Sexual Offender Tracking and Identification Act was passed by Congress in October 1996. This bill required the creation of a national database containing sex offender registration data for all individuals convicted of a sexual offense against a minor and would reside with the Federal Bureau of Investigation (FBI). The purpose was to assist with community notification at both state and federal levels and to improve communication between states for those offenders that move from one place to another. In addition, the Bureau was required to monitor sex offender registration and notification for those states not implementing "minimally sufficient" programs (Baldau, 1999).

In March 1998, in an attempt to assist states in meeting legislative requirements and to participate and benefit from the FBI's database of sex offenders, the Bureau of Justice Statistics (BJS) issued a program announcement for the National Sex Offender Registry Assistance

Program (NSOR-AP). This program provided funding ($25 million) to states to assist them in their efforts. According to Baldau (1999), this program had two goals. The first goal was to help states create an effective, up-to-date and accurate registry, which would aid in their ability to properly disseminate relevant information to the public. The second goal was to establish appropriate interfaces with the national system so that information could be retrieved and tracked from one jurisdiction to another (Baldau, 1999, p.5).

Jessica's Law. On February 23, 2005, nine-year-old Jessica Lunsford vanished in the middle of the night from her grandparents' home in Citrus County, Florida. Three weeks later, John Couey, a convicted sex offender, confessed to the killing. A few days later, police found Jessica's remains and charged Couey with kidnapping, rape and murder. On August 24, 2007, the court sentenced Couey to death (Frank, 2007). Effective September 1, 2005, the Florida Legislature passed Jessica's Law. This law increased mandatory sentences for persons found guilty of lewd and lascivious molestation of a child under 12. Rather, these individuals would be required to serve a minimum of 25 years to life for this type of crime. In addition, this act imposed lifelong electronic monitoring for those released from incarceration, required residency restrictions, and expanded civil commitment.

Adam Walsh Act. Six-year-old Adam Walsh disappeared from a mall in Florida on July 27, 1981. Sixteen days later, the police found his remains. Adam's story is well known because his father, John Walsh, host of *America's Most Wanted*, has been a dedicated advocate for child victims since his son's murder. On the 25th anniversary of his son's death (July 27, 2006), President Bush signed into law the Child Protection and Safety Sex Offender Registration and Notification Act, commonly known as the Adam Walsh Child Protection and Safety Act of 2006. This act amends the Jacob Wetterling Act and calls for the establishment of a comprehensive national system for the registration of sexual offenders with full implementation by 2009. More specifically, this act "increases mandatory sentencing for federal offenders, civil commitment of sex offenders, criminal information record checks, child pornography investigative and prosecutorial resources, requires the creation of a national child abuse registry, and provides grant funding for implementation" (Wright, 2008, p.31). This act also establishes a uniform risk classification system and requires that sex offender information be available in all fifty states via internet. The goal is to have universal access to offender information so that families can keep themselves safer. This act as stated in the statute, is dedicated to seventeen victims – Jacob Wetterling, Megan Kanka, Pam Lychner, Jetseta Gage, Dru Sjodin, Jessica Lunsford, Sarah Lunde, Amie Zyla, Christy Fornoff, Alexandra Zapp, Polly Klaas, Jimmy Ryce, Carlie Brucia, Amanda Brown, Elizabeth Smart, Molly Bish, and Samantha Runnion. Many of these named victims are well known to the public given the incredible amount of media coverage regarding their disappearances and murders. As shown, these cases have greatly influenced legislation.

Media's Influence
The media greatly influences how the public views crime. It conveys a sense of immediacy and according to Garland (2001), it forces the audience to become personally involved with the issue at hand. The media plays an important role in shaping public attitudes and impacting fear, especially regarding how much at risk children are of sexual assault and child molestation. For example, at the passing of Megan's law, there was continuous media coverage. The headlines and attention insisted that children were often not safe within their own communities. Continuing for months around the country, media coverage also caused the public to question how to control and monitor released sex offenders residing in their neighborhoods, especially those that have a history of reoffending. Interestingly, while many believed that child sexual abuse was on the rise, partially due to media exposure, victimization rates were actually declining (Jones & Finkelhor, 2001). The other most notable flaw in public opinion impacted by the media is that strangers commit most of the sex offenses. "Sexual assault committed by a stranger is a tragic but infrequent occurring event" (Wright, 2008, p.21). Media coverage focusing on stranger abductions and killings of children exaggerates this misperception.

Government Incentive
Another powerful influence on the passing of sex offender management laws comes in the form of government pressure. The Violent Crime

Control and Law Enforcement Act of 1994 did not require states to implement a sex registration or community notification system; however, it did provide the stipulation that states that did not execute these programs by September 1997 would lose 10 percent of their allotted share of crime fighting funds (Koenig, 1998; Bedarf, 1995). Not surprisingly, all 50 states established registries. Nonetheless, one major problem was that states did not receive additional financial support in order to fully implement and sustain these services. While the Adam Walsh Act also states that any jurisdiction that fails to comply with the minimum requirements within three years of enactment will lose 10 percent of its federal crime fighting funds each year that it falls short of meeting the minimum requirements, it also offers incentives to those that comply. It offers a bonus payment of a 10 percent increase in funds awarded under the Sex Offender Management Assistance (SOMA) program if the state complies within one year of enactment (Costigliacci, 2008).

Efficacy of Sex Offender Management Laws

There continues to be debate about the efficacy of the myriad of sex offender management laws. Supporters claim that these laws are effective in protecting the public through their impact on increased awareness, providing law enforcement with investigative tools for crime solving, increasing attention on the most dangerous offenders, and their deterrent effect on crime. In some cases, law enforcement officers have reported that notification engages the community in crime prevention strategies, which helps to promote public awareness and safety (Fry-Bowers, 2004). Sex offender statutes allow community members to work amongst themselves and in collaboration with law enforcement to protect their community.

On the other hand, opponents of sex offender legislation report that these statutes do more harm than good to both the offender and the public and are ineffective at protecting potential victims. Those in opposition also assert that these laws are unconstitutional. This section reviews the positions for and against legislation, including the research and theory that supports each position.

Public Protection versus Faulty Assumptions

Those in favor of the laws strongly feel that they increase safety by reducing the likelihood of victimization. In fact, federal legislators have "established the utility of Megan's Law by reference to the Megan Kanka story itself. Had the law been in place before Megan Kanka's murder, she would not have been killed" (Filler, 2001, p.342). Some feel that these statutes empower parents and community members to protect children through awareness – people can protect themselves against danger if they know where and who is likely to attack their family. Knowing who the criminals are may also help with reporting risky behavior (e.g., seeing an ex-offender spending time at a playground), which has the potential to escalate into criminal behavior (Finn, 1997, p.2). In other words, increased awareness helps community members be more vigilant. According to Hier (2008), these laws act as protective measures by providing "communities with information on sex offenders to enable them to engage in 'common sense', responsible practices of harm reduction—avoidance, surveillance, and policing of sex offenders—making risk to the community collectively calculable and governable" (p.185). Furthermore, if law enforcement can keep an eye on offenders and know where offenders are at all times via GPS systems, then the public will be safer because offenders have fewer opportunities to offend. Lastly, residency restrictions also limit the availability of targets, which results in decreased likelihood of reoffending.

However, critics dispute these benefits, reporting that these laws create a false sense of security because they are based on faulty assumptions. These include that most offenders are strangers to their victims, that sex offenders have extremely high recidivism rates, and that the information available to the public is comprehensive so that people believe they know who all the offenders are living in their neighborhoods, which is not the case.

The first concern about sex offender policy is the creation of a false sense of security. The community is often notified about sex offenders who are strangers to their victims, but in most cases, the victim knows the perpetrator. According to Quinn, Forsyth, & Mullen-Quinn (2004), "this false sense of security may actually increase risk to children to the degree that it lowers parental vigilance in monitoring the child's contacts with friends, relatives, and other trusted persons" (Quinn et al., 2004, p.216). In addition, researchers for the National

Incidence Studies of Missing, Abducted, Runaway, and Thrownaway Children (Office of Juvenile Justice and Delinquency) report that offenders abducted 150,000 children in 1999. Of these children, a family member abducted 78% and a non-family member kidnapped 22%. Of the 33,000 children abducted by non-family members, only an estimated 115 were considered the typical stranger crime associated with sex offenders (Wright, 2008, p.22). Other studies also provide supportive evidence to the claim that victims often know their offender. According to Tjaden and Thoennes (2006), results of the National Violence Against Women Survey conducted in November 2000 show that 61.9% of women raped reported the perpetrator was an intimate partner and 21.3% said the assailant was an acquaintance. Only 16.7% said a stranger victimized them. Lastly, the survey inquired about past victimization during childhood and found that of those that reported being a victim of child rape, only 15.7% of the male responders and 10.8% of the female responders said the offender was a stranger. Greenfield (1997) found similar results, reporting that 90% of child rape victims know their offenders. Wright asserts that because most victims know their assailants, one of the central assumptions of registration and notification statutes is undermined – "fear of the unknown offender" (p.21). Another important factor to consider according to Wright (2008) is that society has this image of the brutal stranger rapist, when research also indicates that rape by family members and acquaintances is often as violent (i.e. level of violence and physical injury) as stranger crimes (p.24).

A false sense of security is also derived from the idea that the information about sex offenders on the internet is comprehensive, which is not the case. Sexual offenses are significantly underreported, and those that are reported do not always end in conviction. For example, results of the 1995-1996 National Violence Against Women Survey indicated that 80.9% of rape victims did not report the crime to law enforcement (Tjaden & Thoennes, 2006). A study of college women found that less than 5% had reported the sexual attack to officials (Fisher, Cullen, & Turner, 1999). Some offenders who commit sex crimes plea-bargain down to lesser crimes and then are not required to register (Powers, 2003, p.1066). Furthermore, many offenders who are required to register abscond, particularly once their terms of probation or parole are complete (Meyer & Mohan, 1993).

Additionally, internet registries may only provide information on those classified as the most dangerous offenders. Consequently, individuals may think they are able to retrieve information on all the offenders in their community but they are only accessing information about a small percentage of high-risk offenders. For example, according to data from the Division of Criminal Justice Services, as of June 30, 2008, there were 26,402 sex offenders in the New York State registry with a risk level designation. Of these offenders, 9,873 (37.4%) were considered a. level one offender and therefore no information would be available on the online registry.

Another faulty assumption is that sex offenders have higher recidivism rates than other criminals. Community members may feel safer due to an increased awareness of sex offenders in their community, but other offenders may pose a greater risk to their safety. Sex offenders in particular invoke intense feelings and fear despite research that shows that sex offenders do not have higher recidivism rates than many other types of offenders. In 1950, the New Jersey Commission on the Habitual Sex Offender reported that the sexual recidivism rate for offenders was only seven percent and except for murder, was lower than all other serious offenses (Bedarf, 1995, p.893-894). More recently, Hanson and Morton-Bourgon (2005) conducted a meta-analysis of 82 recidivism studies that followed offenders for an average of five to six years (including 29,450 sexual offenders). They found that on average, 13.7% of offenders sexually recidivated, 14.3% engaged in violent non-sexual recidivism and 14.3% violently recidivated (including sexual and non-sexual violence), and the general (any) recidivism rate was 36.2%. This finding has continuously been supported by research (Miethe et al., 2006). For example, a 2003 report by the Bureau of Justice statistics found that of offenders released in 1994, sex offenders had the lowest reoffense rate at a three-year follow-up (43% compared to 68% of non-sexual offenders). They also found that only 3.5% of sex offenders were reconvicted of another sex crime within three years of release (Langan, Schmitt, & Durose, 2003). In another study, researchers found that some of those with the highest recidivism rates at a three-year follow-up include burglars (74.0%) and larcenists (74.6%), and those in prison for possessing, using, or selling illegal weapons (70.2%). Offenders with the lowest recidivism rates were those in prison for homicide (40.7%), rape (46.0%), and other sexual assaults (41.4%). They also found that only 2.5% of released rapists committed an additional rape within three years (Langan & Levin, 2002). Thus, if decreasing recidivism is the reason for identifying these offenders to the public, then opponents assert that there should also be statutes imposing community notification on those criminals with higher recidivism rates, such as burglars.

A third faulty assumption relates to community notification. People often believe that if they are aware of offenders living in their neighborhoods, than they will be safer. However, there are logistical problems with law enforcement notification. The actual act of community notification is often based on an arbitrary jurisdictional line (i.e. notifying immediate neighbors), so offenders may just evade offending in their immediate living area where their histories are known. For example, in Louisiana, the jurisdictional line for community notification is a one-mile radius from the offenders' residence in a rural area and a three-block radius in an urban or suburban area (Steinbock, 1995). Offenders may just offend outside of their immediate neighborhood, meaning that community notification has little practical use.

A fourth assumption relates to residency restrictions and its ability to protect the public. This legislation aimed to keep predators away from potential victims by limiting where they live. However, researchers from both the Minnesota Department of Corrections and the Colorado Department of Public Safety have found evidence to the contrary. They found that sex offenders that victimize children often choose targets outside of their neighborhoods and that "child sex offenders who recidivate are no more likely to live in close proximity to child congregation locations than offenders who do not recidivate" (Mustaine et al., 2006a, p.178). Furthermore, "recent research indicates that residence restrictions increase transience and homelessness, which may force offenders to move away from supportive environments and employment opportunities," which research shows may ultimately increase recidivism (Mercado, Alvarez, & Levenson, 2008, p.190). Lastly, in a recent study, researchers found that there these restrictions had no effect on where offenders reside. In fact, when a geospatial analysis was performed in two areas, 90-100% of offenders were dispersed within the restricted zones (Berenson & Appelbaum, 2010).

While researchers are often the ones to question sex offender policy, there have been a few legislators to speak out about its impact on creating a false sense of security and ability to protect the public. In New York, while most legislators argued that passing Megan's Law would give meaning to Megan Kanka's life and that children would be safer, Assemblywoman Glick challenged these assumptions:

> I really, in my heart of hearts, believe that we are providing a false sense of security to parents, grandparents, maybe aunts and uncles about how they can do something, they can call a number, they can get some information, and if they can somehow paint a big letter on a particular house, that will prevent somebody from harming some kid (Filler, 2001, p.342).

Effectiveness

Surprisingly, evaluations of sex offender statutes have been limited. There are only a few published studies that exist to date that examine effectiveness - four of which looked at compliance with registration and seven that looked at recidivism. The California Department of Justice was the first to evaluate whether sexual offenders were in fact registering post-incarceration. In 1988, researchers evaluated two years of data and found that in 1973, the compliance rate was 54% and in 1981, it was 72% (Matson & Lieb, 1996). In 1997 and 2006, Washington State's Institute of Public Policy studied compliance rates of released offenders. In the 1997 study, researchers found that the compliance rates were 76% in 1991 and 81% in 1996 (Matson & Lieb, 1996). The Institute engaged in a more in-depth study in 2006 and researchers found that in 1990, 5% of offenders were convicted for failing to register compared to 18% in 1999. Furthermore, those offenders that did not register were also more likely to recidivate and be convicted of a felony, violent felony, and a violent sexual felony (38.5% vs. 22.9%, 15.8% vs. 9.4% and 4.3% vs. 2.8%, respectively). Researchers can interpret this increase in percentages in two different ways. Either the increase in registration and notification laws had a negative effect and people began evading registration or the increase could be the result of more vigilant reporting and tracking. This finding has not been consistently found though. In a recent 2010 study which examined sex offender policy in South Carolina, results showed that registered sex offenders who failed to register were not more sexually dangerous than compliant registrants (Letourneau et al., 2010, p.5). In a telephone survey of 32 states, researchers found that there were very high rates of non-compliance – with California having an estimated 44% non-compliance rate and Massachusetts an estimated rate of 56% (Hannem & Petrunik, 2007). Furthermore, in one survey of all state databases, it was found that as many as 77,000 sex offenders in 32 states had not updated their addresses. In the remaining states, they found that many offenders had completely disappeared. On average, there were 24% missing sex offenders per state (Powers, 2003). Lastly, some areas across the country have conducted some smaller scale studies exploring compliance with registration requirements. For example, in a limited study of the registry in Sacramento County, researchers found that the addresses were incorrect for approximately 80 out of 100 registrants (Bedarf, 1995).

Only six studies exist to date that examine whether community notification is effective in reducing recidivism. In 1988, researchers in California conducted a 15-year follow-up study of sexual offenders who were first arrested in 1973 and found that 49% were rearrested between 1973 and 1988 and 20% of these arrests were for sexual offenses (Matson & Lieb, 1996). Researchers also interviewed 420 state agencies and found that investigators felt that registries were useful in finding sexual offenders who committed additional crimes. However, other research contradicts this finding (Bedarf, 1995).

Researchers at the Washington State Institute of Public Policy have conducted the only two studies in which the recidivism rates of released sex offenders exposed to community notification were compared to those not exposed. Results of their 1995 study showed no difference in recidivism rates for sexual offenses between the two groups. However, although the researchers found that notification did not decrease recidivism, law enforcement captured repeat sexual offenders more quickly (Schram & Milloy, 1995). The study reported that law enforcement apprehended repeat offenders within one year post-release from prison, while before the implementation of notification laws, the average apprehension time for repeat offenders was five years (Fodor, 2001). Apprehending repeat sex offenders quicker may result in fewer sexually assaulted children, which provides some support for notification statutes. In 2005, researchers at the Institute conducted another study examining recidivism rates of those subjected to registration and notification regulation compared to those not exposed and found that although felony recidivism rates did not decrease, violent felony and felony sexual convictions did significantly decrease. Although these results are promising, there is no way of knowing whether the management laws were the cause of the decline in recidivism rates (Barnoski, 2005).

Walker and colleagues (2005) examined registration and notification effects on rates of rape in 10 states. Their findings do little to answer the question of the effectiveness of management laws. Rather, they found that five of the ten states saw a decrease in the rates of rape and only three of the states show a statistically significant decrease. Of the remaining five states, all had an increase in the monthly rate of rape, with one state having a statistically significant increase. The authors concluded that registration and notification statutes "had no systematic influence on the number of rapes committed" in the 10 states examined (Walker, Maddan, Vásquez, VanHouten, & Ervin-McLarty, 2005, p.15).

In another study, Zevitz (2006) examined whether the level of notification may impact recidivism. More specifically, he examined whether extensive notification (high-level) in Wisconsin, including news media releases, posting flyers, door-to-door dissemination, and/or community meetings, had more of an impact on recidivism than low-level notification. His results show that there is no significant effect on reoffending (resentencing to prison for new crime or any violation of a condition of release) between low-and high-level notification. Of the extensive notification group, 48.9% recidivated compared to 49.3% of the limited or low-level notification group. In terms of sexual recidivism, 19% of the high-level notification group recidivated compared to 12% of the low-level notification group (Zevitz, 2006, p. 200). There was also no significant difference between groups on failure time, or time to reoffense.

In one study, Zgoba and colleagues (2008) researched the effects of Megan's Law in New Jersey and found that it had no impact on recidivism. Findings indicated that sex offense arrests were declining at a faster rate prior to the implementation of Megan's Law. Furthermore, there was no reduction in sex offender recidivism or time between release and rearrest (Zgoba, Witt, Dalessandro, & Veysey, 2008).

Finally, most recently, in a study examining the effects of South Carolina's sex offender registration and notification legislation, researchers found a significant deterrent effect when the law was first implemented with approximately 11% reduction in first-time sex crime arrests. However, they also found "no significant decline in the six year period after 1999, which was the year that South Carolina implemented its online sex offender registry, indicating that online notification did not influence general deterrence of adult sex crimes" (Letourneau et al., 2010, p.3). They also report that findings indicate no effect on deterring the risk of sexual recidivism.

In summary, the effectiveness of sex offender statutes is questionable and more research is needed. This need is critical given the alleged impact on public safety and the resources needed to implement and sustain the legal requirements stipulated in the statutes.

Investigative Tools

Proponents of sex offender supervision statutes believe that they enhance law enforcement's ability to monitor criminals living in their jurisdiction. In addition, proponents assert that if a new crime is committed, registries will assist with investigations because there is already a list of potential suspects who live in the area or who have similar crime patterns (i.e. a similar modus operandi). This suspect list saves valuable time when starting an investigation. However, because of inaccurate databases (e.g. poor data entry, lack of resources to maintain their accuracy, and non-compliant offenders), there are questions as to the effectiveness of registries as an investigative tool. According to Jacobs (2003), registries contain much inaccurate information and can become rapidly outdated. According to Bedarf (1995),

> Law enforcement personnel confirm the inadequacies of the registration program in practice. They report being overwhelmed by the volume of information, much of it outdated, that they receive through sex offender registration. The police have neither the time nor the money to check every name on the registry when attempting to solve a sex crime. Nor is the registry helpful in identifying suspects based on location or type of crime, because the list is often incomplete or inaccurate. The result is an unwieldy database with little practical utility (p.901).

Identifying and Classifying Offenders

Criminal justice entities are using risk assessment tools to determine level of risk and community notification. Systems for identifying the most dangerous offenders "can help reduce fiscal and manpower demands while allowing communities to more accurately identify those sex offenders who pose the greatest threat to public safety" (Levenson & Cotter, 2005, p.63). However, prediction of risk is difficult and often inaccurate (Steinbock, 1995). Compounding this problem is that states use various risk assessment tools so that there is no uniform way to classify the risk levels of sex offenders. The Adam Walsh Act will attempt to reduce the problems of risk assessments in that it is requiring a standard tier designation based on the crime committed. It also regulates sentencing and registration requirements based on tier level. According to the Act, this tier system includes:

- Tier I – a sex offender that is not a tier II or tier III offender. This offender must register every year for 15 years with a reduction of five years if he does not reoffend;
- Tier II - a sex offender whose offense is punishable by imprisonment for more than one year and includes offending against a minor (sex trafficking, coercion and enticement, transportation with intent to engage in criminal sexual activity, use of a minor in a sexual performance, solicitation of a minor, and production or distribution of child pornography). A tier II offender is required to register every six months for a mandatory 25 years; and
- Tier III - a sex offender whose offense is punishable by imprisonment for more than one year and includes aggravated sexual abuse or sexual abuse, abusive sexual contact against a minor who has not attained the age of 13 years, and kidnapping a minor (unless committed by a parent or guardian). This offender is required to register every three months for life with the possibility of less time depending on whether he recidivates.

While this act will attempt to create a uniform coding and rating scheme, some researchers feel that this type of assessment is not effective in determining risk. "Offense-based classification schemes, such as those described in recently passed federal legislation (Adam

Walsh Act), are unlikely to be as effective as classification systems that use empirically derived risk assessment mechanisms" (Levenson & D'Amora, 2007, p.188). Levenson and D'Amora (2007) believe that using reliable and valid risk assessment tools, such as the Static-99, will result in classifications that are more accurate. Thus, the question remains as to whether the Adam Walsh Act will result in a useful classification system that will aid in appropriate monitoring.

Theoretical Underpinnings of Sex Offender Legislation

Though most sex offender laws were not created based upon empirical research, there is a theoretical basis for such laws, In particular, registration and community notification laws are based upon the concepts of deterrence, rational choice and routine activities theories. In New York, legislators have argued that Megan's Law enhances safety because it creates fear among offenders due to an increased risk of detection (Filler, 2001). When both law enforcement and those in the community are monitoring an offender's whereabouts and actions, the offender may be more cautious and strive to refrain from behaviors that will cause criminal detention.

Other theoretical perspectives, however, counter the likely benefit of sex offender legislation; in particular, labeling, biobehavioral, strain and social disorganization theories. For example, the stress and isolation caused by legislation may actually have an adverse or paradoxical effect prompting an increase in criminal behavior.

Deterrence, Rational Choice, and Routine Activities Theories

The utilitarian principle is the basis of deterrence theory – punishment is necessary for the greater good of society. Laws and threat of punishment serve as a preventative measure against future criminal acts. The main assumptions of deterrence theory are that people have free will, are able to weight consequences (ones perception of punishment), and the ability to make rational choices to abstain from criminal behavior. Theorists believe that the perception of criminal sanctions, not necessarily objective punishment deters individuals. Human beings are believed to be hedonistic, but rational and able to discern what action(s) will benefit them (Akers, 2000).

According to Bentham and Beccaria, punishment must always fit the crime and should be severe enough only to deter future criminal acts. Severity, certainty and celerity of punishment are all fundamental principles of deterrence theory. The belief is that punishment must be severe (proportionality), certain (risk of penalty), and swift (celerity) in order to deter. For example, if the person believes that punishment for a crime is severe enough, that they are certain to be apprehended or penalized in some way, and if sanctions for the crime will be applied swiftly, then the offender will rationally calculate that more will be lost than gained from committing the crime; thus, deterring the offender.

Deterrence theory is one basis for sex offender management laws. These laws have two types of deterrent effects: general and specific. General deterrence strategies focus on preventing future crime by impacting rational decision-making processes, whereas specific deterrence approaches focus on the use of regulatory laws as a negative sanction. For example, notification statutes instill fear of punishment and shame because offenders are at greater risk of exposure to society for sexual crimes – acting as a general deterrent. Management laws (registration, notification, and GPS) also act as a specific deterrent by encouraging individuals to make a choice not to commit another crime for fear of harsh punishment. The premise is that constant supervision enhances the likelihood that the offender will be apprehended for any further crimes, as well as providing the offender with clear descriptions of what the punishment will be for additional criminal behavior. In many states, mandatory sentencing laws require harsher sentences for those committing sexual crimes, especially for habitual offenders. Thus, offenders are knowledgeable of consequences and are less likely to recidivate. Bachman, Paternoster, and Ward (1992) note that those that lack moral conviction need this type of sanctioned threat in order to refrain from criminal acts (p. 346).

Rational choice theory, which relies on the same underlying assumptions, expanded deterrence theory. Founded on the "expected utility" principle in economic theory, rational choice theorists believe that individuals consciously calculate a cost-benefit-analysis with every decision they make. These individuals then make choices that maximize profits or benefits and minimize costs or losses (Akers, 2000). In other words, individuals choose whichever behavior they feel will provide the most benefit or pleasure and the least amount of pain or punishment (Cornish & Clarke, 1986). Thus, advocates believe that the increased probability of apprehension and the severity of punishment (e.g. mandatory sentencing) given to sex offenders impacts offenders likelihood to offend.

Stemming from rational choice theory is the concept of routine activities. This approach asserts that specific elements have to be in effect in order for crime to occur, including opportunity, suitable targets, and motivated offenders (Cohen & Felson, 1994, p.536). Cohen and Felson (1994) argue that if any one of these elements is missing then criminal behavior will be prevented (p.536). According to the routine activities perspective, "the existence of guardians and guardianship structures" make it more difficult for an offender to commit a crime (Tewksbury, Mustaine, & Stengel, 2008). For example, residency restrictions, GPS monitoring and community notification affect criminal behavior by removing opportunities to reoffend, limiting access to suitable victims and empowering potential victims and their families so that they can guard themselves against possible attack.

Opponents of sex offender legislation have questioned this rationale – if offenders are motivated to offend, will management laws like residency restrictions act as a suitable guardian to prevent the offense? In addition, Bachman and colleagues (1992) have questioned rational choice theory asserting, "Little research to date has been directed at the rational nature of sexual assault, in spite of its theoretical and public policy importance" (Bachman et al., 1992, p.347).

Labeling Theory
Derived from the theory of symbolic interactionism in sociology, labeling theory claims that individuals perceive who they are, based on the perception of others. Labeling is, also known as "looking glass self," a concept originating from the works of Charles Horton Cooley in 1902. An individual becomes or acts in ways that are consistent with how those around him see him – a person's own self-concept are reflections of others' perceptions. Though intended to deter, labeling may bring forth unintended consequences; the person continues or becomes what he is labeled, a self-fulfilling prophecy. According to Akers (2000), "an ironic, unintended consequence of labeling, therefore, is that the person becomes what the sanctioning process meant to prevent, even if he or she did not set out that way" (p.122).

Supporters of sex offender legislation believe that labeling deters offenders. The concept of "naming and shaming" is based on the idea that notifying the public through registries and community notification about potential harm promotes public safety and will discourage offenders from recidivating because they are shamed. They also claim that these laws assist with reintegrative shaming, which is used to effectively communicate that the criminal behavior or act was bad or immoral, but that the offender should be welcomed back and reintegrated into law-abiding society once he has served his sentence. However, in practice, sex offender laws are based more on the concept of disintegrative shaming (McAlinden, 2005). In the name of protecting the public from the high-risk sex offender, offenders are given a "master status" to let everyone know they are dangerous. In general, the community is not willing to forgive the sex offender for his crimes as is expected in reintegrative shaming, and do not want him wandering free amongst law abiding members of society. They treat him as an outcast for fear that he will act out again and hurt their children, further isolating the offender (McAlinden, 2005, p.376). This, in fact, may have a paradoxical effect of provoking recidivism because the offender has taken on a delinquent identity. Additionally, the stigma attached to being labeled as a sex offender may result in absconding from registering or going underground to evade ostracism from the public (Sheppard, 1997).

Strain Theory

"General strain theory recognizes three types of potentially straining relationships: presentation with noxious stimuli, removal of positively valued stimuli, and blockage of achievement of valuable goals" (Botchkovar & Tittle, 2008, p.706). Once released from prison, sex offenders may have good intentions to reintegrate into society, but often find themselves experiencing one or more of these psychological strains. They are often stigmatized, isolated, and lacking support. This causes incredible levels of stress, which may exacerbate the emotional triggers associated with reoffending, including frustration, guilt, or anxiety (Zevitz, 2006, p.194). Thus, researchers, Sample and Streveler, warn that management laws may have latent consequences – offenders may find it more difficult to resist temptations and feel that they have nothing to lose by offending again (Brooks, 1996; Grubin, 1997; Jacobs, 2003; Tewksbury, 2005). Tewksbury (2005) states, "an offender may feel that his case is helpless and he will always be seen in a negative light, and thus reoffending would make little difference to him. In this last case, the chances for recidivism would be greatest" (p.60). Indeed, Zevitz (2006) states that researcher's have found that "stress and isolation experienced by sex offenders under the disclosure spotlight simply reinforces the rejection, stigma, and low self-esteem created by years of imprisonment" (p.194).

Social Disorganization

Registration, notification, and residency restriction statutes make it difficult for offenders to reintegrate back into society due to the barriers they create, thus increasing the likelihood of them failing (Zevitz & Farkas, 2000). There is evidence from various researchers who interviewed sex offenders that they feel socially stigmatized, have been evicted from their residences, have lost relationships, have been subjected to threats and harassment by community members, and that their families have experienced many problems (Levenson, D'Amora, & Hern, 2007; Tewksbury, 2006; Zevitz & Farkas, 2000). These laws have created collateral consequences, including "personal, interactional, economic, or quality of life consequences (Mustaine, Tewksbury, & Stengel, 2006b, p.332). Specifically, they prohibit individuals from finding work after release or losing jobs after it becomes known to employers through community notification that the individual is a sex offender registrant. Furthermore, in some states, the offender is required to notify property owners and the property owner is able to deny rental to the individual. Each of these cases demonstrate the difficulty these offenders have gaining stability in their lives. Interestingly, researchers studying general absconders of parole (not sex offenders) found that the strongest predictors of non-compliance were unstable living environment and frequent unemployment (Williams, McShane & Dolny, 2000). Sex offenders are often forced to move into areas that will accept them. These areas lack needed resources, such as adequate housing and employment opportunities. In one study that examined areas with high concentrations of sex offenders, researchers found that these areas had higher percentages of youth under age 19, greater racial diversity, residents with lower levels of educational attainment, higher rates of poverty and unemployment, homes with lower property values, and fewer owner occupied homes –

each of these findings is associated with areas being considered disorganized (Mustaine et al., 2006b, p.343).

This type of social disorganization has been linked with sexual offenses. For example, according to Mustaine and colleagues (2006b), researchers Baron, Strauss, and Gentry have conducted research that indicates "that higher levels of economic inequality, higher rates of unemployment, and greater degrees of urbanization in a state are all significantly related to rape rates" (p.333). Furthermore, according to McGrath (1991) who looked at sex offenders, men who cannot hold down a job or who are completely unemployed prior to their sex offense are four times more likely to be a treatment failure, also linked with recidivism. This means that the offender is not receiving treatment or the needed support to keep them on track in order to avoid the likelihood of recidivism.

Biobehavioral Theory

Biobehavioralists theorize that sex offenders are at high-risk for reoffending because they have extreme difficulty controlling their behavior or have decreased mental capacity which prohibits them from making rational choices. Sex offender civil commitment laws are grounded in biobehavioral theory. These laws support the belief that not all offenders can voluntarily control their behavior and therefore need confinement for the purposes of treatment. For example, the Adam Walsh Act mandates that jurisdictions establish, enhance, or operate effective civil commitment programs for sexually dangerous offenders. The definition of sexually dangerous person is "a person suffering from a serious mental illness, abnormality, or disorder, as a result of which the individual would have serious difficulty in refraining from sexually violent conduct or child molestation." This act applies to any person convicted of a sexually violent offense or any person deemed by the state to be at high-risk of sexual recidivism against a minor.

Constitutional Challenges

Sex offender management statues have been legally challenged on the grounds that they impose continued punishment after the sex offender has served his sentence. Such punishment would violate the constitutional rights of offenders, including ex post facto clause, double jeopardy (Fifth amendment), cruel and unusual punishment (Eight amendment), and due process (Fourteenth amendment).

Ex Post Facto Clause
Sex offender registration and notification statutes have been challenged according to the Ex Post Facto Clause of the Constitution (Article 1: Section 9). The Ex Post Facto Clause states that laws cannot be applied retroactively if they cause greater punishment than the sentence that was affixed to the original crime (Cullop, 1999). In other words, a legislature cannot increase the penalty on an offender after he has committed a crime (Filler, 2001). Sex offenders have been required to register retroactively even though this stipulation was not part of the original sentence imposed upon them. Eight states require registration for covered convictions prior to 1980. For example, both Hawaii and Mississippi mandate registration for all those convicted of a covered offense, independent of the date of conviction. An additional argument made is whether releasing information to the public about an offenders release inflicts retroactive punishment (Koenig, 1998). Is the "scarlet letter" that community notification imposes on the offender punitive?

The issue of whether these laws inflict retroactive punishment in violation of the Ex Post Facto Clause was brought before the Supreme Court in the Alaska case of *Smith v. Doe*, 538 U.S. 84 (2003). In this case, two offenders convicted of an aggravated sex offense claimed they had already completed their sentence for committing a sexual offense before Megan's Law was enacted; consequently, they believed they should not be required to register. The Court's objective in this case was to determine whether the intention of the legislature was to impose punishment on the offender. The justices held that the intention of the statute was "to create a civil, nonpunitive regime." In regards to the challenge that this law stigmatized the offender and therefore should be considered punishment was also dismissed. The court stated that past techniques:

> Either held the person up before his fellow citizens for face-to-face shaming or expelled him from the community. By contrast, the stigma of Alaska's Megan's Law results not from public display for ridicule and shaming but from the dissemination of accurate information about a criminal record,

most of which is already public (*Smith v. Doe*, 538 U.S. 84, 2003).

The Court also found the statute nonpunitive because the requirement to register is based upon the offender's classification of "sex offender," not on any individual traits. According to Fry-Bowers (2004), the sex offender statute was deemed to have a civil and administrative function and was not a method of punishment, especially given that the implementation of the statute was left up to the Alaska Department of Public Safety. The offender could also move around and change employment. Thus, because there was no direct restraining of the offenders activities, the statute was considered non-punitive.

In the landmark case of *Doe v. Pataki*, 940 F. Supp. 603 (S.D.N.Y. 1996), the U.S. District Court for the Southern District of New York held that the process of community notification violated the Ex Post Facto Clause for offenders that committed their crime prior to the date the law became effective. However, this decision was overturned by the Second Circuit who held that the law did not constitute punishment (*Doe v. Pataki*, 120 F.3d 1263 2d Cir. [1997]). The Second Court made this decision based on two factors, intent and that the sanctions imposed were not punitive and thus, not criminal. The court held, much like the majority of state and federal courts, that registries are regulatory, not punitive.

Double Jeopardy

Sex offenders subject to registration and notification have argued that this legislation punishes defendants twice for the same crime, which the constitution prohibits under the Fifth Amendment. For example, opponents argue that Megan's Law punishes sex offenders through registration requirements, which subjects them to possible ridicule, ostracism, and discrimination. Furthermore, because registries provide information to the public via the internet, offender's information is often available to everyone without restriction, regardless of whether the person is likely to encounter the sex offender. Despite these arguments, in *Smith v. Doe*, 538 U.S. 84 (2003), the court affirmed that registration intends to protect the public, not punish sex offenders. It is regulatory and in the public's best interest. A New York case illustrates a similar example, where the defendant claimed that the new conditions of parole imposed upon him, in addition to needing to comply with registration and notification requirements violated the double jeopardy clause. Again, the court held that there was no violation of the petitioner's rights and that provisions of the Sex Offender Registration Act do not constitute punishment (*M.G. v. Travis*, 236 A.D.2d 163 (1997).

Cruel and Unusual Punishment

Sex offenders have argued that community notification brands or negatively labels an individual causing cruel and unusual punishment in violation of the Eight Amendment. The main argument in these cases is that subjection to community notification and all its negative effects (e.g. vigilantism or invasion of privacy) constitutes additional punishment that lasts longer than the original punishment imposed by the courts (Eyssen, 2001, p.118). There is evidence that notification promotes vigilantism, therefore, causing cruel and unusual punishment (Koenig, 1998; Eyssen, 2001). "Community notification, and the vigilantism it provokes, wrongfully creates an additional form of punishment that tests the threshold of the Cruel and Unusual Punishment Clause of the Constitution" (Eyssen, 2001, p.135). Nonetheless, despite cases of vigilantism, in most rulings the courts have decided that community notification is not punitive, but regulatory and thus, does not constitute cruel and unusual punishment. For example, the New Jersey Supreme Court did not recognize that vigilantism would add excessively to the punitiveness of these statutes (Brooks, 1996). The court felt that law enforcement and laws, which severely punish individuals who behave in this manner, could control vigilantism. (*Doe v. Poritz*, 142 N.J. 1 [1995], *Artway v. Attorney General*, 81 F. 3d 1235, 3d Cir. [1996]).

Due Process

The Fourteenth Amendment specifies equality under the law. Under this amendment, all individuals are entitled to due process rights, meaning that the government is prohibited from depriving individuals of "life, liberty or property," without due process of law. In regards to the Fourteenth Amendment, an argument exists that registration and community notification laws deprive offenders of their rights by labeling them as criminals after they have served their sentence and therefore is a form of punishment.

In *Connecticut Department of Public Safety, v. Doe*, 538 U.S. 1 (2003) the defendant contended that Megan's Law violated his Fourteenth Amendment right to due process. The offender stated that he was no longer a danger to society and thus his designation as a violent offender was false. He also claimed that the requirements imposed upon him were burdensome. The District Court agreed with the plaintiff's due process claim, which ultimately resulted in the shutdown of the Departments sex offender website. A second hearing by the Second Circuit also resulted in justices affirming the ruling. The Court concluded that there was a violation of the sex offender's liberty and that registration violated the Due Process Clause of the Constitution because there was no hearing to determine whether the offender was currently dangerous.

The finding in this case relied on precedent set by the U.S. Supreme Court case, *Paul v. Davis* , 424 U.S. 693 (1976). In this case, an individual, having been arrested for shoplifting, had his picture included in police flyers that were disseminated to merchants. All charges were eventually dismissed, but only after the flyers were already distributed. From this case evolved the "Stigma Plus" test. The Court's decision that harm to a person's reputation alone, "apart from some more tangible interests such as employment, was neither "liberty" nor "property" by itself sufficient" to find that the defendant's right to procedural due process was violated (p.1). The person must demonstrate that he was wronged in two ways, defamation of character was insufficient. However, it was found in *Paul v. Davis*, 424 U.S. 693 (1976) that the burdensome task of registration was sufficient to comprise the plus portion of the test. Kabat (1998) believed that this case could be significant with regard to its implication for sex offenders. Most significant could be that even accused offenders, not yet found guilty could be subjected to community notification. This has yet to be the case, but an interesting argument.

This test has consistently been used by lower courts in deciding whether or not registration and notification statutes are unconstitutional. In *Connecticut Department of Public Safety v. Doe*, 271 F.3d 38 (2001), the offender stated that he was no longer a danger to society and thus, his designation of a violent offender was false. Furthermore, the requirements imposed upon the offender were burdensome and thus, were sufficient to comprise the plus portion of the test. While originally upheld as unconstitutional, in 2003, when the case of *Connecticut Department of Public Safety, v. Doe*, 538 U.S. 1 (2003) was heard by U.S. Supreme Court, officials neglected to use the stigma plus test and overturned the lower courts ruling. The Court concluded that, "mere injury to reputation, even if defamatory, does not constitute the deprivation of a liberty interest." The Court found that there had been no violation because the offender had a trial and was convicted, thus providing him due process. The Court also implied that even if a violation to the offender's right to liberty had occurred, that it would be immaterial to the case because dangerousness was not based on current level, but determined according to the offender's conviction. Thus, the Court ruled only on procedural due process, and allowed for the possibility of a challenge to substantive due process at a later time. Substantive due process concerns an individual's "right to privacy, right to employment, right to personal security, the right to travel, and the right to housing and family relations" (Blair, 2004, p.955). However, if a governmental agency can demonstrate a compelling need for the law, then under strict scrutiny review, the law would be constitutional. This is often where the challenges fall short because states explain that there is a fundamental safety issue at hand when releasing information on these offenders and that there is an interest in public safety and crime prevention.

In regards to whether these statutes invade a person's right to privacy, one of the first questions is whether offenders have the same protections under the law as other individuals. Some argue that once a person engages in a criminal act that is public knowledge, his entitlement to privacy rights is lessened, even if he has already received punishment. The second question is whether a person's right to privacy is violated because of the way the information is packaged. A person's offender status is publicly known at the time of his crime and sentencing, but after he has served his sentence, his personal information coupled with offender status continues to be broadcasted to the public via community notification, diminishing his ability to gain stability in his life and thus, constitutes ongoing punishment.

In 1995, in *Doe v. Poritz*, 662 A. 2d 367 (1995), the defendant asserted that his privacy right's were violated by disseminating his personal information to the public. The court found that sharing information, such as arrest record, name, age, and place of employment was not a violation of privacy because the information was within the public domain and not confidential. The Court further explained that the state had a vested interest in protecting the public which outweighed the privacy interests of the sex offender. However, the court did acknowledge the fact that when a government agency assembles information into one document and then disseminates it, a privacy issue is at hand. That being said, in order for a person's rights to be violated, the person must demonstrate a direct link between the statutes requirements and the outcome or violation of rights. Thus far, courts have found that because the information is public, this link can not be demonstrated. For example, in the case of *Illinois v. Logan* (705 N.E.2d 152, 161) (Ill. App. Ct. 1998) the court found that, "any attendant consequences, such as embarrassment or ridicule, are caused by the offender's status as a felon and not the direct result of the notification" (Blair, 2004, p.965).

One last example of a due process challenge is illustrated in the case *Doe v. Pataki*, 3 F.Supp.2d 456 S.D.N.Y. (1998). In this case, the plaintiffs asserted that administratively assigning a risk level designation deprived them of due process. According to the Court, due process requires that individuals receive a hearing before receiving a risk level classification. This includes providing them the recommended presumptive classification, pre-hearing discovery, and counsel before proceedings begin. Thus, the courts motion was that it is unconstitutional to classify offenders as anything higher than a level one until the court reclassifies them after proceedings that satisfy the requirements of due process.

Examples of Non-constitutional Challenges:
Risk Level. Sex offender risk assessments are a common tool for evaluating a person's risk for recidivism. Researchers and practitioners use risk assessments to decide whether a person has made progress in treatment and for determining the likelihood of reoffending (See Chapter Four). The court system and other criminal justice entities routinely use risk assessments to determine recidivism risk and level of community notification. According to Levenson and Cotter (2005), about half of all states use a three-tiered system to assign risk and decide how and who to notify according to the risk the offender poses to the community (p.50). The information used to establish risk level also varies by state. For example, in New York, each offender is assessed by the Board of Examiners to ascertain his risk level with the

higher number of points indicating higher risk. The Board determines risk level using the following information: the use of force, weapons, use of alcohol or drugs, the victim's age, number of victims, the level of assault or injury to the victim, and relationship to the victim. This assessment tool is used to provide the court with the offenders risk level, level one (low), level two (moderate) and level three (high). However, there are cases that automatically result in a level three designation. These include: (1) the offender having a prior felony conviction for a sex offense; (2) the offender causing serious injury or death to the victim; (3) the offender having threatened to reoffend; or (4) the offender having been assessed as having a psychological, physical, or organic abnormality that decreases his ability to control his behavior (New York County District Attorney Report, 2003).

Although the Board of Examiners uses this tool as the basis for their recommendation to the court during the risk level assessment hearing, there may be departures from the risk level when aggravating or mitigating factors exist and are not taken into account by the tool. The reasoning of the court has been that in the majority of cases, the use of the instrument has provided the proper classification and that departure will be the exception, not the rule (*People v. Guaman*, 8 A.D.3d 545 (2004). In *New York State Board of Examiners of Sex Offenders v. Ransom*, 249 A.D.2d 891 (1998), the Court held that the sentencing court is not bound by the Boards recommendation. The court may use all records to determine the appropriate risk designation. This is also true at risk assessment hearings (*People v. Davis*, NY Slip Op 1150 [2006]).

The Court has also held that there is no statutory time limitation on the criminal history evidence used to assess risk. In the case of *People v. Victor R.*, 186 Misc. 2d 28 (2000), the Supreme Court of New York (Bronx County) used a conviction that occurred 13 years prior to the risk assessment hearing in making a risk level decision. This issue of using past crimes to impact risk level should be less relevant given the Adam Walsh Act, which requires the use of current crime only to assess risk and tier level. However, because only the immediate conviction is used, other appeals may emerge. For example, another concern might be that tier level is not a true indicator of risk for recidivism because it is based on a single variable, the crime for which the person was convicted and no other risk or protective factors.

Furthermore, there is no process for removing oneself from the registry because of a lack of dangerousness or being at low risk of recidivism (Baron-Evans, 2008).

Homeless offenders. Another concern when requiring offenders to register with a current address is that a person may be homeless. In New York, one of the risk assessment questions used to assign risk pertains to adequate housing. In *People v. Ruddy*, NY Slip Op 5607 (2006), the defendant was assigned 10 points for inappropriate housing, which meant he was a level two offender. However, the Court reversed the order because "the evidence presented at the hearing showed that, at the most, the defendant's living situation was uncertain in that he may have been homeless, or was living in a "sober house" in Long Island. This was insufficient as a matter of law to meet the burden of showing, by clear and convincing evidence, that the defendant's living situation was inappropriate." While the Court held that being homeless does not constitute an inappropriate living situation impacting risk, research findings would disagree (Williams et al., 2000). This issue of homelessness may become even more of a problem in that community notification and residency restrictions cause displacement and limits where a person can live.

Juveniles. In New York, the court system has repeatedly upheld that it is permissible to use an offender's youthful offender status when determining risk level (*People v. Irving*, 2007 NY Slip Op 8634, [2007]). In *People v. Pietarniello*, NY Slip Op 6141 (2008), the Court stated, "the offender's age at the commission of his first sex crime, which includes his age at the time of the commission of the instant offense, is a factor associated with recidivism: those who offend at a young age are more prone to reoffend" (p.476-477).

A separate issue involving juvenile offenders and affecting all state legislation may emerge from the requirements set forth by the Adam Walsh Act. Although there have not been any challenges to date, this Act requires that any offender over the age of 14 found guilty of aggravated sexual abuse or sexual abuse be labeled as a Tier III offender. According to Enniss (2008), "in defining juvenile delinquent adjudication as offenses involving aggravated sexual abuse, the Adam Walsh Act unequivocally places juvenile sex-offenders into the third, most severe tier" (p.703-704). Thus, "the fourteen-year-old boy adjudicated delinquent of an attempted sexual act remains on the registry for life" (Baron-Evans, 2008). This undermines and contradicts the underlying presumption that juveniles can be rehabilitated (Trivits & Reppucci, 2002; Zimring, 2004).

In summary, sex offender management laws have been in effect for over 60 years and continue to be supported today as demonstrated by the recent passing of global positioning system surveillance and residency restrictions statutes. As demonstrated from this overview of sex offender management laws, these statutes are highly controversial and the debate of whether these laws promote public safety continues. Although advocates and opponents dispute these laws on many counts, new legislation continues to pass (e.g., the Adam Walsh Act enacted in 2006). While many legislators and community members believe that these laws keep people safe, their true efficacy remains a question. Moreover, because of the possible latent and unintended consequences, the need for additional research is great. Of particular concern is that the belief systems or theory these laws are predicated on may be faulty. Rather, do these laws act as a deterrent, resulting in a decrease in crime by creating safer environments for children and families or actually increase crime due to labeling. Lastly, there is also a concern and debate as to whether these laws are primarily strategies for public safety or punishment and as such, violate individuals' rights. As of now, the true effect of these crime control strategies is not obvious. While research thus far has not shown promising results in their ability to reduce recidivism, research has been limited. Thus, given the potential impact these management laws could have, either positive or negative, it is apparent that much more research is needed.

CHAPTER 6

An Intensive Supervision Program

Sexual violence affects hundreds of thousands of individuals every year in the United States. Managing the perpetrators of these attacks, especially repeat sex offenders, is a challenging problem for the criminal justice system. Once these individuals are no longer incarcerated, it is difficult to monitor their actions. To assist in combating this challenge, the government has passed legislation that sets up a system to supervise offenders in the hopes of deterring any further criminal behavior.

Although national legislation and monitoring systems have been in effect for more than 12 years, there remains an absence of research evaluating sex offender management laws and factors associated with absconding from registration. Understanding the probability of non-compliance and the risk factors associated with it will assist in distinguishing likely offenders. There is also very limited research examining whether these laws are impacting general recidivism or specific types of recidivism, in particular violent or sexual recidivism and those that have completed research show no effect on recidivism (Zgoba et al., 2008). Thus, given the dearth of research in this area, the author conducted an evaluation examining an intensive supervision program and its impact on recidivism. This program was specifically designed to provide intensive supervision to the most dangerous sex offenders residing in New York City.

Program Description

First initiated in July 2003, the program required the establishment of a partnership between many criminal justice agencies to coordinate efforts, increase communication, increase information sharing and improve the tracking of high-risk sex offenders. Targeted efforts have focused on offenders that are categorized as high-risk based on specific criteria, including being classified as a level three offender and having at least one other risk factor making them more likely to reoffend. These risk factors include, but are not limited to offending against a stranger or multiple victims, having a felony conviction history, or committing violent offenses causing serious injury or death against vulnerable victims, such as a child or the physically or mentally handicapped.

In an effort to deter reoffending by these high-risk offenders, the program utilizes a multi-departmental cooperative effort to meet and exceed the legislative requirements imposed by Megan's law. The participating agencies/departments include:

- New York City Criminal Justice Coordinator;
- District Attorney's Offices;
- New York Police Department's Sex Offender Monitoring Unit;
- Administration for Children's Services;
- Division of Criminal Justice Services;
- Office of Court Administration;
- Department of Probation; and
- Division of Parole

The primary goal of the program is to have everyone working together to respond early and quickly when an offender violates Megan's Law or fails to abide by the conditions of probation or parole. In order to do this, Probation, Parole and the New York City Police Department's Sex Offender Monitoring Unit each have a role in providing intensive supervision to offenders within the program, meaning that these agencies make sure that timely annual verifications, address changes, and 90-day visits are completed. In addition, these agencies are responsible for following up and making sure that all level three offenders have verified their address in person every 90-days. If an offender does not register according to requirements set forth in Megan's Law, he is guilty of a class "D" felony.

The specific components of the program are intensive supervision, enhanced prosecution, and improved information sharing. Changes to supervision in the areas of probation and parole include, but are not limited to increased face-to-face contacts per month, curfew enforcement, expedited warrant procedures, and maximum sentences sought for violations. In the area of enhanced prosecution, examples of strategies include, specifically designated Assistant District Attorneys, citywide training to ensure uniformity of prosecution, and a judge designated to hear all program cases. Lastly, in the area of improved information sharing, on a daily basis the Division of Criminal Justice Services notifies the Sex Offender Monitoring Unit of any sexual offender that was arrested the prior day through an Executive Daily Detail Status Report. This report provides information on arresting agency, date, New York State Identification (NYSID) number, offender demographics, and arrest charge. The Monitoring Unit then compares the NYSID numbers of those arrested with those being monitored by the program. Law enforcement then arrests those offenders who have not complied with registration (i.e. known fugitives) and checks the offender's address given at the time of arrest through The New York City Criminal Justice Agency (CJA). This affords law enforcement an opportunity to verify that the address on file is the same address given at time of arrest. Finally, the Administration for Children's Services (ACS) cross-checks all names and addresses of offenders within the program to ensure that offenders are not living with foster children or other children known to ACS.

Each of these features is designed to increase the likelihood of detecting Megan's Law violators. As a result, it is believed that the criminal justice system will rearrest and reconvict more offenders, which will reduce sexual recidivism. Past research conducted by the New York City Criminal Justice Coordinator's office indicated that the intensive tracking mechanism within the program had led to an increase in both arrest rates and incarceration rates of those who were noncompliant with registration. However, there was no research whether the program had an effect on recidivism rates.

Evaluation

At this point in time, to the researchers knowledge, there has not been any evaluations of whether a surveillance program like this one has any effect on reducing crime. This is critically important given the number of intensive supervision policies being implemented today and the resources devoted to those polices. Because this is a new area of study, this research is groundbreaking and can help inform future policy.

To fully understand the impact this program has had on sex offender recidivism, it is imperative that a baseline examination of recidivism be conducted. This is a critical component of any program evaluation model and is necessary to understanding long-term impacts. Thus, this study provides information regarding whether the program monitored all offenders as designed, what recidivism rates were for those offenders in the program compared to non-participant offenders, and the impact offender characteristics and risk factors have had on recidivism, including general, non-compliance, violent, and sexual recidivism.

Research Questions and Hypotheses
The specific research questions and hypotheses addressed include:

Question 1: Has the program. accomplished its goal of monitoring all high-risk offenders?
Hypothesis 1: If a level three offender meets inclusion criteria (independent variable), then the program will monitor him (dependent variable).

Question 2: Do participating offenders have lower rates of reoffending than non-participants?
Hypothesis 2: Offenders monitored by the program (independent variable) will have significantly lower recidivism rates (dependent variable) than non-participants.

Question 3: How many participating offenders have recidivated thus far and for what types of crimes?

Hypothesis 3: If an offender recidivates, then the likelihood of the arrest being for non-compliance will be higher than for violent or sexual recidivism.

Question 4: Are there characteristics that differentiate participating offenders who recidivate from those who do not?

Hypothesis 4: Among participating offenders, general recidivism (dependent variable), will have a significant relationship to and be predicted by various demographic characteristics (independent variables).

Question 5: Can type of recidivistic behavior be predicted by risk factors among participating offenders?

Hypothesis 5: Specific risk factors (independent variables) will be significantly correlated with and predictive of the type of recidivism (dependent variables) among participating offenders.

Question 6: Do violent recidivism rates among offenders monitored by the program vary by sex offender type?

Hypothesis 6: There will be a significant relationship between the type of sexual offender (independent variable) and violent recidivism (dependent variable).

Question 7: Are those offenders that are non-compliant with registration more likely to recidivate?

Hypothesis 7: Among participating offenders, non-compliance recidivism (dependent variable) will be significantly related to general recidivism (independent variable).

Question 8: Are those participating offenders that are non-compliant with registration more likely to commit dangerous or violent crimes than those who are compliant?

Hypothesis 8: Non-compliant participating offenders (independent variable) will commit more violent and/or sexual offenses at time of relapse (dependent variable) than those that are compliant.

Question 9: Among participating offenders that sexually recidivate, is there a difference in length of time to relapse event by type of offender?

Hypothesis 9: Among participating offenders that sexually recidivate, rapists (independent variable) will have a shorter time to relapse (dependent variable) than child molesters (independent variable).

Defining Variables

Due to problems associated with studying recidivism, particularly that it is difficult to correctly interpret and compare findings between studies because researchers operationalize terms differently, it is imperative to specify the concepts that the researcher studied and how the variables were defined and measured when addressing the aforementioned questions and hypotheses.

Sexual Offense (N.Y. Corrections Law Section § 168-a). This state statute defines sexual offenses and other crimes. Some examples include rape, sodomy, sexual misconduct, sexual abuse, aggravated sexual abuse, crimes involving the promotion of sexual performances by a child, kidnapping offenses, and crimes involving prostitution (patronizing a person younger than 18). (See Appendix).

Units of Analysis. This research utilized New York State's sex offender database and the program database to examine individual sex offender information. The individual information collected included all available descriptive data needed to determine recidivism and compliance rates and offender characteristics.

Demographic Information and Criminal History. Variables explored included the following: general demographic information (e.g., date of birth, gender, race/ethnicity), risk level, criminal history information (e.g., date of arrest, type and number of offenses, use of force, sentence length, arresting agency information), and victim information (e.g., number of victims, gender, age).

Risk Levels. In New York State, sex offenders are assessed and given a risk level (one through three), which designates their likelihood of reoffense. These risk assessments are determined upon conviction or prior to release. The data used to make these decisions are the seriousness of the offense, history of offenses, and characteristics of the offender (Tier and Coy, 1997). Level one offenders are considered at low risk to reoffend once released. Information on these offenders is regularly shared only with law enforcement personnel. Offenders rated as moderate risk to reoffend are designated as level two offenders and those who are at a very high risk to reoffend are placed in the third level. In New York, both level two and level three-offender information is disseminated to the public via the internet.

High Risk (level three) Offender. To be included in the program., most individuals are registered level three[3] sex offenders and fall into one of the following categories: (a) victimized a stranger or if the relationship was established for the primary purpose of victimization; (b) has a felony conviction other than the registry offense or has a misdemeanor sex crime conviction; (c) killed or caused serious physical harm to his victim; (d) threatened to reoffend; (e) victimized someone 12 years old or under, 63 years or older, or someone that was physically helpless or mental handicapped; or (f) had two or more victims.

Compliance. Compliant sex offenders are those who registered as mandated, and non-compliant sex offenders are defined as those arrested for failing to register. The criminal justice system interprets an offender's compliance with registration on an individual basis. For example, if an offender is required to register every 90 days and does not do so, he is considered non-compliant and subject to arrest. As a matter of law, all individuals must register within 24 hours of release from prison, detention center, or agency. Any sex offender who moves into the state must register within 30 days of establishing residency and if a sex offender moves out of the state, he is required to send registry information back to New York within 10 days of establishing his new place of residence. Periodic registration is also required depending on

---

[3] If the offender is not a level three, he must meet one of the level three-override criteria (i.e. offenders with a misdemeanor conviction or youth offender adjudication for a sexual crime; those that caused serious physical injury or death during the commission of the crime, and/or recent threat of re-offending)

risk level and offense history. This period ranges from 10 years to lifetime registration.

Recidivism. To measure recidivism, there must be a specified follow-up period, meaning that the program monitored each person for the same amount of time. This is important because the program staff may have monitored one person for three months and another person for two years. This time difference in monitoring would skew results when looking at effectiveness and opportunity to recidivate. This study included only those participating offenders that had a two-year follow-up period. The researcher chose this time frame due to the date the program was implemented (July 2003) and the date that data was requested (July 2005). In addition to time frame, recidivism was defined as having an arrest for any crime. More specifically, recidivism was defined as an: (1) arrest for any new offense (general recidivism), (2) arrest for a violent felony crime (violent recidivism), (3) arrest for a new sexual crime (sexual recidivism), or (4) arrest for failing to register as required by statute (non-compliance recidivism).

Sample
The sample comprises all New York State registered program participants and non-participating sex offenders residing within the New York City jurisdiction as of July 2005. All offenders had been convicted of a sexual crime between January 1996 and July 2005. Information on participating offenders (n=775) was obtained from the Criminal Justice Coordinator's Office and provided to the New York State Division of Criminal Justice Services (DCJS). DCJS then created a link with other databases that contained information on criminal history, sex offenses, and data regarding the victims involved in the registerable offense. While linking these databases the researcher found that there were 14 participating offenders that had invalid identification numbers and an additional 17 offenders that were not in the New York State sex offender registry database. The researcher sent this information back to the Criminal Justice Coordinator's Office, but the office could not correct the data. As a result, there were 744 usable records for the sample of participating offenders. These 744 offenders were then combined with all other non-participating registrants (n=4886) to yield a sample of 5,630 sex offenders.

Figure 1: Sample Breakdown

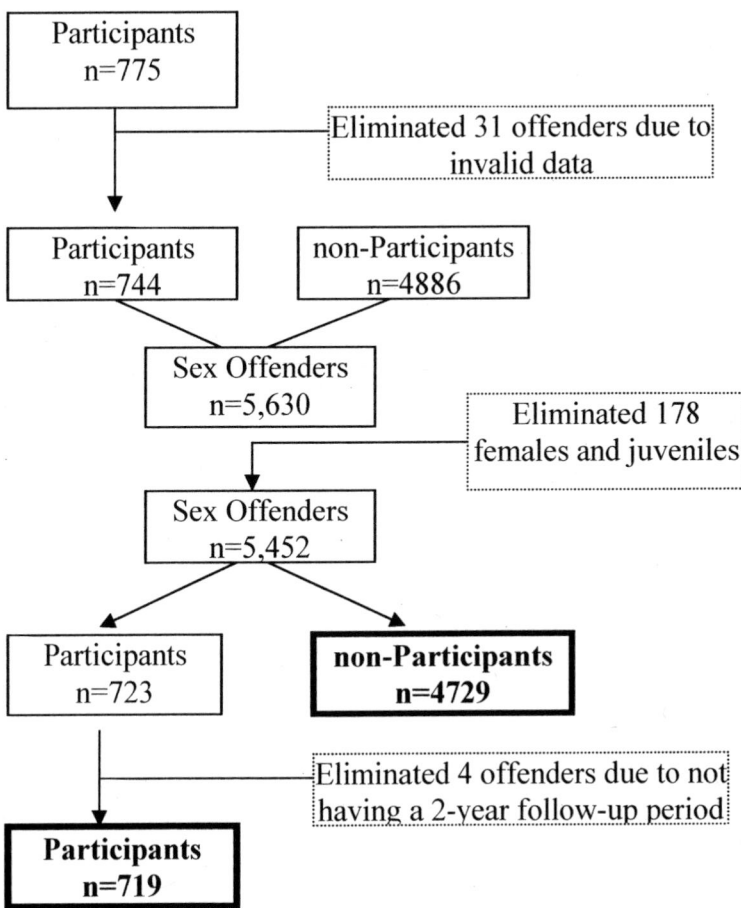

This total sample included males and females, as well as adult and juvenile offenders. The researcher used this entire sample of sex offenders to address the first hypothesis of whether or not the program was monitoring all offenders that fit the criteria for inclusion in the program. The researcher analyzed a slightly smaller sample in an effort to address hypotheses two through nine. More specifically, because prior research suggests that researchers analyze female and juvenile sex offender populations separately and because there was a smaller number of females (1.5% or 80 offenders) and juvenile offenders (1.7% or 98 offenders), these offenders were not included in the overall analyses. To be certain, analyses were conducted to examine their exclusion and no significant differences were found. After eliminating juvenile and female offenders, there were 5,452 offenders, including 723 participating offenders.

To answer hypotheses two through nine, which explore risk factors and recidivism in more depth, only those participating offenders that were monitored by the program for at least two years were examined, leaving a sample of 719 offenders (Figure 1). Having a standardized two-year follow-up period allowed for fair comparisons of recidivism.

Procedure and Data Collection
Data provided by the Criminal Justice Coordinators Office contained New York State Identification (NYSID) numbers. The researcher provided these identification numbers along with registry information on the sex offenders monitored by the program to DCJS. In turn, DCJS provided new unique identifiers that could not be linked with specific sex offenders. This was a method of insuring confidentiality and protection to offenders and their victims. DCJS then provided the researcher with three additional databases, including an offender criminal justice history database, a sex offender registry database, and a victim database. The information requested included the following:

- Risk Level
- Date of arrest
- Birth date
- Marital status
- Race/ethnicity
- Gender
- Criminal history
- Sex offense registration charge
- Treatment Disposition
- Sentence Length
- Number of victims
- Offender relationship to the victim
- Victim age

- Victim gender
- Arresting agency and address of agency

For the entire sample of offenders, the researcher requested criminal justice histories from 1975 through July 2005. This data was collected in order to link criminal history with risk of recidivism (Abel et al., 1988; Barbaree & Marshall, 1988; Dempster & Hart, 2002; Escarela et al., 2000; Hanson & Bussière, 1996 and 1998; Kunselman & Vito, 2002; Långström & Grann, 2000; Prentky & Burgess, 2000; Prentky et al., 1997; Rasmussen, 1999; Scalora & Garbin, 2003). A persons' criminal history included both sealed and unsealed events in order to provide a complete look at historical events over time both prior to and subsequent to the conviction that required his registration. The researcher received data on all offenders who were convicted of a sexual offense and have been required to register by law (See Appendix).[4] Although DCJS staff may be aware of out-of-state criminal histories, which they can run using the Interstate Identification Index administered by the Federal Bureau of Investigation, they do not incorporate this information into their databases. Thus, out-of-state criminal histories were not tracked and therefore missing from the dataset used for this research project. Once these three databases were merged, data was coded and entered into the Statistical Package for the Social Sciences (SPSS) and password protected (Table 9). This ensured confidentiality of all received data.

Data Analysis (See Table 10)
The first step to data analysis involved a basic exploratory examination of the quantity of missing data. At this point, some variables and cases

---

[4] A person given *Youthful Offender* adjudication for a sex offense charge is not subject to the registration requirements since any conviction set aside pursuant to law is not a conviction for purposes of the Sex Offender Registration Act. Juvenile offenders who have been granted *Youthful Offender* status, or who have had their cases removed to family court, have their records of that case sealed and are not subject to the registration and notification requirements of the Sex Offender Registration Act. However, a juvenile offender tried and convicted in adult court would be subject to the registration and notification requirements and were included in the dataset.

had to be eliminated due to omitted data. This included those offenders without a criminal justice history (n=200), as well as the variable victim-offender relationship (missing in 82.3% of program cases). Once the database was in final form, the researcher used several methods of analyses, including cross-tabulations, bivariate correlations, and binary logistic regression.

First, the researcher conducted descriptive analyses. Using cross-tabulations, the frequencies and similarities and differences among demographic and predictor variables were examined across all three sub-samples [(1) all offenders, (2) participating offenders, and (3) non-participating offenders)].

The second form of analyses included bivariate correlations using the chi-square (χ^2) statistic for nominal and dichotomous variables. Examples of these variables include age of the registrant, race/ethnicity, victim characteristics, and risk level. This method was used to measure the significance of the relationships between demographic/predictor variables and recidivism. According to Bachman and Paternoster (1997), the first step in testing a hypothesis is to select an alpha level and obtain the corresponding critical chi-square value using the degrees of freedom (p.306). For example, if the hypothesis to be tested is that age of the registrant and recidivism is not related, the first step is to choose an alpha level. If the chosen level is .05 and a 5 x 2 table is generated, then the degrees of freedom is equal to 4 [(5 - 1) (2-1)] and the critical value is 9.488. If the obtained correlation between age of the registrant and recidivism is $\chi^2 = 14.268$, which is greater than the critical value, then a significant relationship between age and recidivism would be reported and the hypothesis would be rejected.

Next, for the ratio-level variables, independent samples t-tests were conducted to examine the relationships between demographic/predictor variables and recidivism. According to Bachman and Paternoster (1997), when using t-tests, an alpha level and critical value must be determined. The next step is to calculate the test statistic and compare it to the critical value. For example, if the null hypothesis to be tested is that there is no difference between the two means of participating and non-participating offenders in regards to the number of past felony convictions (the means are equal), the first step is to choose an alpha level. If the chosen level is .05 and there are 830 individuals included then the degrees of freedom is equal to 829. The next step is to consider whether the researcher has an idea about the relationship. If she does, then a one-tailed test is chosen. This yields a critical value of *t* equal to 1.645 (t_{crit}=1.645). The value of *t* obtained from the analysis must be equal to or greater than 1.645, or equal to or less than 1.645. If the obtained *t* value is equal to -11.900 (-1.645 < t_{obs}< 1.645) then the means between participating and non-participating offenders in relation to number of past felonies are not equal. Thus, the researcher would fail to reject the null hypothesis. For the purposes of this study, the researcher explored the relationship between each independent variable and recidivism using SPSS, which yielded significance levels and chi-square and t-test results.

The final type of analyses was binary logistic regression. The researcher used the variables that had research to support their inclusion. Regression was an appropriate methodology because there were dichotomous dependent variables (recidivism= Yes or No) and categorical and continuous variables as predictors. The analysis provided an estimated logistic regression coefficient for each independent variable, the standard error of the coefficient, a Wald test for the significance of the estimated partial slope coefficient (*b*), the significance level of the test statistic, and measures of the models goodness of fit (Bachman & Paternoster, 1997, p.573). The Wald test for the significance level has various degrees of freedom dependent on the independent variable – continuous variables have degrees of freedom equaling one, while categorical variables have k-1 degrees of freedom. Thus, the categorical variable level of risk has two degrees of freedom (3 [low, moderate, high] - 1=2). For example:

H^o = Age of the Offender = 0 (null hypothesis)
H^1= Age of the Offender ≠ 0 (research hypothesis) = It is hypothesized that there is a significant relationship between age of the offender and general recidivism.

If the alpha is .05 and the Wald statistic was greater than the critical value, then the researcher would reject the null hypothesis and would not reject the research hypothesis. Thus, in this case if the Wald statistic = 10.165, critical value was 3.841 and the alpha level was .05 then the null hypotheses would be rejected and the researcher would report that there was a significant relationship between age of the offender and general recidivism.

The last measure, the goodness of fit measure, tests the predictive value of the independent variables. Thus, this test examines each individual offender case and finds whether the predicted y value is consistent with the observed y value using estimated probabilities. This gave a percentage of correct predictions. For example, if age of the offender was thought to predict general recidivism and in 20 out of 100 offenders, that finding was correct, then it could be said that using this prediction model resulted in an accurate prediction of whether or not an offender would recidivate 20% of the time. The researcher used this final step of logistic regression to examine the predictor variables for each type of recidivism, including non-compliance with registration, violence, sexual, and general recidivism.

Finally, in testing all hypotheses, the researcher assessed variables that differentiated between recidivists and non-recidivists so that true predictor variables could be ascertained versus problems with sampling. For example, the researcher did not use prior sexual assault as a predictor variable for recidivism because all offenders in the sample have a prior sexual offense (a factor used for inclusion in the program).

Table 9: Coding Scheme

Variables	Coding
Risk Level	1=low, 2=moderate, 3=high, P=pending
Date of arrest	Converted to days
Birth date	Age of registrant in years (under 18=0, 18-29=1, 30-39=2, 40-49=3, 50-59=4, 60 and older=5)
Race/Ethnicity	White non-Hispanic=1, Black non-Hispanic=2, Hispanic=3, Other non-Hispanic=4
Prior criminal history (number of offense(s)	Number of prior arrests (1,2, 3 or more=3), number of past charges (1-5=1, 6-10=2,11-15=3, 16-20=4, 21-25=5, 26-30=6, over 30=7), number of convictions, number of past felony arrests, number of past misdemeanor arrests (0,1,2,3,4, 5 or more=5)
Prior criminal history	Penal Law codes used to determine violent, sexual, and failure to register (No=0, Yes=1)
Type of offender	Extrafamilial child molester=1, Rapists=2, Incest=3, Diverse offender=4
Force	Weapon used during registerable offense (No=0, Yes=1)
Recidivism (general)	Rearrest (No=0, Yes=1)
Recidivism charge(s) (type)	Penal Law codes - coding sexual and failure to register; UCR index crime(s) - coding violent (No=0, Yes=1)
Sentence length	Years (under one year=0, 1-2 years=1, 3-4 years=2, more than 4 years=3)
Number of victims	Number of victims involved in registerable offense (1, 2, 3 or more=3)
Victim(s) age	Age of victim, 12 and younger or aged 63 and older
Victim sex	Male=1, Female=2

Note: Missing data was coded as 999

Table 10: Analyses and Sample Used

Step	Analysis	Sample(s)	Independent Variables	Recidivism Typology*
1	Cross-tabulation	(1) all sex offenders; (2) program offenders; (3) non-program offenders; (4) program offenders with 2 yr. follow-up	All	1, 2, 3, & 4
2	Chi-Square (χ^2) and t-test	(1) All sex offenders; (2) Program offenders; (3) Non-program offenders; (4) Program offenders with 2 yr. follow-up	Dichotomous / Ratio	1, 2, 3, & 4
3	Logistic re-gression	(1) All sex offenders; (2) Program offenders; (3) Non-program offenders; (4) Program offenders with 2 yr. follow-up	All	1, 2, 3, & 4

*Compliance/ non-compliance =1, Violent/ non-violent =2, Sexual/ non-sexual =3, General =4

CHAPTER 7
Impacts of Increased Surveillance

This study addressed nine hypotheses. Before exploring the specific findings, an examination of the samples is critical and provides context for understanding the results. For this reason, the researcher examined a range of demographic and criminal offending variables. The demographic variables included age, gender, and race/ethnicity of offenders. The offending variables included risk level, victim characteristics[5], and criminal history.

Demographic Variables

Age
Table 11 shows the demographic data for all adult male sex offenders in New York City including both participants and non-participants. The age at time of conviction (i.e. offense leading to mandatory registration) varied greatly. The age range for all offenders was 18 to 86 years, with a mean of 33.73 years. Comparing participants and non-participants, the age ranges were 18 to 67 years (mean = 31.39 years, SD = 9.574) for participating offenders and 18 to 86 (mean = 34.09 years, SD = 11.680) for non-participants. The majority (73.2%) were between the ages of 18 and 39 years. This was true for non-participants (72.2%) and even more pronounced in the program sample (80.2%), with the number involved decreasing drastically with age. Using an independent samples t-test to compare the two groups showed a t-value of 6.709, significant at p=.000.

---

[5] All victim characteristic variables are related to the registerable offense. Victim data relating to other offenses was not available.

Table 11: Age

	N	Mean	S.D.	Range	t	df	p
Participants	700	31.39	9.54	18-67	6.79	1053	.000
non-Participants	4,473	34.09	11.60	18-86			

Race/Ethnicity

The majority of participating offenders were a minority, either black non-Hispanic (53.3%) or Hispanic (35.6%). When sub-samples (participants versus non- participants) were examined using a Pearson chi-square analysis, there was a significant difference found (χ^2=30.050, df=3, p=.000) with significantly more minorities in the participating sample (Table 12).

Table 12: Race/Ethnicity

Race/Ethnicity	Total		Participants		non-Participants		χ^2	df	p
	n	%	n	%	n	%			
White non-Hispanic	725	14.0	72	10.3	653	14.6	30.1	3	.000
Black non-Hispanic	2,294	44.3	373	53.3	1,921	42.9			
Hispanic	2,064	39.9	249	35.6	1,815	40.6			
Other non-Hispanic	90	1.7	6	0.9	84	1.9			

Note: Other includes Asian, Indian, and all other races

Offending Characteristics

A comparison between participants and non-participants on characteristics related to offending is shown in Table 13. Variables examined included risk level, victim characteristics, and criminal history.

Risk Level

Those participating in the program were overwhelmingly (90.2%) classified as level three offenders and considered to be at high risk of recidivism. The other 9.8% fit the level three override criteria.

Conversely, among non-participants, the majority (78.4%) were categorized as either level one or level two offenders (Table 13). The breakdowns for the total population of sex offenders in New York City were consistent with statewide percentages. Overall, as of March 29, 2011, 37.7% (n=12,097) of offenders in New York State were considered level one, 35.5% (n=11,387) were level two, 24.8% (n=7,948) were level three, and 2.1% (n=666) of risk assignments were pending (Division of Criminal Justice Services, 2011).

Victim Characteristics
The majority of offenders in this study had one victim, 77.4% of participants and 91.6% of non-participants. The groups differed significantly when the victim number exceeded one (χ^2= 131.404, *df*= 3, p=.000). For example, 18.4% of those in the program victimized two individuals compared to 7.0% of non-participants. While 4.2% of participants offended against three or more victims, only 1.4% of non-participants did the same. There was little difference in victim gender among participating and non-participating offenders, although those offenders in the program were slightly more likely to offend against males and/or offend against both sexes (Table 13).

Criminal History
Program participants were much more likely than non-participants to have prior involvement in the criminal justice system. For instance, 59.9% of participating offenders had a prior misdemeanor arrest compared to 42.4% of non-participants. They were also more likely to have had three or more misdemeanor arrests, 29.1% versus 18.5%. Statistically, the mean number of prior misdemeanor arrests for those in the program was 2.31 (SD = 4.466) compared to 1.48 (SD = 3.564) for non-participants. In addition, 21.9% of participants had a history of three or more misdemeanor convictions compared to only 10.5% of non-participants (μ = 1.82, SD = 4.147 and μ = 0.92, SD = 2.898, respectively). Independent samples t-tests were examined and yielded a t-value of -4.676 (p=.000) for misdemeanor arrests and a t-value of -5.508 (p=.000) for misdemeanor convictions (Table 13).

The number of prior felony arrests also demonstrates the significance and severity of participant's criminal history. Participating offenders were twice as likely to have had three or more felony arrests in the past (49.4% vs. 24.4%, respectively). When means were examined, participating offenders had a mean of 3.44 (S.D. 3.756) prior felony arrests versus 1.72 (S.D. 2.944) for non-participants. The rate of convictions was similar with 52% of those offenders in the program having a felony conviction history compared to 22.3% of those not monitored by the program (μ = .83, SD = 1.024 and μ = .35, SD = .781, respectively). And while 3% of non-participants were convicted of three or more felonies, 7.3% of offenders in the program had such a history. Independent samples t-tests demonstrated a t-value of -11.525 (p=.000) when examining felony arrests and a t-value of -11.900 (p=.000) for felony convictions (Table 13).

Table 13: Offending Characteristics

	Total		Participants		non-Participants	
Risk Level	**n**	**%**	**n**	**%**	**n**	**%**
Level 1	1,817	34.7	13	1.8	1,804	39.8
Level 2	1,799	34.4	50	7.1	1,749	38.6
Level 3	1,410	26.9	635	90.2	775	17.1
Pending	206	3.9	6	0.9	200	4.4
Number of Victims						
1	4,507	89.7	534	77.4	3,973	91.6
2	429	8.5	127	18.4	302	7.0
3 or more	90	1.9	29	4.2	61	1.4
Victim Gender						
Female Only	4,357	89.3	589	86.9	3,768	89.7
Male Only	469	9.6	75	11.1	3 94	9.4
Both Sexes	51	1.0	14	2.1	37	0.9
Number of Prior Misdemeanor Arrests						
0	2,708	55.2	271	40.1	2,437	57.6
1	775	15.8	136	20.1	639	15.1
2	443	9.0	72	10.7	371	8.8
3 or more	978	20.0	197	29.1	781	18.5

Table 13:Offending Characteristics (continued)

	Total		Participants		non-Participants	
	n	%	n	%	n	%
Number of Prior						
Felony Arrests						
0	2,375	48.4	156	23.1	2,219	52.5
1	720	14.7	97	14.3	623	14.7
2	444	9.1	89	13.2	355	8.4
Number of Prior Misdemeanor Convictions						
0	3,326	67.8	343	50.7	2,983	70.6
1	705	14.4	120	17.8	585	13.8
2	282	5.8	65	9.6	217	5.1
3 or more	591	12.0	148	21.9	443	10.5
Number of Prior						
Felony Convictions						
0	3608	73.6	324	47.9	3284	77.7
1	770	15.7	196	29.0	574	13.6
2	348	7.1	106	15.7	242	5.7
3 or more	178	3.6	50	7.3	128	3.0

	N	Mean	S.D.	Range	t	df	p
Misdemeanor Arrests							
Participants	695	2.31	4.466	0-47	-4.676	843	.000
non-Participants	4283	1.48	3.564	0-85			
Misdemeanor Convictions							
Participants	695	1.82	4.147	0-46	-5.508	807	.000
non-Participants	4283	0.92	2.898	0-84			
Felony Arrests							
Participants	695	3.44	3.756	0-32	-11.525	837	.000
non-Participants	4283	1.72	2.944	0-32			
Felony Convictions							
Participants	695	0.83	1.024	0-6	-11.9	829	.000
non-Participants	4283	0.35	0.781	0-6			

Hypothesis Testing

Question 1: Has the program accomplished its goal of monitoring all high-risk offenders?
Hypothesis 1: If a level three offender meets inclusion criteria (independent variable), then the program will monitor him (dependent variable).

Program staff monitored level three sex offenders that met one or more of the following inclusion criteria.

- Victim Relationship (Victim was a stranger to the perpetrator or the perpetrator established the relationship with the victim for the sole purpose of victimization);
- Victim Vulnerability (Victims who were 12 years old or younger, 63 years or older, physically helpless, or mentally incapacitated);
- Multiple Victims (Offenders who offended against more than one victim);
- Felony Convictions (Offenders with any felony convictions); and
- Level Three Overrides (offenders with a misdemeanor sex crime conviction or youth offender adjudication for a sexual crime; those that caused serious physical injury or death during the commission of the crime, and/or recent threat of re-offending)

Program staff did not monitor all high-risk offenders, as shown in Table 15. While the data was unusable or unavailable for many of the criteria listed (either the databases did not capture the variables or had missing values), there was sufficient data to reject the first hypothesis.

Victim Relationship
The relationship to the victim variable was missing for 82.3% of participants (612 cases) and was therefore, not used for in-depth analyses in this study[6]. For level three offenders, the data was missing in 77.9% of non-participant cases and 81.9% of participant cases. However, based on the limited data available, 57 non-participants offended against strangers and thus should have been included in the program sample.

---

[6] Because of the large amount of missing information, this variable is not included in Table 14.

Overall, there were 1,186 (79.7%) cases with missing data, so the number of stranger victimizations for level three offenders may be much higher. While prior research suggests that the majority of offenders assault acquaintances or family members, we also know that sex offenders who victimize strangers are more likely to reoffend (Hanson and Bussière, 1998; Hanson et al., 1993; Lang et al., 1988; Proulx et al., 1997; Scalora and Garbin, 2003).

Victim Vulnerability
When examining the offense that required their registration, level three offenders victimized 1,769 individuals with age ranges from under one years old to 90 years old (n= 814 victims [non-participants] and n=955 victims [participants]). The criterion for monitoring by the program is offending against individual's 12-years-old or younger or 63-years-old or older. Forty-five percent of participants (44.5%, n=251) offended against victims that were 12 years old or younger and 0.9% (n=5) of victims were 63 years or older. Non-participants had a similar rate of offending against children 12 years and younger (43.1%, n=300) and against those ages 63 and older (0.9%, n=6). Findings indicated that at least 292 non-participating offenders committed crimes against the very young or older individuals and should have been monitored by the program. Data addressing the other criterion, namely offending against the physically helpless or mentally incapacitated was not available.

Multiple Victims
While the majority of level three offenders committed crimes against one victim (78.1%, n=1,078), 301 offenders victimized more than one individual, ranging from two (17.3%, n=251) to six victims (0.2%, n=3). Participants were slightly more likely to offend against multiple victims than non-participants, 22.7% (n=143) compared to 21.1% (n=158), respectively. These 158 non-participating offenders should have been included in the program sample given their history of offending against multiple victims.

Felony Convictions
Of the 662 level three program offenders that had known felony histories, 276 (41.7%) had more than one past felony conviction. Eighteen percent (18.1%) of non-participants had a history of more than one felony conviction compared to 22.9% of participants. That is, the

program should have been monitoring 131 additional offenders according to this criterion.

Level Three Overrides

There were 141 (9.7%) level three offenders with a history of at least one misdemeanor sex crime prior to the registerable offense. Of these offenders, 52.5% were non-participants and therefore should have been monitored by the program (9.2%, n=74). Within the participating sample, 10.2% (n=67) of offenders had a history of a misdemeanor sex crime. The database of offenders did not include information on whether or not the individual had Youth Offender adjudication status for a sexual crime, whether the individual caused serious physical injury or death during the commission of the sex crime or whether there was a recent threat of re-offending.

In summary, as shown in Table 14, numerous non-participating offenders met criteria for inclusion in the program. These criteria were not mutually exclusive; there was some overlap among offenders meeting these criteria. Considering this, further analyses demonstrated that participants should have been monitoring an additional 516 offenders because they were level three offenders and met at least one of the inclusion criteria. Rather, 57 offenders met criteria for victimizing a stranger, 131 offenders had a past felony conviction, 158 offenders victimized more than one person, 292 offenders victimized a vulnerable person (12-years-old and younger or 63-years-old and older) and there were 74 offenders that were not level three offenders, but had a misdemeanor sex crime conviction (i.e. level three override). Finally, because some of the data was missing, the number of offenders that should have been monitored may actually be much higher. For example, there was no data available on offending against other types of vulnerable victims - those that were considered physically helpless or mentally incapacitated. The reasons for the apparent misclassification of more than 500 offenders are unknown.

Table 14: Inclusion Criteria

	Participants		non-Participants				
	n	%	n	%	χ^2	df	p
Victim Vulnerability							
Children 12 years and younger	251	44.5	300	43.1	.248	1	.618
Ages 63 and older	5	0.9	6	0.9			.593
Multiple Victims							
One victim	487	77.3	591	78.9	.571	3	.903
More than one victim	143	22.7	158	21.1			
Felony Convictions							
More than one past felony conviction	145	22.9	131	18.1	7.275	4	.122
Level Three Overrides							
More than one misdemeanor sex crime	67	10.2	74	9.2	.390	1	.532

Question 2: Do participating offenders have lower rates of reoffending than non-participants?

Hypothesis 2: Offenders monitored by the program (independent variable) will have significantly lower recidivism rates (dependent variable) than non-participants.

The program does intensive monitoring, which means that according to situational crime prevention theories, those supervised more closely should have fewer chances to recidivate. In an effort to test whether the program had an impact on recidivism a comparison group was needed. Prior analyses indicated that there were non-participating offenders (n=516) that should have been included in the study sample. Therefore, there was well-established evidence that a comparison group was available for this analysis. First, chi-square and independent samples t-tests were run to explore differences between all program offenders (n=719) and the sample of non-participating. offenders (n=516) using variables believed to impact recidivism, including:

- Race/Ethnicity
- Age of the offender

- Weapon use during SOR event (proxy for use of force)
- History of violent felony offense
- Number of past charges and number of past arrests
- Number of past felony arrests
- Number of past misdemeanor arrests
- Sentence Length

There was only one variable that indicated a significant difference between comparison groups - history of violence (i.e. violent felony offense) (p=.020). However, because this variable has been linked to recidivism in the past, a random selection of 75% of the total sample was taken in order to create two well-matched comparison groups. Selecting a random sample resulted in the elimination of 362 offenders, leaving a sample of 873 offenders (participants=496 and non-participants=377). In the end, after exploring differences using chi-square and t-tests, the comparison groups did not significantly differ (p<.05) on any variable (Table 15).

Table 15: Demographic and Risk Factors by Comparison Groups

	Participants (n=496)		non-Participants (n=377)	
	n	**%**	**n**	**%**
Race/Ethnicity				
White non-Hispanic	52	10.5	36	9.5
Black non-Hispanic	269	54.2	211	56.0
Hispanic	175	35.3	130	34.5
History of violent felony offense				
Yes	388	78.2	289	76.7
No	108	21.8	88	23.3
Force used during SOR* offense				
Yes	94	19.4	53	15.1
No	390	80.6	299	84.9
Age of the Offender				
18-29	56	11.3	47	12.5
30-39	154	31.0	108	28.6
40-49	199	40.1	137	36.3
50-59	63	12.7	59	15.6
60 and older	24	4.8	26	6.9

Table 15: Demographic and Risk Factors by Comparison Groups (continued)

	Participants (n=496)		non-Participants (n=377)	
	n	**%**	**n**	**%**
Number of past arrests				
0	41	8.3	24	6.4
1-10	320	64.5	252	66.8
11-20	100	20.2	79	21.0
21-30	26	5.2	18	4.8
More than 30	9	1.8	4	1.1
Number of past felony arrests				
0	63	12.7	45	11.9
1	76	15.3	55	14.6
2	59	11.9	48	12.7
3	57	11.5	37	9.8
4	51	10.3	44	11.7
5 or more	190	38.3	148	39.3
Number of past misdemeanor arrests				
0	138	27.8	99	26.3
1	94	19.0	71	18.8
2	64	12.9	52	13.8
3	44	8.9	42	11.1
4	52	10.5	29	7.7
5 or more	104	21.0	84	22.3
Minimum Sentence Length				
Up to one year	36	9.6	18	7.3
1-2 years	90	24.1	64	25.9
3-4 years	67	17.9	29	11.7
4-5 years	44	11.8	28	11.3
5-6 years	42	11.2	25	10.1
6-7 years	28	7.5	24	9.7
More than 7 years	67	17.9	59	23.9

*SOR=Sex Offense Registry

Table 16: Chi-square and Independent Samples T-test Results for Comparison Groups by Demographic and Risk Factors

			χ^2	df	p
Race/Ethnicity			.342	2	.843
History of violent felony offense			.302	1	.582
Force used during SOR* offense			2.679	1	102
Number of past misdemeanor arrests			3.413	5	.637
Number of past felony arrests			1.290	5	.963
Age of the Offender	Mean	S.D.	t	df	p
Participants	43	9.692	1.010	871	.313
Non-Participants	44	10.700			
Number of past arrests					
Participants	8	8.237	-.100	871	.920
Non-Participants	8	7.378			
Minimum Sentence Length					
Participants	1307	1566.387	1.833	619	.067
Non-Participants	1305	1217.288			

* SOR=Sex Offense Registry

Using matched comparison groups, rates of recidivism were explored. First, when general recidivism rates were examined, there were no significant differences in rates of recidivism (χ^2= 2.060, df=1, p=.151). To explore in more detail, other types of recidivism were also examined, including sexual, violent, violent sexual, and failing to register or non-compliance. Further analysis of specific types of recidivism showed that there were no differences in sexual recidivism (χ^2= .033, df=1, p=.856), violent recidivism (χ^2= .098, df=1, p=.755), violent sexual recidivism (χ^2= 1.139, df=1, p=.286) or non-compliance (χ^2= .581, df=1, p=.446). Thus, the hypothesis that participating offenders would have significantly lower recidivism rates than non-participating offenders was rejected.

Table 17: Recidivism Among Comparison Groups

	Participants		non-Participants				
	n	%	n	%	χ^2	*df*	p
Recidivism: General							
No	395	72.4	256	67.9	2.06	1	0.151
Yes	137	27.6	121	32.1			
Recidivism: Sexual							
No	480	96.8	364	96.6	0.033	1	0.856
Yes	16	3.2	13	3.4			
Recidivism: Violent							
No	470	94.8	359	95.2	0.098	1	0.755
Yes	26	5.2	18	4.8			
Recidivism: Violent Sexual							
No	485	97.8	367	97.3	1.139	1	0.286
Yes	11	2.2	10	2.7			
Recidivism: Non-compliance							
No	465	93.8	358	95.0	0.581	1	0.446
Yes	31	6.3	19	5.0			

Question 3: How many participating offenders have recidivated thus far and for what types of crimes?

Hypothesis 3: If an offender recidivates, then the likelihood of the arrest being for non-compliance will be higher than for violent or sexual recidivism.

This analysis examined the number of offenders that were rearrested after the date the program went into effect (July 1, 2003). Of all participating offenders, 27.1% (n=195) were rearrested within the two-year follow-up period (Figure 2). Of the 195 offenders that recidivated, 76 offenders were arrested for failing to register, violent recidivism, and/or sexual recidivism, leaving 119 offenders that were arrested for various other crimes. Moreover, of these offenders, there were 436 arrests for various crimes, with number of arrests ranging from one to 17.

Overall, rates of violent, sexual, and non-compliance recidivism are quite low. As shown in Figure 3, only 5.4% (n=39) of all program offenders were rearrested for a violent felony offense (measured using arrests for violent felony offenses comprising all index crimes, including murder, non-negligent manslaughter, rape, robbery, and aggravated assault) and/or failing to register as required by Megan's Law. This is in comparison to 2.8% (n=20) who were arrested for an additional sexual crime. An exploratory analysis showed that of those offenders that failed to register, 66.7% (n=26) were child molesters, 17.9% (n=7) were rapists and 15.4% (n=6) were diverse and other types of offenders. Of those that violently reoffended, 66.7% (n=26) were child molesters, 20.5% (n=8) were rapists and 12.8% (n=5) were diverse and other types of offenders. Lastly, of those that sexually recidivated, 65% (n=13) were child molesters, 25% (n=5) were rapists and 10% (n=2) were diverse offenders.

There were 39 participating offenders arrested for failing to register; 36 offenders were arrested only once, two offenders were arrested twice, and one offender had three arrests for failing to register. The 39 offenders arrested for a violent felony after program implementation were arrested 50 times, with six offenders committing more than one violent offense. Thirty-three offenders committed a single violent felony offense, two were arrested twice, three were arrested three times, and one offender was arrested four times for violent crimes. Of the 20 offenders rearrested for committing another sexual crime, only one offender had two arrests for such a crime.

In summary, of all participating offenders that recidivated, non-compliance rates were the same as violent recidivism rates and although not statistically significant, non-compliance recidivism rates did exceed sexual crime recidivism rates (5.4% compared to 2.8%, respectively), which indicate that there was sufficient evidence to partially reject the third research hypothesis.

Figure 2: Recidivism: Arrests of Participants

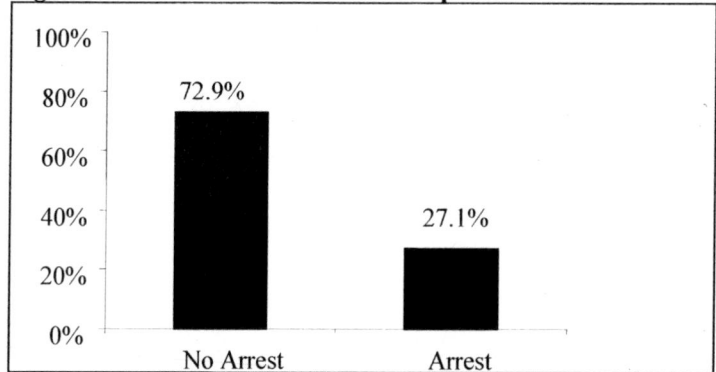

Figure 3: Recidivism Type: Arrests of Participants

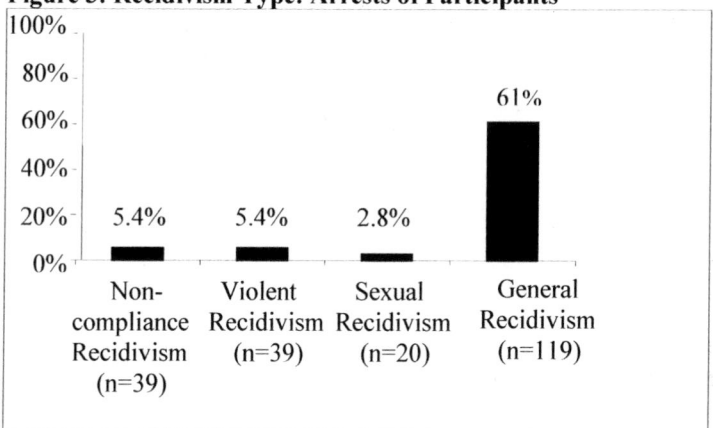

Note: Types of recidivism are not mutually exclusive.

Question 4: Are there characteristics that differentiate participating offenders who recidivate from those who do not?

Hypothesis 4: Among participating offenders, general recidivism (dependent variable), will have a significant relationship to and be predicted by various demographic characteristics (independent variables).

To examine hypothesis four, the researcher explored specific demographic and offending characteristics believed to be related to and predictive of general recidivism. More specifically, the researcher examined (a) age of offender, (b) marital status, (c/d) prior criminal history (number of charges, types of crimes), (e) use of force, (f) number of victims, (g) offender relationship to the victim, (h) victim age, (i) victim sex, (j) sentence length, and (l) type of community supervision.

Indeed, using a Pearson chi-square analysis, some characteristics differentiated participants that recidivate from those that do not. The total number of victims was significantly related to general recidivism (χ^2= 8.402, df= 3, p=.038). Age of the offender was also significantly related to recidivism (χ^2= 14.014, df= 4, p=.007). The recidivism rate was greatest for offenders between ages 18 and 29 years old (34.1%), after which it steadily declined and then dropped quickly after age 60 (5%). This decrease in offending over the life course, or "aging out," is characteristic of most offenders. When examining criminal history variables, there were a number of significant relationships. The number of past charges was highly correlated with general recidivism (χ^2= 128.761, df= 6, p=.000), as was the number of prior arrests (χ^2= 54.351, df= 3, p=.000), and a history of a violent felony offense (χ^2= 15.081, df= 1, p=.000). In general, the number of felony and misdemeanor arrests were both significantly related to recidivism (χ^2= 46.818, df= 5, p=.000 and χ^2= 61.778, df=5, p=.000, respectively). Of those offenders that did not have a history of a felony arrest (n=91), 89% did not recidivate after program monitoring began. Also important to note, of those that were first time offenders, most did not recidivate after monitoring began (89.6%). First-time offenses were also significantly related to recidivism (χ^2=24.222, df=4, p=.000) (Table 18). As show in Figure 4, in general, as the number of felonies increased, so did the recidivism rate. Those offenders with the highest recidivism rate (53.1%) had eight past felony arrests. This same pattern (i.e. increasing recidivism rates) was also seen when examining past misdemeanor arrests – as the number of past arrests increased, so did the percent recidivating. Those offenders with the most extensive misdemeanor arrest histories (i.e. 11 or more misdemeanor arrests) had the highest recidivism rate at 65.1%.

Victim gender was also significantly related to general recidivism (χ^2= 11.730, df= 2, p=.003). Of those who offended against a female during their registerable offense, 29.2% recidivated after program monitoring began, compared to an 11.8% recidivism rate for those that offended against a male, and a 13.3% rate for those that offended against both sexes.

Other variables used in the analysis included risk level, race/ethnicity, offender typology, age of the victim, use of a weapon (used as a proxy measure for force), and minimum sentence length. When these variables were examined as risk factors for recidivism, the hypothesis was rejected. Using chi-square analyses, data indicated that no relationship existed between recidivism and certain offender characteristics. Specifically, there was no relationship between recidivism and offender risk level ($\chi^2 = 1.527$, $df = 2$, p=.466), race/ethnicity ($\chi^2 = 6.291$, $df = 3$, p=.098), and typology ($\chi^2 = 4.595$, $df = 3$, p=.204). There was also no relationship between recidivism and offending against a victim 12-years-old and younger ($\chi^2 = 0.006$, $df = 1$, p=.937), offending against a victim aged 63 years and older (Fisher's exact test, two-tailed, p=1.000), weapon use ($\chi^2 = 1.051$, $df = 1$, p=.305), and minimum sentence length received ($\chi^2 = 0.539$, $df = 3$, p=.910). The recidivism rate for those that served less than a year was no different than for those that had a minimum sentence of four years or more (27.6% compared to 27.4%, respectively). Victim/offender relationship, marital status and treatment disposition variables were not available and thus not utilized in this analysis.

The researcher then performed logistic regression to determine the significant predictors of general recidivism in participating offenders. Various models were examined using different criminal history variables, such as the number of misdemeanor and felony arrests prior to implementation, history of arrest(s) for a violent felony, typology of sexual offender (i.e. child molester, rapist, diverse offender), number of past charges, and number of past arrests. While each of these criminal history variables were significantly related to recidivism, the criminal history variable that best predicted recidivism was number of past charges. The odds of rearrest increase by a factor of 2.38 for each unit increase in the number of past criminal charges. In other words, as the number of past charges increased, so did the offenders risk of rearrest.

Table 18: Risk Factors and General Recidivism

	Arrest=Yes		Arrest=No		χ^2	df	p
	n	%	n	%			
Risk Level					1.527	2	0.466
Level 1	3	23.1	10	76.9			
Level 2	11	20.4	43	79.6			
Level 3	180	27.9	466	72.1			
Race/Ethnicity					6.291	3	.098
White non-Hispanic	13	18.1	59	81.9			
Black non-Hispanic	109	28.5	273	71.5			
Hispanic	73	28.7	181	71.3			
Other	0	0.0	7	100.0			
Age of the Offender					14.014	4	.007
18-29	29	34.1	56	65.9			
30-39	62	29.1	151	70.9			
40-49	81	28.4	204	71.6			
50-59	21	21.9	75	78.1			
60 and older	2	5.0	38	95.0			
Typology					4.595	3	0.204
Child Molester	130	25.1	387	74.9			
Rapist	39	31.7	84	68.3			
Diverse	9	29.0	22	71.0			
Other	16	37.2	27	62.8			
Victim Vulnerability					0.006	1	0.937
Children 12 yrs and younger	74	26.8	202	73.2			
Ages 63 and older	1	20.0	4	80.0			1.000
Multiple Victims					8.402	3	.038
One victim	156	28.6	390	71.4			
Two victims	25	19.4	104	80.6			
Three Victims	3	15.8	16	84.2			
More than three victims	5	50.0	5	50.0			
Victim Gender Choice					11.73	2	.003
Females	175	29.2	425	70.8			
Males	9	11.8	67	88.2			
Both Genders	2	13.3	13	86.7			
First Time Offenders					24.222	4	.000

Table 18: Risk Factors and General Recidivism (continued)

	Arrest=Yes		Arrest=No		χ^2	df	p
	n	**%**	**n**	**%**			
Number of Past Charges					128	6	.000
1-5	29	10.0	262	90.0			
6-10	47	24.4	146	75.6			
11-15	45	41.7	63	58.3			
16-20	27	45.8	32	54.2			
21-25	22	71.0	9	29.0			
26-30	12	80.0	3	20.0			
Over 30	13	59.1	9	40.9			
History of Violent Felony Arrest	172	30.5	392	69.5	15	1	.000
Number of Past Felonies Arrests					46	5	.000
0	10	11.0	81	89.0			
1	13	12.0	95	88.0			
2	18	19.8	73	80.2			
3	23	31.1	51	68.9			
4	23	30.3	53	69.7			
5 or more	108	38.7	171	61.3			
Number of Past Misdemeanors Arrests					61	5	.000
0	24	12.2	173	87.8			
1	26	19.0	111	81.0			
2	30	29.7	71	70.3			
3	18	28.6	45	71.4			
4	27	36.5	47	63.5			
5 or more	70	52.4	77	52.4			
Force Used in SOR* offense					1.051	1	0.305
Weapon used in SOR* offense	41	30.4	94	69.6			
Minimum Sentence Length					0.539	3	0.91
Under one year	21	27.6	55	72.4			
1-2 years	68	28.0	175	72.0			
3-4 years	44	30.8	99	69.2			
More than 4 years	57	27.4	151	72.6			

*SOR=Sex Offense Registry

Figure 4: Percent of Participants Recidivating by Felony and Misdemeanor History

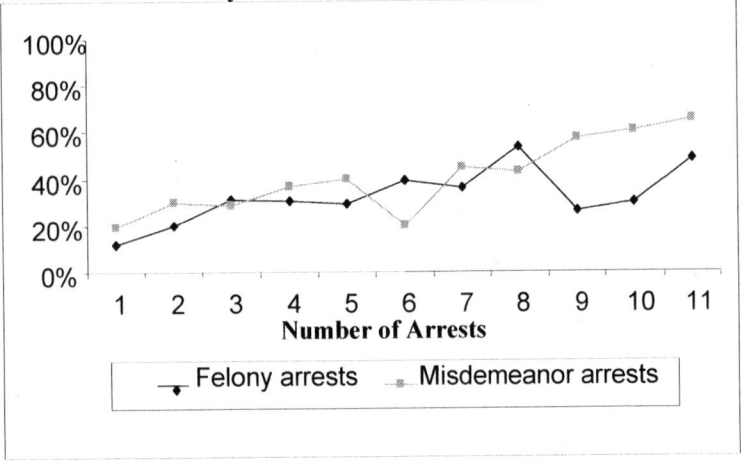

Table 19 summarizes the results of each variable hypothesized to predict recidivism. As shown, overall, age of offender and prior criminal history (past number of charges) were significant predictor variables in the model of general recidivism. Victim age, victim gender, total number of victims, minimum sentence length, and use of force were not significant predictors in this model. While many of these variables were significant predictors in other models, the model shown in Table 19 was selected because it explains the greatest amount of variance ($R^2=.245$). This model correctly predicted 75% of the cases. Of those variables that are significantly predictive of recidivism, increasing values of age correspond with decreasing odds of recidivism. Furthermore, as the number of past charges increase, the odds of recidivism also increases.

Table 19: Logistic Regression: Predictors of General Recidivism

Age of the Offender	B	S.E.	Wald	df	Sig.	Exp(B)
	-.408	.126	10.462	1	.001	.665
Children 12 years and younger	-.115	.220	.273	1	.601	.891
Ages 63 and older	.095	1.167	.007	1	.935	1.100

Table 19: Logistic Regression: Predictors of General Recidivism (continued)

	B	S.E.	Wald	df	Sig.	Exp(B)
Victim Gender	-.389	.337	1.334	1	.248	.678
Total Number of Victims	.362	.194	3.498	1	.061	1.436
Minimum Sentence	.165	.118	1.935	1	.164	1.179
Force Used in SOR* offense	-.015	.283	.003	1	.956	.985
Number of Past Charges	.865	.103	70.358	1	.000	2.375
Constant	-2.584	.475	29.634	1	.000	.075

SOR=Sex Offense Registry;   Nagelkerke R Square = .245

Question 5: Can type of recidivistic behavior be predicted by risk factors among participating offenders?

Hypothesis 5: Specific risk factors (independent variables) will be significantly correlated with and predictive of the type of recidivism (dependent variables) among participating offenders.

The researcher hypothesized that specific risk factors would be significantly correlated with and predictive of the type of recidivism among participating offenders, namely, (a) non-compliant, (b) violent, and/or (c) sexual recidivism. More specifically, it was hypothesized that (a) age of offender, (b) marital status, (c) sentence length, (d) treatment disposition, and (e) type of community supervision would be related to non-compliance. Second, (a) prior criminal history (number of charges, types of crimes), (b) use of force, (c) number of victims, and (d) offender relationship to the victim would be related to violent recidivism. Lastly, (a) prior criminal history (number of charges, types of crimes), (b) use of force, (c) offender relationship to the victim, (d) victim age, and (e) victim sex would be associated with sexual recidivism.

In analyzing data for hypothesis five, a Pearson's chi-square analysis was conducted to examine risk factors associated with various types of recidivism. In the majority of past studies examined, researchers either did not distinguish between types of recidivism or focused only on one specific type, such as sexual recidivism. Because there are differences in rates of various types of recidivism, it is important to examine what types of factors may impact these rates.

Non-compliance Recidivism

First, it was hypothesized that age of offender, marital status, sentence length, treatment disposition, and type of community supervision would be related to non-compliance. Findings indicated that age of the offender and the minimum sentence length received for the registry offense were not significantly related to failing to register (non-compliance recidivism) ($\chi^2=4.080$, $df=4$, p=.395, $\chi^2=2.239$, $df=2$, p=.326, respectively). Marital status, treatment disposition, and type of community supervision were not collected in the criminal database and therefore were not available for inclusion in this analysis.

Table 20: Risk Factors and Non-compliance Recidivism

	Arrest=Yes		Arrest=No		χ^2	df	p
	n	%	n	%			
Age of the Offender					4.080	4	.395
18-29	6	7.1	79	92.9			
30-39	13	6.1	200	93.9			
40-49	17	6.0	268	94.0			
50-59	3	3.1	93	96.9			
60 and older	0	0.0	40	100			
Minimum Sentence Length					2.239	2	.326
2 years or less	11	5.8	178	94.2			
3-4 years	10	6.2	152	93.8			
More than 4 years	6	3.1	188	96.9			

Logistic regression was then performed to predict non-compliance recidivism. Using the variables age of the offender and minimum sentence length at time of the offender's registerable offense, a regression model was analyzed. Results indicate that only age of the offender (p=.031) was predictive of non-compliance recidivism (i.e. failing to register) within this model. Minimum sentence length (p=.302), was not predictive and thus the first part of the research hypothesis was partially rejected.

However, because this model was not very strong ($R^2 = .034$) an exploratory analysis was performed to detect if there was in fact a model that helped predict who will fail to register. The best-fit-model included number of past charges and age of the offender ($R^2 = .189$), both which were significantly predictive of non-complaint recidivism (p=.000 and p=.009, respectively). The odds of failing to register increase as the number of past criminal charges increases, and increasing values of age correspond with decreasing odds of recidivism (Table 21).

Table 21: Logistic Regression: Predictors of Non-compliance Recidivism

	B	S.E.	Wald	df	Sig.	Exp(B)
Force Used in SOR* offense	.842	.443	3.611	1	.057	2.320
Number of Past Charges	.984	.231	18.133	1	.000	2.674
History of Violent Felony Arrest	-.418	.752	.309	1	.579	.659
Age of the Offender	-.694	.264	6.901	1	.009	.499
Minimum Sentence received for SOR* offense	-.018	.172	.011	1	.916	.982
Constant	-3.622	.873	17.228	1	.000	.027

*SOR=Sex Offense Registry; Nagelkerke R Square = .189

Violent Recidivism

Second, it was hypothesized that prior criminal history, use of force, number of victims, and offender relationship to the victim would be related to violent recidivism. Criminal history was examined by looking at number and types of crimes committed in the offender's past. Two significant relationships were found when examining those with a history of committing a violent felony offense. Having a violent past criminal history did increase the likelihood of committing a violent felony offense after monitoring began ($\chi^2=6.582$, $df=1$, p=.010). Of those that had a history of violence, 5.4% violently recidivated. Ninety-five percent of offenders that violently recidivated had a history of violence. The number of past charges in a person's history was also significantly related to violent recidivism (χ^2=17.449, *df*=3, p=.001).

To examine the relationship between past number of arrests and violent recidivism, a recode needed to be done because of small cell counts. Further analyses using a Pearson chi-square indicated that the number of arrests was not significantly related to violent recidivism (χ^2=1.004, *df*=2, p=.605). Chi-square analyses also indicated that type of crime, namely number of misdemeanors (χ^2=5.218, *df*=5, p=.390) and felonies (χ^2=9.886, *df*=5, p=.079) were also not significantly related to violent recidivism.

Use of weapon during the commission of the registerable offense was used as proxy measure for use of force. Findings indicate that use of a weapon was significantly related to violent recidivism (χ^2=8.637, *df*=1, p=.003). Interestingly, of those that used a weapon in the past, only 5.3% (n=37) committed a violent crime after monitoring began. This rate is similar to the overall rate of violent recidivism (5.4%).

The number of individuals the offender victimized during the offense requiring registration was not related to violent recidivism (χ^2=1.246, *df*=2, p=.536). Relationship to these victims as a factor related to further violence could not be assessed due to missing data.

Table 22: Risk Factors and Violent Recidivism

	Arrest=Yes		Arrest=No		χ^2	*df*	p
	n	%	n	%			
History of Violent Felony Arrest	39	5.4	680	94.6	6.582	1	.010
Number of Past Charges					17.449	3	.001
1-5	6	2.1	285	97.9			
6-10	9	4.7	184	95.3			
11-15	12	11.1	96	88.9			
More than 15	12	9.4	115	90.6			
Number of Prior Arrests					1.004	2	0.60
1-10	25	5.3	448	94.7			
11-20	9	6.3	134	93.7			
More than 20	4	8.7	42	91.3			

Table 22: Risk Factors and Violent Recidivism (continued)

	Arrest=Yes		Arrest=No		χ^2	df	p
	n	%	n	%			
Number of Past Misdemeanors					5.218	5	0.39
Arrests							
0	6	3.0	191	97.0			
1	6	4.4	131	95.6			
2	7	6.9	94	93.1			
3	3	4.8	60	95.2			
4	6	8.1	68	91.9			
5 or more	11	7.5	136	92.5			
Number of Past Felonies Arrests					9.886	5	.079
0	2	2.2	89	97.8			
1	1	0.9	107	99.1			
2	5	5.5	86	94.5			
3	4	5.4	70	94.6			
4	7	9.2	69	90.8			
5 or more	20	7.2	259	92.8			
Force Used in	37	5.3	663	94.7	8.637	1	.003
SOR* offense							
Multiple Victims					1.246	2	0.536
One victim	28	5.1	518	94.9			
Two victims	7	5.4	122	94.6			
Three or more	4	9.1	40	90.9			

SOR=Sex Offense Registry

Logistic regression was then conducted to determine a best-fit model for predicting violent recidivism. Multiple models were analyzed using different variables for prior criminal history and the model that included use of force, number of victims involved in the registerable offense, number of charges, types of crimes, number of past arrests, and history of violence was most predictive (R^2=.141). Table 23 shows the best-fit model and includes force or use of a weapon (p=.018), number of past charges (p=.000), number of past arrests (p=.003) and history of a violent felony arrest (p=.028), which were all significantly related to and predictive of violent recidivism.

Table 23: Logistic Regression: Predictors of Violent Recidivism

	B	**S.E.**	**Wald**	***df***	**Sig.**	**Exp(B)**
Force Used in SOR* offense	0.874	0.370	5.591	1	.018	2.398
Total Number of Victims	0.359	0.272	1.743	1	.187	1.432
Number of Past Charges	1.463	0.369	15.694	1	.000	4.320
Number of Past Misdemeanor Arrests	-.166	.142	1.375	1	.241	.847
Number of Past Felony Arrests	-.265	.188	1.974	1	.160	.768
Number of Past Arrests	-1.367	.468	8.535	1	.003	.255
History of Violent Felony Arrests	2.012	.918	4.808	1	.028	7.477
Constant	-5.772	.874	43.610	1	.000	.003

SOR=Sex Offense Registry; Nagelkerke R Square = .141

Thus, the second part of this hypothesis was only partially rejected. As hypothesized, having a violent past criminal history, number of past charges and use of force did increase the likelihood of committing a violent felony offense after monitoring began. However, type of crime (misdemeanors and felonies) and number of victims was not significantly related to violent recidivism, resulting in the researcher rejecting these assumptions.

Sexual Recidivism

Finally, it was hypothesized that prior criminal history, use of force, offender relationship to the victim, victim age, victim sex, and treatment disposition would be associated with sexual recidivism. Fisher's Exact test was used to examine many of the prior criminal history variables given the small number of offenders that sexually recidivated. These variables included history of violence, number of prior arrests, number of past felony arrests, and use of a weapon (proxy measures for use of force). The only variable significantly related to sexual recidivism was the use of a weapon (Fisher's exact test, two-tailed, p=.017). A chi-square analysis was completed to examine past number of misdemeanor arrests and its relationship with sexual recidivism and no significant relationship was found.

Age of the victim, categorized by program criteria (12-years-old and under or 63- years-old and older), was surprisingly not related to sexual recidivism (χ^2=.013, *df*=1, p=.909 and two-tailed, p=1.000, respectively). Lastly, given past research findings, it was also notable that victim gender ("both sexes" not used given small cell counts) was also not related to recidivism among this sample (Fisher's exact test, two-tailed, p=.152).

Table 24: Risk Factors and Sexual Recidivism

	Arrest=Yes		Arrest=No		χ^2	*df*	p
	n	%	n	%			
History of Violent Felony Arrest	19	3.4	545	96.6			.094
Number of prior Arrests							0.714
1	1	1.3	76	98.7			
2 or more	18	3.1	567	96.9			
Number of Past Misdemeanors Arrests					.566	1	0.452
0	4	2.0	193	98.0			
1 or more	16	3.1	506	96.9			
Number of Past Felonies Arrests							0.496
0	1	1.1	90	98.9			
1 or more	19	3.0	609	97.0			
Force Used in SOR* offense	8	5.9	127	94.1			.017
Victim Age							0.909
Children 12 years and younger	8	2.9	268	97.1	0.013	1	
Ages 63 and older	0	0.0	5	100.0			1.000
Victim Gender							0.152
Female Only	19	3.2	581	96.8			
Male Only	0	0.0	76	100.0			

SOR=Sex Offense Registry

Logistic regression was then used to explore whether these variables were predictive of sexual recidivism. The best-fit model consisted of weapon use (proxy for force), victim gender choice, and history of a violent felony offense. However, as shown in Table 25, no significant relationships were found.

Table 25: Logistic Regression: Predictors of Sexual Recidivism

	B	S.E.	Wald	*df*	Sig.	Exp(B)
Force Used in SOR* offense	.867	.496	3.053	1	.081	2.379
Victim Gender Choice	-17.311	4628.904	.000	1	.997	.000
History of Violent Felony Arrest	1.387	1.036	1.794	1	.180	4.004
Constant	-4.933	1.017	23.503	1	.000	0.007

*SOR=Sex Offense Registry; Nagelkerke R Square = .068

In summary, the only significant relationship found between the risk factors chosen and sexual recidivism was use of force and when using this variable in a regression analysis, it was not significant at the .05 level. Thus, the hypothesis that number and types of prior arrests, (misdemeanors and felonies), use of force, victim age, and victim sex would be significantly related and predictive of sexual recidivism was rejected. Relationship to the victim and treatment disposition were not collected by the criminal justice agency and/or there were missing cases which did not permit their inclusion in this analysis.

Question 6: Do violent recidivism rates among offenders monitored by the program vary by sex offender type?
Hypothesis 6: There will be a significant relationship between the type of sexual offender (independent variable) and violent recidivism (dependent variable).

To examine violent recidivism in more depth, it was hypothesized that the type of sexual offender within the program, (1) rapist, (2) extrafamilial child molester, (3) incest offender, or (4) diverse offender, would be significantly related to violent recidivism. More specifically, it was thought that offenders who recidivate will be more likely to have a diverse history of sex crimes. In addition, rapists will be more likely to violently recidivate than other types of offenders.

In order to test the sixth hypothesis, the researcher had to construct an offender typology variable. To that end, each participating offender's entire criminal history was examined using the detailed information from the SOR offense, as well as general penal code information found in past history. Those offenders that had a history of offending against only children (under the age of consent, 17) were coded as extrafamilial child molesters. If the age of the victim was missing, but the crime involved a sexual offense that was specific to a child, they were classified as a child molester (e.g., Penal Code §130.60, second-degree sexual abuse with a person less than 14 years). Because the relationship variable was missing in 82% of cases, all offenders received a classification as child molester if they offended against a child and the charge was not for incest (Penal Code §255.25). Offenders that had a charge of incest were coded as such. Although these offenders victimized children, they were examined separately based on past research that has found that incest offenders have lower sexual recidivism rates than other types of offenders (Hanson and Bussière, 1998; Quinsey, 1977). However, there were only three incest offenders in the program sample and therefore the researcher removed them from further analysis.

If an offender had an arrest for rape, the researcher classified him as a rapist. Rapists were mainly charged under Penal Code §130.35 (first-degree rape). However, if the crime under Penal Code §130.35 included a child, namely first-degree rape – having intercourse with a person under age 11 or the actor being over age 17 years and the victim being 13 years old or younger, the offender was coded as a child molester.

Diverse offenders were those that had a history of offending against both adults and children. It was important to examine these offenders separately given past research that suggests that the diversity of sex offenses committed by the offender is related to recidivism (Abel et al., 1988). Lastly, those offenders that did not fit within the above categories were coded into an "other" group. Crimes committed might include kidnapping or sexual misconduct.

A Pearson chi-square analysis was executed to explore the relationship between type of offender (excluding incest offenders) and violent recidivism. The majority of offenders were coded as child molesters (72.4%, n=517), followed by rapists (17.2%, n=123), other offenders (6%, n=43), and diverse offenders (4.3%, n=31). Of these offenders, 39 (5.5%) committed a violent felony offense after monitoring began. Violent felony offenses included all violent index offenses (murder, nonnegligent manslaughter, rape, robbery, and aggravated assault).

The researcher believed that recidivism rates would be higher for offenders who had a diverse history of sex crimes. In addition, rapists would be more likely to violently recidivate than other classifications of offenders. In order to conduct a chi-square analysis to explore the significance of this relationship, the group of "other" offenders, those that did not fit within the main typologies, was eliminated due to a small cell count. Although diverse offenders also had a small cell count, this group was needed in order to examine the significance and assist in testing the hypothesis.

First, the rate of violent offenses, measured by having a violent felony arrest after the program began, was not significantly related to sex offender type (χ^2=.501, df=2, p=.778) and therefore the hypothesis was rejected. Notably, violent reoffending rates were low, regardless of offender typology (Table 26).

Table 26: Percent of Participating Offenders that Violently Recidivate by Typology

Sex Offender Typology	Violent Recidivism	
	n	%
Child Molester	26	5.0
Rapist	8	6.5
Diverse	2	6.5
Other	3	7.0

To explore whether or not the researcher could predict violent recidivism given the various types of sex offenders, logistic regression was performed. Analyses indicated that typology of offenders did not predict violent recidivism among participating offenders (Table 27), which is not surprising given the low rates of violent reoffending.

However, an unforeseen finding was that the percentage of child molesters violently recidivating was similar to rapists, which is highly unusual given past research findings.

Table 27: Logistic Regression: Violent Recidivism and Sex Offender Typology

	B	S.E.	Wald	df	Sig.	Exp(B)
Child Molester	-.264	.758	.121	1	.728	.768
Rapist	.009	.817	.000	1	.992	1.009
Diverse	.034	.943	.001	1	.971	1.034
Constant	-2.708	.596	20.626	1	.000	.067

Nagelkerke R Square = .002

Question 7: Are those offenders that are non-compliant with registration more likely to recidivate?

Hypothesis 7: Among participating offenders, non-compliance recidivism (dependent variable) will be significantly related to general recidivism (independent variable).

In order to examine the relationship between non-compliance and general recidivism (arrested for any crime except failure to register), a Pearson's chi-square analysis was performed. Analyses indicated that there was a significant relationship between these two variables (χ^2=110.811, df=1, p=.000). Of those offenders that were arrested for failing to register (non-compliance recidivism) after the program began, all were rearrested for an additional crime, with a range of one to 11 arrests after implementation. There was also a significant relationship between arrest for non-compliance and the number of crimes after monitoring began (χ^2=18.696, df=3, p=.000). Of non-compliant recidivists, 23.1% committed one crime with the remaining 76.9% committing more than one crime after the program began (Table 28). Thus, the researcher failed to reject this hypothesis given the significant relationship between variables.

Table 28: Non-compliant Recidivism by Number of General Recidivism Arrests

Non-Compliant Recidivism	General Recidivism (Arrests)							
	0		1		2		3 or more	
	n	%	n	%	n	%	n	%
No	524	77.1	96	14.1	28	4.1	32	4.7
Yes	0	0.0	9	23.1	13	33.3	17	43.6

Question 8:   Are those participating offenders that are non-compliant with registration more likely to commit dangerous or violent crimes than those who are compliant?

Hypothesis 8:   Non-compliant participating offenders (independent variable) will commit more violent and/or sexual offenses at time of relapse (dependent variable) than those that are compliant.

Twenty-one percent (n=8, 20.5%) of offenders that were non-compliant committed a violent felony offense after the program began compared to 4.6% of compliant offenders.   There was a significant relationship between violent recidivism and non-compliance (Fisher's exact test, two tailed, p=.001).   However, there was not a significant relationship between non-compliance and sexual recidivism (Fisher's exact test, two tailed, p=1.000). To explore violence and sexual recidivism in more depth, violent sexual recidivism was examined and no significant relationship was found (Fisher's exact test, two tailed, p=.545).   Thus, the researcher failed to reject the research hypothesis for violent recidivism and non-compliance with registration, but rejected that there was a significant relationship between non-compliance and sexual recidivism.

Question 9:   Among participating offenders that sexually recidivate, is there a difference in length of time to relapse event by type of offender?

Hypothesis 9:   Among participating offenders that sexually recidivate, rapists (independent variable) will have a shorter time to relapse (dependent variable) than child molesters (independent variable).

There were only 20 offenders that sexually recidivated after the program began, including 12 child molesters, five rapists, two diverse offenders, and one incest offender. In order to address hypothesis nine, relapse time and typology of offender data needed to be collapsed and a Fisher's exact test was utilized because the incidence of sexual recidivism was very low. Only data for child molesters and rapists was analyzed. Length of time to relapse (meaning time between registerable offense and first new arrest) was broken down into two categories: rearrest within 0 to 5 years and rearrest after five years. Using these breakdowns, results indicated that there was not a significant difference between child molesters and rapists and their time to relapse (Fisher's exact tests, two-tailed, $p=.515$). Thus, the hypothesis that rapists would have a shorter time to relapse than child molesters was rejected. In fact, of the five rapists that did sexually recidivate, none relapsed in the first five years compared to three of the 12 child molesters.

Summary
After analyzing the descriptive data available, many interesting and important findings emerged. First, the program did not monitor all offenders that met criteria for inclusion. Second, results show that there were no significant differences in rates of general recidivism, sexual, violent, violent sexual or non-compliance recidivism between participants and non-participants. Thus, the immediate impact of the program is questionable. When examining participants only, there were also many interesting findings. For example, although the rates of non-compliance recidivism, violent recidivism and sexual recidivism were low, analyses indicated that specific offender characteristics were significantly related to and predictive of recidivism – an important finding for those working with offenders.

CHAPTER 8

Implications and Recommendations

The research was based upon three policy-based questions: (1) Is the program monitoring all those offenders that it should? (2) Are offenders that are being intensely monitored by the program less like to recidivate? and (3) Are there specific offender characteristics that have an effect on recidivism?

A review of past literature indicated that many sex offender programs are implemented and legislation is signed into law as the result of fear that if sex offenders are not monitored closely, then they are sure to reoffend. The problem is that little empirical support for these policies exists and few are subject to research and evaluation. This dearth of scientific support for sex offender monitoring legislation is intriguing, particularly since sex offender legislation is increasing in scope and severity. Too often city and state agencies invest their limited resources into programs and services that are not effective or into programs that have not yet been evaluated. Like other intensive supervision programs, it was unknown whether the program would reduce recidivism. However, the staff of the Criminal Justice Coordinator's Office was unique in that they sought an evaluation of the program to determine its effect on its stated objectives before considering its continuation or expansion.

Key Findings

Many key findings emerged that impact the aforementioned policy-based questions. First, 516 non-participants met the inclusion criteria for the program, but were not subjected to this intensive supervision program – the reason for their elimination is unknown. Although their omission was questionable, it did afford the opportunity to do a comprehensive, well-matched comparison study of the program's impact on recidivism. Results indicated that there was no significant difference between those monitored and those not monitored in terms of recidivism, including general, non-compliant, violent, or sexual recidivism.

When examining just those offenders in the program, there were numerous findings to consider. First, 27.1% of participants were arrested during the period of intensive supervision. However, the rates of arrest for specific types of recidivism, such as failing to register (non-compliance recidivism), violent recidivism and sexual recidivism were much lower than arrests for other types of offenses (e.g., drug-related offenses). Analyses showed that some characteristics differentiated those offenders that recidivated and those that did not. For example, the total number of victims attacked during the registerable offense, age of the offender, the number of criminal records, victim gender, number of past charges before entering the program, number of past misdemeanor and felony arrests, and history of violence were all significantly related to general recidivism. Furthermore, the best prediction model for general recidivism included age of offender, total number of victims, and prior criminal history (i.e. past number of charges). This finding was expected given past research (Barbaree & Marshall, 1988; Dempster & Hart, 2002; Långström & Grann, 2000; Prentky et al., 1997).

Secondly, predictive risk factors for specific types of reoffending were explored. Non-compliance recidivism was examined and, surprisingly, age of the offender and the minimum sentence length were not significantly related to or predictive of failing to register as suggested by past research (Farrell, 2002; Kunselman & Vito, 2002). However, an exploratory analysis did show that when age of the offender was coupled with number of past charges, both were significantly predictive of non-compliance recidivism. In terms of violent recidivism, having a violent past criminal history, number of past charges and use of a force (i.e. used a weapon) were significantly related to violent recidivism. Findings from researchers in the field support these results (Barbaree & Marshall, 1988; Dempster & Hart, 2002; Hanson & Bussière, 1998; Gendreau et al., 1996; Långström &

Grann, 2000; Proulx et al. 1997). However, unexpectedly, number of victims, number of arrests and types of crimes, namely number of misdemeanors and felonies were not related to violent recidivism (Freeman & Sandler, 2008). Also surprising was the data indicating that sex offender typology did not predict violent recidivism among participating offenders (Olver & Wong, 1006). Moreover, an additional finding emerged that the percentage of child molesters violently recidivating was similar to rapists – a highly unusual finding (Hanson & Bussière, 1998). Lastly, in regards to sexual recidivism, findings indicated that prior criminal history, measured by past criminal arrests, misdemeanor or felony arrests, use of a weapon, and age and gender of the victim were not related to recidivism – an unexpected finding given past research (Barbaree & Marshall, 1988; Dempster & Hart, 2002; Långström & Grann, 2000; Prentky et al., 1997). However, caution should be given in interpreting these findings since only a small number of offenders violently or sexually recidivated. The fact that victim sex was not related is of real interest since past research has repeatedly shown that offenders who target males are more likely to sexually recidivate (Hanson & Bussière, 1998; Hanson & Harris, 2001a; Roberts et al., 2002; Wilson et al. 2000).

Lastly, several other important findings emerged. A significant relationship exists between non-compliance and general recidivism (arrests for any crime). There was also a significant relationship between arrest for non-compliance and the number of crimes after program monitoring began. A significant relationship between non-compliance and violent recidivism also existed, a finding that is supported by past research. In 2006, the Washington Institute of Public Policy conducted a study and found that those offenders that did not register were more likely to recidivate and be convicted of a felony and violent felony offense – 38.5% vs. 22.9% and 15.8% vs. 9.4%, respectively. However, as found in this study, there was no significant relationship between non-compliance and sexual recidivism, a finding that is contradictory to what was found in the Institute's study, which found that 4.3% of those that absconded committed a violent sexual felony compared to 2.8% of those that were compliant.

Policy Considerations

These key findings raise important programmatic and policy considerations:

(1) Not all offenders who met criteria were included in the program;

(2) Non-compliance, violent and sexual recidivism rates were low; and

(3) There were no significant differences in general, non-compliance, violent and sexual recidivism rates between offenders who were and were not monitored.

Non-monitored Offenders

The inclusion criteria to be monitored by the program included being designated as level three offenders and (1) offending against strangers, vulnerable victims, or having multiple victims, or (2) having a history of a felony conviction or a sex offense misdemeanor conviction, or (3) having committed crimes that resulted in the death or serious injury of the victim.

After analyzing the available data, an additional 516 offenders should have been monitored by the program. Considering there were only 717 participants, including these additional offenders would have nearly doubled the program size. The finding that many offenders were omitted has many implications, namely possible selection bias, dangerous offenders not being monitored, and issues with resource allocation.

The first issue is possible selection bias. The fact that the program was not closely monitoring all like offenders may set the stage for constitutional challenges. The constitutional violation most evident is equal protection under the Fourteenth Amendment. For example, if there was selection bias or other problems with identifying offenders where one group was being subjected to intense monitoring while another group that met criteria was not, then the fairness of the program comes into question. Also, because this program mandated intensive supervision to ensure compliance with Megan's Law (e.g., increased face-to-face contacts with probation and parole staff, enhanced address verification), challenges may also surface in regards to the ex post facto clause, double jeopardy, and/or cruel and unusual punishment. However, it is unlikely that the court would entertain these challenges given past court decisions where it was found that sex offender management laws are constitutional and not a means of punishment (e.g. *Smith v. Doe*, 538 U.S. 84 [2003]; *Doe v. Pataki*, 120 F.3d 1263 2d Cir. [1997]; *M.G. v. Travis*, 236 A.D.2d 163 [1997]). Nonetheless, if it did entertain these challenges, it is doubtful that the court would determine this program to be unconstitutional because of its regulatory function. In other words, the court would probably find as it has in the past, that the subjection to increased monitoring is a protection to society, not a punishment.

The second issue is that many dangerous offenders as defined by program criteria were not subjected to intensive monitoring. This may have implications regarding chance for rearrest, reconviction, and ultimately recidivism. For example, although these missed offenders were still subjected to level three registration requirements (e.g., 90-day address verification, parole/probation), they were not exposed to the additional intensive monitoring. This would include increased number of required meetings between parole and probation officers (if relevant), mandated curfews (if relevant), and/or enhanced address verification tactics (e.g., general arrest checks with DCJS, improved information sharing between ACS and DCJS). In other words, if these non-monitored offenders were included, there may be a greater probability they would be apprehended quicker for violating Megan's Law and may have less opportunity to reoffend – ultimately decreasing likelihood of recidivism. This assumption is supported by a study done at the Washington State Institute of Public Policy, which found that offenders that did not register were more likely to recidivate and to be convicted of a felony, violent felony, and/or a violent sexual felony. While results of the current study indicated that this was not the case (i.e. there was no difference in recidivism rates between participants and non-participants), there is no way of knowing whether monitoring these missed offenders within the program may have affected the findings of this study.

Third, an expansion of the program would also have resource implications. If the program staff needed to monitor these additional 516 offenders, the offender population would almost double from 719 to 1,235 offenders. When the program was first implemented, the Police Department's Sex Offender Monitoring Unit was doubled in order to monitor up to 900 offenders who qualified for inclusion. This included forming an apprehension unit with six new investigators/detectives designated as staff to track down those offenders who failed to register or check in every 90 days, and to conduct home-visits to verify registrants' addresses. Thus, if the program substantially increased, it would require increased funding and resources for additional specially-designated ADAs, city-wide training to ensure uniformity of prosecution, additional members for the apprehension team, and additional parole and probation officers.

Recommendation – If intensive supervision of offenders continues under the current program, then all offenders who fit the criteria should be included.

Recidivism Rates

Arrests rates were used to measure recidivism among sex offenders and 27.1% (n=195) of participants were rearrested within a two-year follow-up period. Of these offenders, there were 436 arrests for various crimes, with a range of one to 17 arrests per offender. Only 5.4% (n=39) of all participants were rearrested for failing to register as required by Megan's Law, 5.4% (n=39) of offenders were rearrested for a violent felony offense[7] and 2.8% (n=20) were arrested for an additional sex crime. Among those offenders that failed to register, 66.7% (n=26) were child molesters, 17.9% (n=7) were rapists and 15.4% (n=6) were diverse and other types of offenders. Of those that violently reoffended, 66.7% (n=26) were child molesters, 20.5% (n=8) were rapists and 12.8% (n=5) were diverse and other types of offenders. Lastly, of those that sexually recidivated, 65% (n=13) were child molesters, 25% (n=5) were rapists and 10% (n=2) were diverse offenders. In each case, child molesters were more likely to recidivate than other types of offenders - a finding that has not been supported by past research. For example, child molesters have been found to be less likely to violently recidivate than other types of sexual offenders (Hanson & Bussière, 1998).

Because the number of offender's recidivating is small, findings should be viewed with caution. Nonetheless, these findings demonstrate that these high-risk offenders may be more likely to

---

[7] Violent felony offenses comprise all violent index crimes, including murder, non-negligent manslaughter, rape, robbery, and aggravated assault.

engage in generalized criminality and are less likely to be arrested for sexual or violent crimes as often implied by politicians and the media. This concept of the generalist offender has been supported by past research (Hanson & Morton-Bourgon, 2004; Lussier, 2005; Soothill et al., 2000). Indeed, Hanson and colleagues conducted a meta-analysis and found that sex offenders had a much higher general recidivism rate than sexual recidivism rate (Hanson & Morton-Bourgon, 2007). Moreover, when a sample of program participants was compared to a well-matched comparison group, recidivism rates did not significantly differ by type of recidivism, 26.9% vs. 32% for general recidivism, 5.4% vs. 5.6% for non-compliance recidivism, 5% vs. 6.1% for violent recidivism, and 2.2% vs. 3.2% for sexual recidivism, respectively. Thus, the fact that many participants did not differ in rates of reoffending and that they engaged in continued criminal behavior indicates that they may be career criminals, especially since they continued their criminal behavior despite knowing they were under increased surveillance. These findings indicate some questionability about the program's impact on reducing recidivism. In should also be noted that since the time data was collected for this study, the program has expanded and all sexual offenders are now subjected to increased monitoring – making a longer term follow-up that much more critical.

However, it must also be noted that the low violent and sexual recidivism rates made it difficult to statistically determine what offender characteristics to look for in those that do recidivate and if the follow-up period were longer, as suggested by recidivism literature, then differences may have been noticed (Barbaree & Marshall, 1988; Furby et al., 1989; Langevin et al., 2004; Soothill & Bibbens, 1978). For example, Barbaree and Marshall (1988) note that the longer the follow-up period, the more likely it is that the researchers will find evidence of recidivism. In their own study, they found a recidivism rate that increased from 12.5% (one to two years) to 64.3% (more than four years) for child molesters. Typology of sex offender is also critical when studying recidivism due to documented differences in base rates of sexual offending and relapse. For example, in one meta-analytic study, Hanson and Bussière (1998) examined 61 studies with a total of 23,393 offenders. They found that the rearrest rates, defined as those rearrested or reconvicted for a sex offense over a four-five year period, were 18.9% for rapists and 12.7% for child molesters. When the researchers examined rates for those who committed non-sexual violent crimes, the rates were 22.1% for rapists and 9.9% for child molesters.

Recommendation – Continue to follow participants for at least an additional three years given that past research shows that sexual and violent recidivism rates increase over time. When further analyses are completed, typologies should be examined in order to distinguish any differences in recidivism and whether the program has more of an impact or is more effective for one type of offender over another. Continued follow-up is imperative because at this point it is unclear whether rates will continue to increase as indicated by past research (Barbaree & Marshall, 1988; Furby et al., 1989; Langevin et al., 2004; Soothill & Bibbens, 1978), or whether rates will stay consistently low, which may demonstrate program effectiveness in decreasing recidivism rates among the most dangerous offenders. In addition, given the cost and needed resources of implementing such a program, understanding whom it benefits most and when it is most beneficial is critically important to getting the best return on investment. Moreover, given the need for increased funding to implement the program with an additional 516 offenders, the researcher suggests revising whom and when individuals should be monitored based on other findings of low recidivism rates. The researcher recommends that the Criminal Justice Coordinator's Office establish criteria for length of intensive monitoring. For instance, if an offender has not reoffended or violated conditions of the program within five years, then the offender should be removed from the program with regular level three monitoring continuing.

Effectiveness

After comparing recidivism rates using a well-matched randomly selected comparison group, offenders that were monitored by the program were not significantly less likely to recidivate (general, violent and sexual recidivism) than those not monitored. There was also no difference in their rate of compliance with registration requirements. These findings have various implications, including whether or not the program should be continued given the lack of evidence for its effectiveness, poor return on investment, and risk of creating a false sense of security for the public.

Given that recidivism was not affected, the most significant question now is whether the program will be effective in reducing recidivism long-term. While it is a significant that data did not indicate a reduction in recidivism rates for those who were monitored in the program; it must be kept in mind that the program had only been in effect for two years. Because the first year of the program was largely devoted to its implementation, it may have a greater effect on recidivism after being in place longer. The low rates of reoffending in both groups are not surprising and an increase in recidivism in both the intensely (participants) and less-intensely (non-participants) monitored groups would be expected after several years (Barbaree & Marshall, 1988; Furby et al., 1989; Langevin et al., 2004; Soothill & Bibbens, 1978). Furthermore, because data was not available regarding length of incarceration and/or institutionalization, there may be differing recidivism rates simply based on opportunities to reoffend. In other words, after offenders were convicted and sentenced for recidivating during the two-year follow-up period, exact amount of time spent incapacitated was not available. Thus, a full understanding of opportunities for reoffense after the first case of recidivism is limited. Lastly, because data was not collected on program implementation, such as whether offenders were intensely monitored as prescribed by the program design (i.e. doing a process evaluation), it is also difficult to obtain a true measure of program efficacy. There is no way of knowing whether the program was implemented with fidelity. For instance, did all the parole and probation contacts occur as prescribed? Did address checks occur as prescribed? These are the types of questions that needed to be answered in order to know for sure whether the outcomes are valid.

Second, because there are questions about its effectiveness, another concern is whether the resources allocated to this program are necessary. If the program does not significantly reduce recidivism, then can these resources be better allocated for other types of crime control? Given limited resources, perhaps the program may be more useful in targeting a specific type of offender or those with specific criminal background characteristics. For instance, data indicated that absconding from registration, number of past charges, and history of using force were significantly related to violent recidivism. Thus, if resources are limited, a particular focus on non-compliant offenders or those with certain risk factors may be most cost effective.

Finally, one may question whether this program may be creating a false sense of security. There is a widespread national trend to implement harsher sentences and stricter monitoring policies for sex offenders in an attempt to reduce recidivism. However, the effect this may have on reducing recidivism is questionable given the results of this and other studies. In particular that there were no differences in recidivism rates among those monitored and those not monitored, as well as that not all high risk offenders were monitored and included in the program (n=516).

In general, opponents of sex offender legislation believe that it gives people a false sense of security (Filler, 2001; Quinn et al., 2004). At this time it is unclear whether this program has an impact in this regard. Until these offenders and those that should have been monitored are followed for a longer time, we will not know whether this program is effective and whether or not the public should feel safer in their communities.

Recommendation – Risk factors for inclusion in the program should be reevaluated given that the data in this study indicated that there are specific characteristics predictive of reoffending. This will also be important when exploring the return on investment and performing a cost benefit analysis. Until a full program evaluation is done after five years, it will not be clear whether the program is in fact effective at reducing recidivism.

Limitations

As with most recidivism studies, this research project has limitations that need to be noted. These include the issue of underreporting, the use of a non-random design, agency data, generalizability, and a short follow-up timeframe.

Underreporting
Past findings indicate that many offenses do not come to the attention of officials (Fisher, Cullen, & Turner, 1999; Tjaden & Thoennes, 2006). For instance, victims do not report all crimes to law enforcement and the police do not apprehend all offenders; thus, ever truly knowing recidivism rates and time to recidivism is unlikely. However, not

having complete and inclusive data should not limit the efforts of researchers in this area. In fact, the researcher believes that continued research will increase knowledge of sex offenders and recidivistic behavior, which may lead to increased awareness and reporting. In addition, gaining knowledge about this and other intensive supervision programs may impact future research and policy and may increase the arrest and conviction rates of offenders.

Non-Experimental Design
There was no possibility of using an experimental design whereby offenders could be randomly assigned to supervision by the program versus standard supervision. Thus, the observed outcomes of the program evaluation could be the result of extraneous variables or events. That being said, well-matched comparison group studies are the second best alternative to randomized control trials. Thus, because a carefully matched comparison group was randomly selected from offenders that should have been monitored, it is believed that the outcomes found are valid.

Agency Data
There are limitations inherent in analyzing data collected by others. The first and often a major problem was recordkeeping. Many preliminary studies of other state databases showed high levels of missing, incomplete or erroneous data. Sex offender databases require more time and resources than are typically available in order to verify and update information (Bedarf, 1995). Another problem was that the researcher was confined to studying only the variables collected by DCJS and the program, which meant ignoring other intervening variables that may have impacted recidivism. For example, more detailed information about treatment would have been beneficial, but was not available. Another major issue was the lack of data regarding institutionalization and incarceration within the two-year follow-up. Because there was no way to tell whether participants or non-participants had periods of incapacitation, offenders may have had different opportunities to offend, thus skewing the data. Although these important factors may have impacted recidivism rates and outcomes in the study, this limitation could not be controlled. Conversely, the variables chosen and available for use in this study were essential to understanding risk of recidivism. In addition, the data

used for this study is what is readily available to criminal justice agencies and personnel who will be making decisions about risk, and many research studies have supported their importance in the past.

Generalizability

This study examined adult male sex offenders and therefore, the results may not be applicable to juvenile and female sex offenders. Due to the program's capacity for monitoring only those sex offenders within its jurisdiction, generalizability is also affected, namely generalizability to rural, non-metropolitan areas or other areas of the country. Offenders in this study were also primarily level three offenders. This means that the findings may not generalize to sex offenders that are assigned a lower risk for reoffense or do not meet inclusion criteria.

Although the results are not generalizable to some populations and areas, the findings should be similar to what would be found when examining recidivism for level three (high-risk) sex offenders nationally if risk level designations are the same. Thus, if the criteria used to designate an offender as "high-risk," are similar in another state, then results should be similar and would be generalizable.

Follow-up Timeframe

Lastly, this research is a descriptive study evaluating recidivism of offenders monitored by the program, which was only in effect for two years. Therefore, the follow-up period was limited and may have affected the outcomes. Because there is evidence that recidivism rates increase after longer follow-up periods, the rates should be expected to increase if the observation period is extended to five years (Barbaree & Marshall, 1988; Furby et al., 1989; Langevin et al., 2004; Soothill & Bibbens, 1978). Nevertheless, as a first step to understanding the impact of this supervision policy, a preliminary examination of recidivism was needed and provided interesting and useful data, as well as raised important questions. In addition, having a baseline to compare future rates of recidivistic behavior is critical for an accurate evaluation of this programs impact longitudinally.

Summary

This research is a starting point for understanding sex offender registration compliance and contributes to a surprisingly limited number of published studies evaluating sex offender management statutes. Problems with compliance with sex offender registration have been documented in the past. However, to date there have been limited research studies examining the characteristics of those who are compliant versus those that are not. Furthermore, there has been no research to date examining a program like this one and whether intensive supervision of high-risk sex offenders in the community has an impact on recidivism. There is also little information available on what characteristics are likely to be related to and predictive of recidivism for those under intensive supervision. Understanding the characteristics of those who are noncompliant and/or recidivate may influence supervision procedures and budgetary expenditures. Knowledge gained from this research is invaluable to criminal justice professionals and agencies, including law enforcement, court administrators, supervisory units, and policy makers and legislators. It provides a better understanding of which registrants pose a greater risk and where to focus financial and human resources. This is important because if policymakers know whom to monitor, the result may be a more focused approach to supervision resulting in a decrease in recidivism, an increase in safety for communities, as well as possible cost savings. In conclusion, this research builds on past literature of understanding risk factors related to recidivism and is one of the first studies to examine whether differential monitoring and supervision of offenders has an impact of reoffense rates.

Appendix

Registerable offenses

Article	Class	Crime	Definition
120.70	E Felony	Luring a Child	A person who lures a child into a motor vehicle, aircraft, watercraft, isolated area, or building for the purpose of committing the following crime(s) against a child (unde17 years): Murder (125.25, 125.27); sexual offense (Article 130); prostitution (230.30, 230.33), sex trafficking (230.34); incest (255.25, 255.26, 255.27; and child pornography (263.05, 263.10, 263.15)
130.20	A Misdemeanor	Sexual misconduct	A person who engages in sexual intercourse, deviant or otherwise, without the other person's consent; A person who engages in intercourse with an animal or dead human body

Registerable offenses (continued)

Article	Class	Crime	Definition
130.25	E Felony	Rape in the third degree	A person who engages in sexual intercourse with a person to whom he is not married and who is incapable of consent by some reason other than age (under 17 years) or who is 21 years or older and engages in intercourse with a person to whom he is not married and is under 17 years old
130.30	D Felony	Rape in the second degree	A person who is 18 years old or older and engages in intercourse with a person to whom he is not married and is under 14 years old
130.35	B Felony	Rape in the first degree	A person who engages in sexual intercourse with a person by forcible compulsion or who is incapable of consent due to being physically helpless or who is under 11 years old
130.40	E Felony	Sodomy in the third degree	A person who engages in deviant sexual intercourse with another person who is incapable of consent by some reason other than age (under 17 years) or who is 21 years or older and engages in deviant intercourse with a person who is under 17 years old

Registerable offenses (continued)

Article	Class	Crime	Definition
130.45	D Felony	Sodomy in the second degree	A person who is 18 years old or older and engages in deviant intercourse with a person who is under 14 years old
130.50	B Felony	Sodomy in the first degree	A person who engages in deviant sexual intercourse with another person by forcible compulsion or who is incapable of consent due to being physically helpless or who is under 11 years old
130.52	A Misdemeanor	Forcible Touching	A person who intentionally and for no legitimate purpose forcibly touches the sexual parts of another person for the purpose of degrading or abusing such person or for the purpose of gratifying the actors sexual desire
130.53	E Felony	Persistent Sexual Abuse	A person who has been convicted of sexual abuse in the second or third degree and has been convicted of such crimes two or more times in separate criminal proceedings within the previous ten year period

Registerable offenses (continued)

Article	Class	Crime	Definition
130.55	B Misdemeanor	Sexual abuse in the third degree	A person who subjects another person to sexual contact without consent and the victim is less than 17 years, but more than 14 years old and the offender is less than five years older
130.60	A Misdemeanor	Sexual abuse in the second degree	A person who subjects another person to sexual contact who is incapable of consent by some reason other than age (under 17 years) or is under 14 years old
130.65	D Felony	Sexual abuse in the first degree	A person who subjects a person to sexual contact by forcible compulsion or who is incapable of consent due to being physically helpless or who is under 11 years old
130.65-a	E Felony	Aggravated sexual abuse in the 4th degree	A person who inserts a foreign object in the vagina, urethra, penis or rectum of a person incapable of consent by some reason other than age (under 17 years) or inserts a finger into the vagina, urethra, penis or rectum of a person causing physical injury and the person is incapable of consent by some reason other than age (under 17 years)

Registerable offenses (continued)

Article	Class	Crime	Definition
130.66	D Felony	Aggravated sexual abuse in the 3rd degree	A person who inserts a foreign object in the vagina, urethra, penis or rectum of a person by forcible compulsion or who is incapable of consent - physically helpless or who under 11 years old
130.67	C Felony	Aggravated sexual abuse in the 2nd degree	A person who inserts a finger into the vagina, urethra, penis or rectum of a person causing physical injury by forcible compulsion or who is incapable of consent - physically helpless or who is under 11 years old
130.70	B Felony	Aggravated sexual abuse in the 1st degree	A person who inserts a foreign object in the vagina, urethra, penis or rectum of a person causing physical injury by forcible compulsion or who is incapable of consent - physically helpless or who is under 11 years old.
130.75	B Felony	Sexual conduct against a child in the 1st degree	A person who engages in two or more acts of sexual conduct (sexual intercourse, deviant sexual intercourse or aggravated sexual conduct) over a period of at least three months with a child less than 11 years old.

Registerable offenses (continued)

Article	Class	Crime	Definition
130.80	D Felony	Sexual conduct against a child in the 2nd degree	A person who engages in two or more acts of sexual conduct over a period of at least three months with a child less than 11 years old
130.90	D Felony	Facilitating a sex offense with a controlled substance	A person who knowingly and unlawfully possesses a controlled substance and administers it to another person without her consent with the intent to commit a felony sexual offense
130.91	Various Felonies	Sexually Motivated Felony	A person who commits one of the following offenses for the purpose of sexual gratification: assault (120.05-07, 120.10); stalking (120.60); manslaughter (125.15, 125.20); murder (125.25-27); kidnapping (135.20-25); burglary (140.20, 140.25, 140.30); arson (150.15, 150.20); robbery (160.05, 160.10, 160.15, prostitution (230.30, 230.32-33); disseminating indecent material to minors (235.22); pornography (263.05, 263.10, 263.15)

Registerable offenses (continued)

Article	Class	Crime	Definition
130.95	A II Felony	Predatory sexual assault	A person who causes serious physical injury/ uses or threatens immediate use of a dangerous instrument during the commission of rape in the first degree, criminal sexual act in the first degree, aggravated sexual abuse in the first degree, course of sexual conduct against a child in the first degree; a person who commits one of these crimes against one or more additional persons; a person who has previously been convicted of one of these crimes, incest, or use of a child in a sexual performance
130.96	A II Felony	Predatory sexual assault against a child	A person who is 18 years old or older and commits rape in the first degree, criminal sexual act in the first degree, aggravated sexual abuse in the first degree, or course of sexual conduct against a child in the first degree against a child 12 years old or younger
135.05	A Misdemeanor	Unlawful imprison-ment in the 2nd degree	A person who restrains another person
135.10	E Felony	Unlawful imprison-ment in the 1st degree	A person who restrains another person under circumstances which expose them to a risk of serious physical injury

Registerable offenses (continued)

Article	Class	Crime	Definition
135.20	B Felony	Kidnapping in the 2nd degree	A person who abducts another person
135.25	A-I Felony	Kidnapping in the 1st degree	A person who abducts another person (1) with the intent of compelling a third person to pay or deliver money or property as ransom, (2) and restrains the person longer than twelve hours with intent to: (a) Inflict physical injury upon her or violate or abuse her sexually; (b) Accomplish or advance the commission of a felony; (c) Terrorize her or a third person; or (d) Interfere with the performance of a governmental or political function; or (3) The person abducted dies during the abduction or before he is able to return to safety
230.04	A Misdemeanor	Patronizing a prostitute in the 3rd degree	A person who patronizes a prostitute
230.05	E Felony	Patronizing a prostitute in the 2nd degree	A person over eighteen years of age who patronizes a prostitute under fourteen years of age
230.06	D Felony	Patronizing a prostitute in the 1st degree	A person who patronizes a prostitute under eleven years of age

Registerable offenses (continued)

Article	Class	Crime	Definition
230.30	C Felony	Promoting prostitution in the 2nd degree	A person who (1) advances prostitution by compelling a person by force or intimidation to engage in prostitution, or profits from such coercive conduct, or (2) Advances or profits from prostitution of a person under sixteen years of age
230.32	B Felony	Promoting prostitution in the 1st degree	A person who advances or profits from prostitution of a person under eleven years old
230.33	B Felony	Compelling prostitution	A person over twenty-one years of age who compels a person under sixteen years old to engage in prostitution by using force or intimidation
230.34	B Felony	Sex trafficking	A person who intentionally advances or profits from prostitution by (1) unlawfully providing a narcotic, concentrated cannabis, methadone, gamma-hydroxybutyrate (GHB) or flunitrazepan to a person to impair her judgment; (2) making material false statements, misstatements, or omissions to induce or maintain the person's engagement in prostitution; (3) withholding, destroying, or confiscating any passport, immigration document, or other gov. identification

Registerable offenses (continued)

Article	Class	Crime	Definition
230.34	B Felony	Sex trafficking	document with the intent to impair the person's freedom of movement; (4) requiring that prostitution be performed to retire, repay, or service a debt; (5) using force or engaging in any scheme, plan or pattern to compel the person to engage in prostitution by instilling fear that if the person does not comply, the result will be (a) physical injury or death (b) damage to property c)accusation of a crime or causing criminal charges or deportation proceedings to be instituted; (d) exposure e) testifying or refusing to testify with respect to another's legal claim or defense; (f) using or abuse his position as a public servant by performing some act within or related to his or her official duties, or by failing or refusing to perform an official duty,(g) performing any other act which is calculated to harm the person with respect to her health, safety, or immigration status

Registerable offenses (continued)

Article	Class	Crime	Definition
235.22	D Felony	Disseminating indecent material to minors in the 1st degree	A person who disseminates information to a minor which depicts/describes, either in words/images actual/ simulated nudity, sexual conduct or sadomasochistic abuse; he intentionally uses any computer system to initiate/engage in communication with a person who is a minor to invite or induce a minor to engage in sexual intercourse/oral sexual conduct/ anal sexual conduct/ sexual contact with him, or to engage in a sexual performance or conduct for his benefit
250.45	E Felony	Unlawful surveillance in the 2nd degree	A person who for no legitimate purpose, or for amusement, entertainment, or profit, or for the purpose of degrading or abusing a person, or for his or another person's sexual arousal or gratification, intentionally uses or installs an imaging device to view, broadcast or record a person dressing or undressing or the sexual or other intimate parts of such person at a place and time when such person has a reasonable expectation of privacy, without such person's knowledge or consent

Registerable offenses (continued)

Article	Class	Crime	Definition
250.50	D Felony	Unlawful surveillance in the 1st degree	A person who commits the crime of unlawful surveillance in the second degree and has been previously convicted within the past ten years of unlawful surveillance in the first or second degree
255.25	E Felony	Incest (committed prior to 11/1/06) **OR** Incest in the 3rd degree	A person who marries or engages in sexual intercourse or oral or anal sexual conduct with a person to whom he is related whether through marriage or not, as an ancestor, descendant, brother, sister, uncle, aunt, nephew or niece
255.26	D Felony	Incest in the 2nd degree	A person who commits rape in the second degree or criminal sexual act in the second degree against a person to whom he is related whether through marriage or not, as an ancestor, descendant, brother, sister, uncle, aunt, nephew or niece
255.27	B Felony	Incest in the 1st degree	A person who commits rape in the first degree or criminal sexual act in the first degree against a person to whom he is related whether through marriage or not, as an ancestor, descendant, brother, sister, uncle, aunt, nephew or niece

Registerable offenses (continued)

Article	Class	Crime	Definition
263.05	C Felony	Use of a child in a sexual performance	A person who employs, authorizes or induces a child under seventeen years of age to engage in a sexual performance or who is the parent, legal guardian or custodian of a child and consents to the child's participation in a sexual performance
263.10	D Felony	Promoting an obscene sexual performance by a child	A person who produces, directs or promotes any obscene performance which includes sexual conduct by a child under seventeen years of age
263.11	E Felony	Possessing an obscene sexual performance by a child	A person who knowingly has in his possession or control any obscene performance which includes sexual conduct by a child under sixteen years of age
263.15	D Felony	Promoting a sexual performance by a child	A person who produces, directs or promotes any performance which includes sexual conduct by a child under seventeen years of age
263.16	E Felony	Possessing a sexual performance by a child	A person who knowingly has in his possession or control any performance which includes sexual conduct by a child under sixteen years of age

Registerable offenses (continued)

Article	Class	Crime	Definition
263.30	B Felony	Facilitating a sexual per-formance by a child with a controlled substance or alcohol	A person who knowingly and unlawfully possesses a controlled substance and (1) administers that substance to a person under seventeen years of age without such person's consent, and intends, attempts, or commits a felony against the person (specifically 263.05, 263.10, or 263.15), or (2) administers alcohol to a person under seventeen years of age without the person's consent, and intends, attempts, or commits a felony against the person (specifically 263.05, 263.10, or 263.15)

Note: Quoted in whole or part from Looseleaf Law Publications (1996-97), DCJS (2008) and Findlaw (2008).

Bibliography

Abel, G. G., Becker, J. V., Mittelman, M., Cunningham-Rathner, J., Rouleau, J. & Murphey, W. (1987). Self-reported sex crimes of nonincarcerated paraphiliacs. *Journal of Interpersonal Violence*, 2, 3-25.

Abel, G., Becker, J., Cunningham-Rathner, J., Mittelman, M. & Rouleau, J. (1988). Multiple paraphilic diagnoses among sex offenders. *Bulletin of the American Academy of Psychiatry and the Law*, 16, 153-168.

Abel, G. G., Gore, D. K., Holland, C. L., Camp, N., Becker, J., & Rathner, J. (1989). The measurement of the cognitive distortions of child molesters. *Annals of Sex Research*, 2, 135-152.

Abel, G., Mittelman, M. & Becker, J. (1985). Sexual offenders: Results of assessment and recommendations for treatment. In M. H. Ben-Aron, S.J. Hucker, & C.D. Webster. (Eds.). *Clinical Criminology: Current Concepts*. Toronto: M&M Graphics, 191-205.

Abel, G.G., Mittleman, M.S., Becker, J.V., Rathner, J., & Rouleau, J.L. (1988). Predicting child molesters response to treatment. *Annals of New York Academy of Sciences*, 528, 223-234.

Adam Walsh Child Protection and Safety Act (2006). 42 U.S.C. Section 16901.

Adams, D. (2002, March). *Summary of state sex offender registries, 2001*. Bureau of Justice Statistics. U.S. Department of Justice.

Ahlmeyer, S., Heil, P., McKee, B., & English, K. (2000). The impact of polygraphy on admissions of victims and offenses in adult sexual offenders. *Sexual Abuse: A Journal of Research and Treatment*, 12,123-138.

Akers, R. L. (2000). (Third Edition). *Criminological theories: Introduction, evaluation, and application*. Roxbury Publishing Company. Los Angeles, California, Pp. 310.

American Psychiatric Association. (1994). *Diagnostic and statistical manual of mental disorders* (4th ed.). Washington, DC: Author.

Andrade, J. T. (2008). The inclusion of antisocial behavior in the construct of psychopathy: A review of the research. *Aggression and Violent Behavior,* 13(4), 328-335.

Arrigo, B.A. & Shipley, S. (2001). The confusion over psychopathy (I): historical considerations. *International Journal of Offender Therapy and Comparative Criminology,* 45, 325-344.

Artway v. Attorney General, 81 F. 3d 1235, 3d Cir. (1996)

Austin, J. Peyton, J. & Johnson, K. D. (2003, January). *Reliability and validity study of the Static-99/RRASOR sex offender risk assessment instruments.* Institute on Crime, Justice and Corrections United States. NCJ 221278.

Bachman, R. & Paternoster, R. (1997). *Statistical methods for criminology and criminal justice.* The McGraw-Hill Companies. Pp. 704.

Bachman, R., Paternoster, R. & Ward, S. (1992). The rationality of sexual offending: Testing a deterrence/rational choice conception of sexual assault, *Law and Society Review,* 26(2), 343-372.

Baldau, V. B. (1999, August). *Summary of state sex offender registries: Automation and operation.* U.S. Department of Justice, Office of Justice Programs, Bureau of Justice Statistics. NCJ 177621

Bandura, A. (1974, December). Behavior theory and the models of man. *American Psychologist,* 29(12), 859-869.

Barbaree, H. E. (1991). Denial and minimization among sex offenders: Assessment and treatment outcome. *Forum on Correctional Research,* 3, 300-333.

Barbaree, H. E., Baxter, D. J. & Marshall, W. L. (1989). The reliability of the rape index in a sample of rapists and nonrapists. *Violence and Victims,* 4, 299-306.

Barbaree, H. E. & Marshall, W. L. (1988). Deviant sexual arousal, offense history, and demographic variables as predictors of reoffense among child molesters. *Behavioral Sciences & the Law,* 6(2), 267-280.

Barbaree, H. E., Seto, M. C., Langton, C. M. & Peacock, E. J. (2001, August). Evaluating the predictive accuracy of six risk assessment instruments for adult sex offenders. *Criminal Justice and Behavior,* 28(4), 490-521.

Barnoski, R. (2005). *Sex offender sentencing in Washington State: Has community notification reduced recidivism?* Olympia: Washington State Institute for Public Policy.

Baron-Evans, A. (2008, June). Rethink misguided sex offender registration and notification act. *Federal Sentencing Reporter,* 20(5), 357-362.

Basile, K.C., Chen, J., Black, M.C., & Saltzman, L.E. (2007, August). Prevalence and characteristics of sexual violence victimization among U.S. adults, 2001-2003. *Violence & Victims*, 22(4), 437-448.

Bauer, H. (2003). Richard von Krafft-Ebing's psychopathia sexualis as sexual sourcebook for Radclyffe Hall's the well of loneliness. *Critical Survey*, 15(3), 23-38.

Bedarf, A.R. (1995, May). Comment: Examining sex offender community notification laws. *California Law Review*, 83 Calif. L. Rev. 885.

Berenson, J. & Appelbaum, P. (2010, June 14). A Geospatial Analysis of the Impact of Sex Offender Residency Restrictions in Two New York Counties. *Law and Human Behavior*, 1-12.

Bickley, J. & Beech, A. (2001). Classifying child abusers: Its relevance to theory and clinical practice. *International Journal of Offender Therapy and Comparative Criminology*, 45(1), 51-69.

Blair, M. (2004, Summer). Wisconsin's sex offender registration and notification laws: Has the Wisconsin legislature left the criminals and the constitution behind? *Marquette Law Review*, 87, 939-990.

Bootzin, R.R. Acocella, J. R. & Alloy, L. B. (1993). *Abnormal psychology: Current perspectives.* Sixth Edition. McGraw-Hill, Inc.

Botchkovar, E. & Tittle, C.R. (2008, September). Delineating the scope of reintegrative shaming theory: An explanation of contingencies using Russian data. *Social Science Research*, 37(3), 703-720

Bourke, M. L. & Donohue, B. (1996). Assessment and treatment of juvenile sex offenders: An empirical review. *Journal of Child Sexual Abuse*, 5(1), 47-70.

Briere, J. N. (1992). Child abuse trauma: Theory and treatment of the lasting effects. Newbury Park, CA. Sage Publishing.

Broadhurst, R. & Loh, N. (2003). The probabilities of sex offender re-arrest. *Criminal Behaviour and Mental Health*, 13, 121-139.

Brooks, J. H. & Reddon, J. R. (1996). Serum testosterone in violent and nonviolent young offenders. *Journal of Clinical Psychology*, 52(4), 475-483.

Brownmiller, S. (1975). *Against our will: Men, women and rape.* Simon and Schuster, New York, New York.

Buffalo News. (1994, August 17). *Communities need to know about sex predators nearby; there should be warning about worst ex-cons.* City Edition, Editorial. Pg. 2.

Buffalo News. (1994, November 22). *Give communities the facts when sex offenders move in; parents need to know when danger may be near.* City

Edition, Editorial. Pg.2.

Burdon, W.M. & Gallagher, C.A. (2002, February). Coercion and sex offenders: Controlling sex-offending behavior through incapacitation and treatment. *Criminal Justice and Behavior,* 29(1), 87-109.

Burnham, J. C. (1973). The Progressive Era revolution in American attitudes toward sex. *Journal of American History,* 59, 885–908.

Byrnes, C.T. (1998). Putting the focus where it belongs: Mens rea, consent, force, and the crime of rape. 10 *Yale Journal of Law and Feminism* Yale 277.

Call, J.E., Nice, D. & Talarico, S.M. (1991, December). An analysis of state rape shield laws. *Social Science Quarterly,* 72(4), 774-788.

Carich, M. S. Newbauer, J. F. & Stone, M. H. (2001, Spring). Sexual offenders and contemporary treatments. *The Journal of Individual Psychology,* 57(1), 3-17.

Catalano, S. M. (2006, September). *Criminal victimization 2005.* U.S. Department of Justice Office of Justice Programs. Bureau of Justice Statistics. National Crime Victimization Survey. NCJ 214644.

Catalano, S. M. (2004, September). *Criminal victimization 2003.* U.S. Department of Justice Office of Justice Programs. Bureau of Justice Statistics. National Crime Victimization Survey. NCJ 205455.

Chard-Wierschem, D. (1995). *Comparison of temporary release absconders and nonabsconders: 1993-94.* New York: New York Department of Corrections.

Chesire, J. D. (2004). Review, critique, and synthesis of personality theory in motivation to sexually assault. *Aggression and Violent Behavior,* 9, 633-644.

Cohen, S. (1972) *Folk devils and moral panics: The construction of the mods and rockers.* London: MacGibbon & Kee.

Cohen, L. E. & Felson, M. (1994). Social *change and crime rate trends: A routine activities approach.* In Theories of Deviance (Fourth Edition). Traub, S. H. and Little, C. B. (Eds.). F. E. Peacock Publishers, Inc. Itasca, Illinois.

Coleman, J.C., Butcher, J. N., & Carson, R. C. (1984). *Abnormal psychology and modern life.* Seventh Edition. Scott, Foresman and Company

Connecticut Department of Public Safety v. Doe, 271 F.3d 38, [63] (2d Cir. 2001)

Connecticut Department of Public Safety v. Doe, 538 U.S. 1, 123 S. Ct. 1160 (2003)

Conrad, P. & Schneider, J.W. (1994). Medicine *as an institution of social* control: Consequences for society. In Traub, S.H. and Little, C.B. (Eds.) Theories of Deviance (Fourth Edition). F.E. Peacock Publishers, Inc. Itasca, Illinois. Pp. 485-519.

Cornish, D.B. & Clarke, R.V. (Eds). (1986). *The reasoning criminal: Rational choice perspectives on offending.* New York: Springer.

Costigliacci, S.J. (2008, January). Protecting our children from sex offenders: Have we gone too far? *Family Court Review*, 46, 180.

Craissati, J. & Beech, A. (2003, May). A review of dynamic variables and their relationship to risk prediction in sex offenders. *Journal of Sexual Aggression*, 9(1), 41-55.

Craissati, J., McClurg, G., & Browne, K. D. (2002). Characteristics of perpetrators of child sexual abuse who have been sexually victimized as children. *Sexual Abuse: A Journal of Research and Treatment*, 14, 225–240.

Cullop, F. G. (1999). *The constitution of the United States: An introduction (Revised & Updated Edition).* New York: New American Library.

Curnoe, S. & Langevin, R. (July 2002). Personality and deviant sexual fantasies: An examination of the MMPIs of sex offenders. *Journal of Clinical Psychology*, 58(7), 803-815.

Danni K & Hampe G.D. (2000). An analysis of predictors of child sex offender types using presentence investigation reports. *International Journal of Offender Therapy and Comparative Criminology*, 44, 490-504.

Dempster, R. J. & Hart, S. D. (2002). The relative utility of fixed and variable risk factors in discriminating sexual recidivists and nonrecidivists. *Sexual Abuse: A Journal of Research and Treatment*, 14(2), 121-138.

Dickey, R., Nussbaum, D., Chevolleau, K., & Davidson, H. (2002). Age as a differential characteristics of rapists, pedophiles, and sexual sadists. *Journal of Sex & Marital Therapy*, 28, 211-218.

Division of Criminal Justice Services (n.d.). Registered sex offenders by county. Retrieved March 30, 2011 from http://criminaljustice.state.ny.us/nsor/stats_by_county.htm.

Division of Criminal Justice Services (n.d.). Predatory sexual assault laws of New York, 2006 Chapter 107. Retrieved April 18, 2008 from http://criminaljustice.state.ny.us/legalservices/ch107_predatorysexualassa ult.htm

Doe v. Pataki, 940 F. Supp. 603 (S.D.N.Y. 1996)

Doe v. Pataki, 120 F.3d 1263 2d Cir. (1997)

Doe v. Pataki, 3 F.Supp.2d 456 (S.D.N.Y. 1998)

Doe v. Poritz, 662 A.2d 367 (N.J. 1995)

Doe v. Poritz, 142 N.J. 1 (1995)

Doren, D. M. (2002). *Evaluating sex offenders: A manual for civil commitments and Beyond*, Sage Publications, Inc., California, 4-11, 146-149.

Doren, D. M. (2004, August). Toward a multidimensional model for sexual recidivism risk. *Journal of Interpersonal Violence*, 19(8), 835-856.

Douglas, J. E., & Olshaker, M. (1998). *Obsession: The FBI's legendary profiler probes the psyches of killers, rapists, and stalkers and their victims and tells how to fight back*. New York: Scribner.

Durling, C. (2006, Fall). Never going home: Does it make us safer? Does it make sense? Sex offenders, residency restrictions, and reforming risk management law. *Journal of Criminal Law & Criminology*, 97(1), p317-363.

English, K., Pullen, S., & Jones, L. (1997, January). *Managing adult sex offenders in the community-a containment approach*. U.S. Department of Justice, Office of Justice Programs, National Institute of Justice.

Enniss, B. (2008). Note: Quickly assuaging public fear: how the well-intended Adam Walsh Act led to unintended consequences. *Utah Law Review*, 697-717.

Escarela, G., Francis, B., & Soothill, K. (2000, December). Competing risks, persistence, and desistance in analyzing recidivism. *Journal of Quantitative Criminology*, 16(4), 385-414.

Eyssen, A. B. (2001). Comment: Does community notification for sex offenders violate the eight amendments prohibition against cruel and unusual punishment? A focus on vigilantism resulting from "Megan's Law." 33 *St. Mary's Law Journal*, 101-142.

Farrall, S. (2002, July). Long-term absences from probation: officers' and probationers' accounts. *The Howard Journal*, 41(3), 263-278.

Farley, L. G. (2008, Winter). Note: The Adam Walsh Act: The scarlet letter of the twenty-first century. 47 *Washburn Law Journal*, 471-503.

Feller, R. D. (1992, March). Sexual aggression in a male sex offender population as a function of hostility, attitudes toward women, levels of empathy, and alcoholism. *Dissertation Abstracts International*, 52(9-B), 4962-4963.

Filler, D.M. (2001, Spring). Making the case for Megan's law: A study in legislative rhetoric. *Indiana Law Journal*. 76 Ind. L.J. 315.

FindLaw (n.d.). New York State Consolidated Laws; Article 130: Sexual Offenses. Retrieved April 18, 2008 from http://caselaw.lp.findlaw.com/nycodes/c82/a29.html.

Finkelhor, D. (1984). *Child sexual abuse. New theory and research.* New York. The Free Press.

Finn, P. (1997, February). *Sex offender community notification.* U.S. Department of Justice. Office of Justice Programs. National Institute of Justice.

Fishbein, D. H. (1994). *Biological perspectives in criminology.* In Traub, S.H. and Little, C.B. (Eds.) Theories of Deviance (Fourth Edition). F.E. Peacock Publishers, Inc. Itasca, Illinois. Pp. 435-485.

Fishbein, D. (2001). *Biobehavioral perspectives in criminology.* Wadsworth. Pp.139.

Fisher, B. S., Cullen, F. T., & Turner, M. G. (1999). *The extent and nature of the sexual victimization of college women: A national-level analysis* (Final report submitted to the National Institute of Justice, NCJ 179977).Washington, DC: U. S. Department of Justice.

Fisher, B., Cullen, F. T. & Turner, M. G. (2000, December). *The sexual victimization of college women.* U.S. Department of Justice. Office of Justice Programs. National Institute of Justice. NCJ 182369. U.S. Government Printing Office. Washington, D.C.

Firestone, P., Bradford, J. M., McCoy, M., Greenberg, D. M., Curry, S. & Larose, M. R. (2000). Prediction of recidivism in extrafamilial child molesters based on court-related assessments. *Sexual Abuse: A Journal of Research and Treatment,* 12(3), 203-221.

Firestone, P., Nunes, K.L., Moulden, H., Broom, I. & Bradford, J.M. (2005, June). Hostility and recidivism in sexual offenders. *Archives of Sexual Behavior,* 34(3), 277-283.

Flack, C. (2005, Fall). Chemical castration: An effective treatment for the sexually motivated pedophile or an impotent alternative to traditional incarceration. *The Journal of Law in Society,* 7(1), 173-195.

Flowe, H. D. Ebbesen, E. B. & Putcha-Bhagavatula, A. (2007). Rape shield laws and sexual behavior evidence: Effects of consent level and women's sexual history on rape allegations. *Law and Human Behavior,* 31(2), 159-175.

Fodor, M.D. (2001). *Megan's Law: Protection or privacy.* Enslow Publishers, Inc. New Jersey.

Frank, J. (2007, August 27). Jessie's killer gets death. *St. Petersburg Times,* Pp. 1.

Freedman, E. B. (1987, June). "Uncontrolled desires": The response to the sexual psychopath., 1920-1960. *The Journal of American History,* 74(1), 83-106.

Freeman, N. J. & Sandler, J. C. (2008). Female and male sex offenders: A comparison of recidivism patterns and risk factors. *Journal of Interpersonal Violence, 23,* 1394-1413.

Freeman-Longo, R. E., Bird, S., Stevenson, W. F., & Fiske, J. A. (1995). *1994 nationwide survey of treatment programs and models: Serving abuse-reactive children and adolescents and adult sex offenders.* Brandon, VT.: Safer Society Press.

Fry-Bowers, E. K. (2004, Summer). Controversy and consequence in California: Choosing between children and the constitution. 25 *Whittier Law Review.* 889.

Furby, L., Weinrott, M. R. & Blackshaw, L. (1989). Sex offender recidivism: A review. *Psychological Bulletin, 105,* 3-30.

Gallagher, C. A., Wilson, D. B., Hirschfield, P., Coggeshall, M. B., & MacKenzie, D. L. (1999). A quantitative review of the effect of sex offender treatment on sexual reoffending. *Corrections Management Quarterly,* 3(4), 19-29.

Garland, D. (2001).*The culture of control: Crime and social order in contemporary society.* Chicago: University of Chicago Press.

Gendreau, P., Little, T., & Goggin, C. (1996, November). A meta-analysis of the predictors of adult offender recidivism: What works! *Criminology,* 34(4), 575-607.

Gerardin, P. & Thibaut, F. (2004). Epidemiology and treatment of juvenile sexual offending. *Paediatric Drugs,* 6, 79-91.

Gordon, L. (1988, Spring). The politics of child sexual abuse: Notes from American history. *Feminist Review,* 28, 56-64.

Gottfredson M. R. & Hirschi, T. (1990). *A general theory of crime.* Stanford University Press, Stanford, California.

Greenfield, L. A. (1997). *Sex offenses and offenders: An analysis of data on rape and sexual assault.* Washington DC: U.S. Department of Justice, Office of Justice Programs, Bureau of Justice Statistics.

Grossman, L.S., Martis, B., & Fichtner, C.G. (1999, March). Are sex offenders treatable? A research overview. *Psychiatric Services,* 50(3), 349-361.

Groth, A. N. (1979). *Men who rape: The psychology of the offender.* Plenum Press, New York.

Groth, A.N., Hobson, W.F., & Gary, T.S. (1982). The child molester: Clinical observations. *Social Work & Human Sexuality, 1,* 129-144.

Grubin, D. (1997, June-September). Inferring predictors of risk: Sex offenders. *International Review of Psychiatry,* 9(2/3), 225-233.

Guttmacher M. & Weihofen, H. (1952, July-August). Sex offenses. *The*

Journal of Criminal Law, Criminology, and Police Science, 43(2), 153-175.

Hall, G. C. N. (1995). Sex offender revisited: A meta-analysis of recent treatment studies. *Journal of Consulting and Clinical Psychology*, 63, 802-809.

Hannem, S. & Petrunik, M. (2007, June). Circles of support and accountability: A community justice initiative for the reintegration of high risk sex offenders. *Contemporary Justice Review*, 10(2), 153-171.

Hanson, R. K. (1997). *The development of a brief actuarial risk scale for sexual offense recidivism* (User report 1997-04). Ottawa: Department of the Solicitor General of Canada.

Hanson, R. K. & Bussière, M. T. (1996). *Predictors of sexual offender recidivism: A meta-analysis.* User Report 1996-04. Ottawa: Department of the Solicitor General of Canada.

Hanson, R. K. & Bussière, M. T. (1998). Predicting relapse: A meta-analysis of sexual offender recidivism studies. *Journal of Counseling and Clinical Psychology*, 66(2), 348-362.

Hanson, R. K. & Harris, A. J. R. (2001a). A structured approach to evaluating change among sexual offenders. *Sexual Abuse: A Journal of Research and Treatment*, 13(2), 105-120.

Hanson, R. K. & Harris, A. J. R. (2001b). The Sex Offender Need Assessment Rating (SONAR): A method for measuring change in risk levels 2000-1. Corrections Research Department of the Solicitor General of Canada. Public Works and Government Services Canada. Cat. No.: JS42-88/1999E. ISBN: 0-662-28407-0

Hanson, R. K., & Morton, K. E. (2003, June). *Recidivism risk factors for sexual offenders: An updated meta-analysis.* Paper presented at the Annual Convention of the Canadian Psychological Association, Hamilton, Ontario.

Hanson, R. K. & Morton-Bourgon, K.E.. (2004). *Predictors of sexual recidivism: An updated meta-analysis 2004-02.* Public Works and Government Services Canada. Retrieved May 1, 2009 from http://www.static99.org/pdfdocs/hansonandmortonbourgon2004.pdf

Hanson, R. K. & Morton-Bourgon, K.E.. (2005). The characteristics of persistent sexual offenders: A meta-analysis of recidivism studies. *Journal of Consulting and Clinical Psychology*, 73(6), 1154-1163.

Hanson, R. K., & Morton-Bourgon, K. E. (2007). *The accuracy of recidivism risk assessments for sexual offenders: A meta-analysis.* Corrections User

Report No 2007-01. Ottawa: Public Safety and Emergency Preparedness Canada.

Hanson, R. K., Steffy, R. A., & Gauthier, R. (1993, August). Long-term recidivism of child molesters. *Journal of Consulting and Clinical Psychology*, 61(4), 646-652.

Hanson, R.K. & Thornton, D. (2000). Improving risk assessments for sex offenders: A comparison of three actuarial scales. *Law and Human Behavior*, 24(1), 119-136.

Hare, R. D., (1996). Psychopathy: A clinical construct whose time has come. *Criminal Justice and Behavior*, 23, 25-54.

Harris, G. T., Rice, M. E., & Cormier, C. A. (1991, December). Psychopathy and violent recidivism. *Law and Human Behavior*, 15(6), 625-637.

Hazelwood, R., & Burgess, A. W. (1987). *Practical aspects of rape investigation: A multidisciplinary approach*. New York: Elsevier.

Hier, S. P. (2008, May). Thinking beyond moral panic: Risk, responsibility, and the politics of moralization. *Theoretical Criminology*, 12(2), 173-190.

Hill, A., Briken, P., Kraus, C., Strohm, K. & Berner, W. (2003). Differential pharmacological treatment of paraphilias and sex offenders. *International Journal of Offender Therapy and Comparative Criminology*, 47(4), 407-421.

Holmes, S.T. & Holmes, R. M. (2002). (Second Edition). *Sex crimes: Patterns and behavior*. Sage Publications, Inc. CA.

Howells, K. (1981). Adult sexual interest in children: Considerations relevant to theories of etiology. In M. Cook & K. Howells (Eds.), *Adult sexual interest in children*. London: Academic Press.

Hudson, S. M., Ward, T., & McCormack, J. C. (1999, August). Offense pathways in sexual offenders. *Journal of Interpersonal Violence*, 14(8), 779-798.

Illinois v. Logan (705 N.E.2d 152, 161) (Ill. App. Ct. 1998)

Jacob Wetterling Crimes Against Children and Sexually Violent Offender Registration Act, *42 U.S.C. 14071 § 170101 (2000)*

Jacobs, D. (2003, February). Sex offender registration: Why sex offender notification won't keep our children safe. *Corrections Today*, 65(1), p.22.

Jenkins, P. (1998). *Moral panic: Changing concepts of the child molester in modern America*. New Haven, CT: Yale University Press.

Jenkins, P. (2001). *How Europe discovered its sex offender crisis*. In J. Best (ed.), How claims spread: Cross-national diffusion of social problems. Hawthorne Creek, NY: Aldine.

Johnson, K. (2002, Summer/Fall). States' use GPS offender tracking systems.

Journal of Offender Monitoring, 15(2), 21-26.

Jones, K. D. (1999, December). The media and Megan's law: Is community notification the answer? *Journal of Humanistic Counseling, Education, and Development*, 38 (2), 80-89.

Jones, L. & Finkelhor, D. (2001, January). *The decline in child sexual abuse cases*. U.S. Department of Justice, Office of Justice Programs, Office of Juvenile Justice and Delinquency Prevention. Retrieved February 18, 2001 from http://www.ncjrs.org/pdffiles1/ojjdp/184741.pdf#search ='child%20sexual%20abuse%20and%201990's.

Kabat, A.R. (1998, Winter). Note: Scarlet letter sex offender databases and community notification: Sacrificing personal privacy for a symbol's sake. *American Criminal Law Review*. 35 Am. Crim. L. Rev. 333.

Kennedy, H. (2001). Research and commentaries on Richard von Krafft-Ebing and Karl Heinrich Ulrichs. *Journal of Homosexuality*, 42(1), 165-178.

Klein, R. (2008). An analysis of thirty-five years of rape reform: A frustrating search for fundamental fairness. 41 *Akron Law Review* 981.

Knight, R.A. (1999, March). Validation of a typology for rapists. *Journal of Interpersonal Violence*, 14(3), 303-330.

Knight, R. A., Carter, D. L., & Prentky, R. A. (1989, March). A system for the classification of child molesters: Reliability and application. *Journal of Interpersonal Violence*, 4(1), 3-23.

Koenig, W. P. (1998, Winter). Does congress abuse its spending clause power by attaching conditions on the receipt of federal law enforcement funds to a state's compliance with Megan's Law?" *Journal of Criminal Law & Criminology*, 88(2), 721-766.

Kunselman, J. C. & Vito, G. F. (2002, Fall). Questioning mandatory sentencing efficiency: A case study of persistent felony offender rapists in Kentucky. *American Journal of Criminal Justice*, 27(1), 53-68.

Lang, R. A., Pugh, G. M., & Langevin, R. (1988). Treatment of incest and pedophilic offenders: A pilot study. *Behavioral Sciences and the Law*, 6, 239-255.

Langan, P. & Levin, D. J. (2002, June). *Recidivism of prisoners released in 1994*. Bureau of Justice Statistics Special Report. NCJ 193427. Washington, DC: U.S. Department of Justice.

Langan, P. A., Schmitt, E. L. & Durose, M. R. (2003, November). *Recidivism of sex offenders released from prison in 1994*. Bureau of Justice Statistics Special Report. NCJ 198281. Washington, DC: U.S. Department of Justice.

Langevin, R., Curnoe, S., Fedoroff, P., Bennett, R., Langevin, M., Peever, C., Pettica, R., & Sandhu, S. (2004, October). Lifetime sex offender recidivism: A 25-year follow-up study. *Canadian Journal of Criminology & Criminal Justice,* 46(5), 531-552.

Långström, N. & Grann, M. (2000, August). Risk for criminal recidivism among young sex offenders. *Journal of Interpersonal Violence,* 15(8), 855-871.

Langton, C.M.; Barbaree, H.E.; Seto, M.C.; Peacock, E.J., Harkins, L. & Hansen, K.T. (2007, January). Actuarial assessment of risk for reoffense among adult sex offenders: Evaluating the predictive accuracy of the Static-2002 and five other instruments. *Criminal Justice and Behavior,* 34(1), 37-59.

Letourneau, E.J., Levenson, J.S., Bandyopadhyay, D., Sinha, D. & Armstrong, K.S. (2010, September). *Evaluating the Effectiveness of Sex Offender Registration and Notification Policies for Reducing Sexual Violence against Women.* National Institute of Justice.

Levenson, J. S., Brannon, Y., Fortney, T., & Baker, J. (2007). Public perceptions about sex offenders and community protection policies. *Analyses of Social Issues and Public Policy,* 7(1), 1-25.

Levenson, J. S. & Cotter, L. P. (2005, February). The effect of Megan's law on sex offender reintegration. *Journal of Contemporary Criminal Justice,* 21(1), 49-66.

Levenson, J.S., & D'Amora, D.A. (2007). Social policies designed to prevent sexual violence: The emperor's new clothes? *Criminal Justice Policy Review,* 18(2), 168–199.

Levenson, J. S., D'Amora, D. A., & Hern, A. L. (2007). Megan's Law and its impact on community re-entry for sex offenders. *Behavioral Sciences & the Law,* 25(4), 587-602

Lev-Wiesel, R. & Witztum, E. (2006). Child molesters vs. rapists as reflected in their self-figure drawings: A pilot study. *Journal of Child Sexual Abuse,* 15(1), 105-117.

Lisak, D. (1991, Winter). Sexual aggression, masculinity, and fathers. *Signs: Journal of Women in Culture and Society,* 16(2), 238-262.

Lombroso, C. (1911). *Crime: Its causes and remedies.* Translation by Henry P. Horton. Introduction by Maurice Parmelee. Boston: Little, Brown, & Co. Pp.151-174, 365-428.

Looseleaf Law Publications (1996-97). *Penal law and criminal procedure law of the State of New York.* Looseleaf Law Publications, Inc.

Lussier, P. (2005, July). The criminal activity of sexual offenders in adulthood: Revisiting the specialization debate. *Sexual Abuse: A Journal of Research and Treatment,* 17(3), 269-292.

Maletzky, B. M. & Field, G. (2003). The biological treatment of dangerous sexual offenders, a review and preliminary report of the Oregon pilot Depo-Provera program. *Aggression and Violent Behavior,* 8, 391-412.

Maletzky, B. M. (1991). *Treating the sexual offender.* Newbury Park, CA: Sage.

Marshall, W. L. (1989). Intimacy, loneliness and sexual offenders. *Behaviour Research and Therapy,* 27, 491–503.

Marshall, W. L. (1996). Assessment, treatment, and theorizing about sex offenders. *Criminal Justice and Behavior,* 23(1), 162-199.

Marshall, W. L. & Barbaree, H. E. (1988). The long-term evaluation of a behavioral treatment program for child molesters. *Behaviour Research & Therapy,* 26(6), 499-511.

Marshall, W. L. & Barbaree, H. E. (1990). Outcome of comprehensive cognitive-behavioral treatment programs. In Marshall, W. L., Laws, D. R., and Barbaree H. E. (Eds). *Handbook of sexual assault: Issues, theories, and treatment of offenders.* New York: Plenum. Pp.368-385.

Marshall, W. L. & Pithers, W. D. (1994). A reconsideration of treatment outcome with sex offenders. *Criminal Justice and Behavior,* 21, 10-27.

Martin, K., Vieraitis, L. M. & Britto, S. (2006, April). Gender equality and women's absolute status: A test of the feminist models of rape. *Violence Against Women,* 12 (4), 321-339.

Matson, S. & Lieb, R. (1996). *Sex offender registration: A review of state laws.* Washington State Institute of Public Policy, 10.

McAlinden, A. (2005, January). The use of 'shame' with sexual offenders. *Britain Journal of Criminology,* 45, 373-394.

McCabe, M. P. & Wauchope, M. (2005, April). Behavioral characteristics of men accused of rape: Evidence for different types of rapists. *Archives of Sexual Behavior,* 34(2), 241-253.

McGrath, R.J. (1991). Sex-offender risk assessment and disposition planning: A review of empirical and clinical findings. *International Journal of Offender Therapy and Comparative Criminology,* 35(4), 328-350.

Mercado, C. C., Alvarez, S. & Lenvenson, J. (2008, June). The impact of specialized sex offender legislation on community reentry. *Sexual Abuse,* 20(2):188-205.

Meyer, J. and Mohan, G. (1993, December 15). *Flawed system hampers valley molester search.* The Los Angeles Times.

M.G. v. Travis, 236 A.D.2d 163 (1997)

Miethe, T. D., Olson, J., & Mitchell, O. (2006). Specialization and persistence in the arrest histories of sex offenders: A comparative analysis of alternative measures and offense type. *Journal of Research in Crime and Delinquency.* 43: 204-229

Money, J. (2003, August). History, causality, and sexology. *Journal of Sex Research,* 40(3), 237-239.

Mustaine, E. E., Tewksbury, R., & Stengel, K. M. (2006a). Residential location and mobility of registered sex offenders. *American Journal of Criminal Justice,* 30, 177–192.

Mustaine, E. E., Tewksbury, R., & Stengel, K. M. (2006b, May/June). Social disorganization and residential locations of registered sex offenders: Is this a collateral consequence? *Deviant Behavior,* 27(3), 329-350.

New York City CompStat Unit. (n.d.) Patrol services bureau, city wide crime statistics weekly, 13, 4. Retrieved February 18, 2006 from http://www.ci.nyc.ny.us/html/nypd/html/pct/cspdf.html.

New York City CompStat Unit. (n.d.) Patrol services bureau, city wide crime statistics weekly, 15, 14. Retrieved April 12, 2008 from http://www.ci.nyc.ny.us/html/nypd/html/crime_prevention/crime_statistics .shtml.

New York County District Attorney Report. (2003, February 7). *Megan's law.* Criminal Justice Commissioners Office. Office of the Mayor: New York City.

New York State Board of Examiners of Sex Offenders v. Ransom, 249 A.D.2d 891 (1998).

Olver, M. E., & Wong, S. C. P. (2006). Psychopathy, sexual deviance, and recidivism among sex offenders. *Sexual Abuse: A Journal of Research and Treatment,* 18, 65-82.

Padgett, K. G., Bales, W. D., & Blomberg, T. G. (2006). Under surveillance: An empirical test of the effectiveness and consequences of electronic monitoring. *Criminology Public Policy,* 5(1), 61-91.

Parkinson, P. N. Shrimpton, S., Oates, R. K. Swanston, H. Y. &. O'Toole, B. I. (2004). Nonsex offences committed by child molesters: Findings from a longitudinal study. *International Journal of Offender Therapy and Comparative Criminology,* 48(1), 28-39.

Paul v. Davis, 423 U.S. 693 (1976)

People v. Davis, NY Slip Op 1150 (2006)

People v. Guaman, 8 A.D.3d 545 (2004)

People v. Irving, 2007 NY Slip Op 8634 (2007)

People v. Pietarniello, NY Slip Op 6141 (2008)

People v. Ruddy, NY Slip Op 5607 (2006)

People v. Victor R., 186 Misc. 2d 28 (2000)

Powers, P. A. (2003). Making a spectacle of panopticism: A theoretical evaluation of sex offender registration and notification. *New England Law Review*, 38, 1049.

Prentky, R. A. & Burgess, A. W. (2000) *Forensic management of sexual offenders*. Kluwer Academic/ Plenum Publishers. Pp.331

Prentky, R. A., Knight, R. A, & Lee, A. F. S. (1997). Risk factors associated with recidivism among extrafamilial child molesters. *Journal of Consulting and Clinical Psychology*, 65(1), 141-149.

Proulx, J., Paradis, Y., McKibben, A., Aubut, J., & Quimet, M. (1997). Static and dynamic predictors of recidivism in sexual aggressors. *Sexual Abuse: A Journal of Research and Treatment*, 9, 7-27.

Proulx, J., Perrault, C., & Oimet, M. (1999). Pathways in the offending process of extra-familial child molesters. *Sexual Abuse: A Journal of Research and Treatment*, 11, 117-129.

Purvis, M. & Ward, T. (2006, May/June). The role of culture in understanding child sexual offending: Examining feminist perspectives. *Aggression and Violent Behavior*, 11(3), 298-312.

Quinn, J., Forsyth, C., & Carla Mullen-Quinn, C. (2004, May). Societal reaction to sex offenders: A review of the origins and results of the myths surrounding their crimes and treatment amenability. *Deviant Behavior*, 25(3), 215-232.

Quinsey, V. (1977). The assessment and treatment of child molesters: A review. *Canadian Psychological Review*, 18, 204-220.

Quinsey, V.L. (1986). Men who have sex with children. In D Wetstub (Ed). *Law and mental health international perspectives* (Vol 2), New York Pergamon Press

Quinsey, V. L., Harris, G. T., Rice, M. E., & Cormier, C.A. (1998). *Violent offenders: Appraising and managing risk*. Washington, DC: American Psychological Association.

Quinsey, V. L., Rice, M. E., & Harris, G. T. (1990). Psychopathy, sexual deviance, and recidivism among sex offenders released from a maximum security institution. *Penetanguishene Research Report*, 7, 1.

Rada, R. T., Laws, D. R. & Kellner, R. (1976, July-August). Plasma testosterone levels in the rapist. *Psychosomatic Medicine*, 38(4), 257-268.

Rada, R. T., Laws, D. R., Kellner, R., Stivastava, L., & Peake, G. (1983). Plasma androgens in violent and nonviolent sex offenders. *Bulletin of the American Academy of Psychiatry and the Law*, 11, 149-158.

Rand, M. & Catalano, S. (2007, December). *Criminal victimization 2006.* U.S. Department of Justice Office of Justice Programs. Bureau of Justice Statistics. National Crime Victimization Survey. NCJ 219413.

Rasmussen, L. A. (1999, January). Factors related to recidivism among juvenile sexual offenders. *Sexual Abuse: Journal of Research & Treatment*, 11(1), 69-86.

Rice, M. E., Quinsey, V. L. & Harris, G. T. (1991). Sexual recidivism among child molesters released from a maximum security institution. *Journal of Consulting and Clinical Psychology*, 59, 381-386.

Richards, H. J., Washburn, J. J., Craig, R., Taheri, A. & Yanisch, D. (2004). Typing rape offenders from their offense narratives. *Individual Differences Research*, 2(2), 97-108.

Robertiello, G. & Terry, K.J. (2007). Can we profile sex offenders? A review of sex offender typologies. *Aggression and Violent Behavior*, 12(5), 508-518.

Roberts, C.F., Doren, D. M., & Thornton, D. (2002, October). Dimensions associated with assessments of sex offender recidivism risk. *Criminal Justice & Behavior*, 29(5), 569-589.

Rothman, E. & Silverman, J. (2007). The effect of a college sexual assault prevention program on first-year students' victimization rates. *Journal of American College Health*, 55(5), 283-290.

Russell, D. E. H. (1975). *The politics of rape.* New York: Stein and Day.

Saleh, F.M. & Guidry, L. L. (2003). Psychological and biological treatment and considerations for the paraphilic and nonparaphilic sex offender. *The Journal of the American Academy of Psychiatry and the Law*, 31, 486-493.

Sample, L. L., & Bray, T. M. (2003). Are sex offenders dangerous? *Criminology and Public Policy*, 3(1), 59–82.

Scalora, M. J. & Garbin, C. (2003). A multivariate analysis of sex offender recidivism. *International Journal of Offender Therapy and Comparative Criminology*, 47(3), 309-323.

Schram, D. & Milloy, C. (1995). *Community notification: A study of offender characteristics and recidivism.* Washington State Institute for Public Policy. Retrieved October 12, 2003 from http://www.wsipp.wa.gov/rptfiles/chrrec.pdf.

Schwaner, S. (1997). They can run, but can they hide? A profile of parole violators at large. *Journal of Crime and Justice*, 20(2), 19-32.

Schweitzer, R. & Dwyer, J. (2003, November). Sex crime recidivism: Evaluation of a sexual offender treatment program. *Journal of Interpersonal Violence,* 18(11), 1292-1310.

Scully, D. & Marolla, J. (1984, June). Convicted rapists' vocabulary of motive: Excuses and justifications. *Social Problems,* 31(5), 530-544.

Serin, R. C., Malcolm, P. B., Khanna, A., & Barbaree, H. E. (1994). Psychopathy and deviant sexual arousal in incarcerated sexual offenders. *Journal of Interpersonal Violence,* 9, 3-11.

Seto, M. C. & Barbaree, H. E. (1999, December). Psychopathy, treatment behavior, and sex offender recidivism. *Journal of Interpersonal Violence,* 14(12), 1235-1248.

Sheppard, J. (1997, November). Double punishment. *American Journalism Review,* 19(9), 36-42.

Simon, L. M. J. (2000). An examination of the assumptions of specialization, mental disorder, and dangerousness in sex offenders. *Behavioral Sciences and the Law,* 18, 275-308.

Simon, L. M. & Zgoba, K. (2006). Sex crimes against children: Legislation, prevention and investigation. In Richard Wortley and Stephen Smallbone (eds.), Situational Prevention of Child Sexual Abuse. *Crime Prevention Studies,* vol. 19. Monsey, N.Y.: Criminal Justice Press.

Sjöstedt, G., Långström, N., Sturidsson, K. & Grann, M. (2004, October). Stability of modus operandi in sexual offending. *Criminal Justice and Behavior,* 31(5), 609-623.

Smallbone, S. & Wortley, R. (2000). *Child sexual Abuse in Queensland: Offender characteristics and modus operandi.* Brisbane, Australia: Queensland Crime Commission.

Smith, P., Gendreau, P. & Swartz, K. (2009), Validating the principles of effective intervention: A systematic review of the contributions of meta-analysis in the field of corrections. *Victims and Offenders,* 4(2), 148-169.

Smith v. Doe, *538 U.S. 84, 123 S.Ct. 1140 (2003)*

Snyder, H. N. (2000, July). *Sexual assault of young children as reported to law enforcement: Victim, incident, and offender characteristics.* U.S. Department of Justice. National Center for Juvenile Justice.

Snyder, H. N., & Sickmund, M. (1999, September). *Juvenile offenders and victims: 1999 national report.* U.S. Department of Justice. National Center for Juvenile Justice.

Soothill, K. & Francis, B. (1998, September). Poisoned chalice or just deserts? (The Sex Offenders Act 1997). *The Journal of Forensic Psychiatry,* 9(2), 281-293.

Soothill, K., Francis, B., Sanderson, B., & Ackerley, E. (2000). Sex offenders: Specialists, generalists-or both? A 32-year criminological study. *British Journal of Criminology*, 40, 56-67.

Spitzberg, B. (1999). An analysis of empirical estimates of sexual aggression victimization and perpetration. *Violence and Victims*, 14(3), 241-260.

Stalans, L. J. (2004, October). Adult sex offenders on community supervision: A review of recent assessment strategies and treatment. *Criminal Justice and Behavior*, 31(5), 564-608.

Stark, C.A. (1997, Summer). Is pornography an action? The causal vs. the conceptual view of pornography's harm. *Social Theory & Practice*, 23(2), 277-306.

Steinbock, B. (1995, Summer/Fall). A policy perspective. *Criminal Justice Ethics*, 14(2), 4-9.

Sturgeon, V. H., & Taylor, J. (1980). Report of a five-year follow-up study of mentally disordered sex offenders released from Atascadero State Hospital in 1973. *Criminal Justice Journal*, 4, 31-63.

Sutherland, E. (1950, September). The diffusion of sexual psychopath laws. *The American Journal of Sociology*, 56(2), 142-148.

Sykes, G. M. & Matza, D. (1957, December). Techniques of neutralization: A theory of delinquency. *American Sociological Review*, 22(6), 664-670.

Tedeschi J.T. & Felson, R.B. (1994). *Violence, aggression, & coercive actions*. American Psychological Association. Washington, D.C.

Terry, K. J. (2006). *Sexual offenses and offenders: Theory, practices, ad policy*. Belmont, CA: Thomson Learning/Wadsworth.

Tewksbury, R. Mustaine, E. & Stengel, K. M. (2008, January). Examining rates of sexual offenses from a routine activities perspective. *Victims & Offenders*, 3(1), 75-85.

Tewksbury, R. (2005). Collateral consequences of sex offender registration. *Journal of Contemporary Criminal Justice*, 21(1), 67-81

Tewksbury, R. (2006). Sex offender registries as a tool for public safety: Views from registered offenders. *Western Criminology Review*, 7, 1–8.

Tier, R. & Coy, K. (1997). The treatment of sex offenders: Approaches to sexual predators: Community notification and civil commitment. *New England Journal on Criminal and Civil Confinement*, 405-424.

Tjaden, P. & Thoennes, N. (2000, November). Full *report of the prevalence, incidence, and consequences of violence against women: Findings from the national violence against women survey.* Washington, D.C., National Institute of Justice; Publication NCJ 183781. Retrieved April 24, 2009 from http://www.ncjrs.gov/pdffiles1/nij/183781.pdf.

Tjaden P. & Thoennes N. (2006). *Extent, nature, and consequences of rape victimization: Findings from the national violence against women survey.* Washington, DC: National Institute of Justice; Publication NCJ 210346.

Traub, S.H. & Little, C.B. (Eds.) (1994). *Theories of deviance* (Fourth Edition). F.E. Peacock Publishers, Inc. Itasca, Illinois. Pp. 431-435.

Trivits, L.C. & Reppucci, N.D. (2002). Application of Megan's law to juveniles. *American Psychologist,* 57, 690-704.

Turner, J. S. & Helms, D. B. (1991). *Lifespan development.* (Fourth Edition). Holt, Rinehart, and Winston, Inc. Pp. 28-67.

U.S. Department of Health and Human Services. (2010). *Child maltreatment 2009.* Administration for Children and Families, Administration on Children, Youth and Families Children's Bureau. Retrieved January 15, 2011 from http://www.acf.hhs.gov/programs/cb/pubs/cm09/cm09.pdf

U.S. Department of Justice. (2008, September). *Crime in the United States 2007: Uniform crime reports.* Federal Bureau of Investigation. U.S. Government Printing Office. Washington, D.C.

Walker, J.T., Maddan, S., Vásquez, B. E., VanHouten, A. C., & Ervin-McLarty, G. (2005). *The influence of sex offender registration and notification laws in the United States.* Arkansas Crime Information Center. Retrieved October 18, 2008, from http://www.acic.org/statistics/Research/SO_Report_Final.pdf

Ward, T. & Beech, A. (2006, January). An integrated theory of sexual offending. *Aggression and Violent Behavior,* 11(1), 44-63.

Ward, T., & Gannon, T. A. (2006). Rehabilitation, etiology, and self-regulation: The comprehensive lives model of treatment for sexual offenders. *Aggression & Violent Behavior,* 11, 77-94.

Ward, T., & Siegert, R. J. (2002). Toward and comprehensive theory of child sexual abuse: A theory knitting perspective. *Psychology, Crime, and Law,* 9(4), 319–351.

Weinrott, M. R. & Saylor, M. (1991, September). Self-report of crimes committed by sex offenders. *Journal of Interpersonal Violence,* 6(3), 286-300.

Williams, F. P., McShane, M.D., & Dolny, H. M. (2000, March). Predicting parole absconders. *The Prison Journal,* 80(1), 24-38.

Wilson, R.J., Stewart, L., Stirpe, T., Barrett, M., & Cripps, J. E. (2000, April). Community-based sex offender management: Combining parole supervision and treatment to reduce recidivism. *Canadian Journal of Criminology,* 177-188.

Winick, B. J. (1998, March-June). Sex offender law in the 1990s: A therapeutic jurisprudence analysis. *Psychology, Public Policy, and Law,* 4(1-2), 505-570.

Wolfgang, M. E., Figlio, R. M. & Sellin, T. (1972) *Delinquency in a British cohort.* Chicago: Univ. of Chicago Press.

Wright, R. G. (2008). Sex offender post-incarceration sanctions: Are there any limits? *New England Journal on Criminal and Civil Confinement,* 34(1), 17-50.

Zevitz, R. G. (2006). Sex offender community notification: Its role in recidivism and offender reintegration. *Criminal Justice Studies,* 19(2), 193-208.

Zevitz, R.G. & Farkas, M.A. (2000). Sex offender community notification: Managing high risk criminals or exacting further vengeance? *Behavioral Sciences & the Law,* 18(2-3), 375-391.

Zgoba, K., Witt, P., Dalessandro, M., & Veysey, B. (2008, December). *Megan's law: Assessing the practical and monetary efficacy.* National Institute of Justice. NIJ 225370. Retrieved April 24, 2009 from http://www.ncjrs.gov/pdffiles1/nij/grants/225370.pdf

Zimring, F.E. (2004). *An American travesty: Legal responses to adolescent sex offending.* Chicago, IL: University of Chicago Press.

Index

A

Acquaintances, 6, 18, 89-90
*Adam Walsh Child Protection and
    Safety Act (2006).* 42 U.S.C.
    Section 16901, 81-83, 86-87,
    96-97, 103, 110-111
Antisocial personality, 26
Anger excitation rapist, 35-36
Anger rapist, 28, 34, 41
Anger retaliatory rapist, 35-37
Artway v. Attorney General 81 F.
    3d 1235, 3d Cir. (1996), 106
Assessments, 51, 62-67, 77
Aversion therapy, 72-73

B

Biobehavioral theory, 103
Biological positivism, 20-21
Biological theory, 20
Biological treatment, 22, 68
Brownmiller, Susan, 31

C

Castration, 16, 21, 26, 68-69
Catholic church, 6, 18
Child molester, 19, 29-30, 32, 42-

Cognitive restructuring, 73-74
Community notification, 61, 78-
    81, 83-85, 87, 91-92, 94, 96,
    98, 102, 104-111
Community Protection Act, 83
*Connecticut Department of
    Public Safety v. Doe,* 271
    F.3d 38, [63] (2d Cir. 2001),
    107
*Connecticut Department of
    Public Safety v. Doe,* 538
    U.S. 1, 123 S. Ct. 1160
    (2003), 106-107
Constitutional challenges, 103-
    109
Covert sensitization,72-73
Cruel and Unusual Punishment,
    103, 105-106

D

Deterrence theory, 98-99
Distortions, 29-30, 32-33, 71-73
Doe v. Pataki, 940 F. Supp. 603
    (S.D.N.Y. 1996), 104
Doe v. Pataki, 120 F.3d 1263 2d
    Cir. (1997), 105,166

49, 53-54, 57-58, 76, 78, 157-161, 165, 168-169

Child pornography, 2, 4, 86, 97, 177 (see pornography)

Civil commitment, 16-17, 79, 82-83, 86, 103

Cognitive behavioral theory, 25

Douglas and Olshaker- typology, 37, 40, 42

Due Process, 103, 106-109

E

Eugenics, 21, 33

Exhibitionism, 3, 23

Exploitative rapist, 37, 42

Ex Post Facto Clause, 103-105, 166

F

Feminist theory, 30-31

Fish, Albert, 15-16

Fixated child molester, 43

Forcible rape, 6

Frank, Leo, 15

Freud, Sigmund, 26, 29

Fullmer, Stephanie, 3

G

Galton, Francis, 21

Generalist, 52-54, 168

Global Positioning System, 79, 81, 111

Goring, Charles, 22

Groth- typology, 27-29, 34-35, 40-44, 47-49

Doe v. Pataki, 3 F.Supp.2d 456 (S.D.N.Y. 1998), 109

Doe v. Poritz, 662 A.2d 367 (N.J. 1995), 108

Doe v. Poritz, 142 N.J. 1 (1995), 106

Double jeopardy, 103, 105, 166

Homeless offenders, 92, 110-111

Homosexuality, 10-11, 13

Hoover, J. Edgar, 16

I

Illinois v. Logan (705 N.E.2d 152, 161) (Ill. App. Ct. 1998), 108

Imaginal desensitization, 72-74

Incest, 4, 10, 17, 26-27, 54, 64, 78, 126, 157-158, 161, 177, 182, 187

Integrated theory, 32

J

Jack the Ripper, 14

Jacob Wetterling Crimes Against Children and Sexually Violent Offender Registration Act, *42 U.S.C. 14071 § 170101 (2000)*, 83-84, 86

Jessica's law, 83, 85-86

Juveniles, 111

K

Knight and Prentky- typology, 38, 41-42, 53

Knight, Carter and Prentky-typology, 24, 43-45, 47-49

H

Hazelwood and Burgess-typology, 35-38, 40-42
Hickey, Frank, 14-15
High contact molester, 45-48
High fixation molester, 45, 48

Low fixation molester, 45, 48

M

Masochism, 12, 23-24
Masturbatory reconditioning, 72, 74
McMartin case, 18
Media's influence, 87
Megan's Law, 18, 83-84, 87, 92, 95, 104, 106, 114, 142, 166-168
M.G. v. Travis, 236 A.D.2d 163 (1997), 105, 166
MMPI, 61-62, 66
MnSOST-R, 61, 63, 66
Moral panic, 9, 14

N

National Crime Victimization Survey, 4-5, 51
National Institute of Justice, 4
New York State Board of Examiners of Sex Offenders v. Ransom, 249 A.D.2d 891 (1998), 110

O

Opportunistic rapist, 38, 42, 53

Krafft-Ebing, Richard von, 12

L

Labeling theory, 100-101
Lombroso, Cesare, 21-22
Low contact molester, 46-48
Pedophilia, 13, 18-19, 23, 43, 48, 70
Penile Plethysmography, 85, 87
People v. Davis NY Slip Op 1150 (2006), 110
People v. Guaman 8 A.D.3d 545 (2004), 110
People v. Irving 2007 NY Slip Op 8634 (2007), 111
People v. Pietarniello NY Slip Op 6141 (2008), 111
People v. Ruddy NY Slip Op 5607 (2006), 110-111
People v. Victor R. 186 Misc. 2d 28 (2000) , 110
Pervasively angry rapist, 38-39, 41
Pinel, Phillip, 12
Polygraph, 61, 63, 66
Pornography, 2, 4, 11, 31, 33, 86, 97, 177, 181 (See Child pornography)
Power assertive rapist, 35-36, 40
Power rapist, 28, 34-35, 40, 42
Power reassurance rapist, 35-37, 40
Prevalence rates, 4-7, 24, 51-52, 56, 59
Progressive Era, 9-10
Psychoanalytic theory, 25-28
Psychological theory, 25-30
Psychological treatment, 71-76

P

Pam Lyncher Act, 83, 85
Paraphilia, 3, 12, 23-24, 26, 65
Pathways Model, 32
Paul v. Davis 423 U.S. 693 (1976), 106-107
PCL-R, 61-62, 66
157, 177-178, 182, 187
Rape shield laws, 11
Rapists, (see Rape)
Rational choice theory, 99-100
Recidivism, 51, 79, 82-95, 109-113, 119-122, 125-127, 137-161, 163-175
Registration, 4, 6, 78-80, 83-87, 90, 93-99, 101, 103, 105-107, 119, 152, 160, 170
Regressed child molester, 44
Relapse prevention, 71-72, 75
Residency Restrictions, 79, 81, 86, 89, 92, 99-100, 111
Risk factors, 56-67
Risk level, 80, 90, 96-97, 109-110, 118, 130-132, 145-146
Risk management statutes, 79-112
Routine activities theory, 81, 98-99
RRASOR, 51, 57, 62-67

S

SACJ-Min, 62, 65-67
Sadism, 12, 23-24, 45, 49
Sadistic rapist, 28, 35-37, 40-42
Sex offender legislation, 16, 53, 79-112
Sexual abuse, 1-2, 5-7,, 10, 17-18, 23, 29, 31-32, 87, 179-1890, 182
Sexual deviancy, 12-18

Psychopathy statutes, 17
Public lewdness, 3

R

Rape, 4-7, 11, 17, 19, 24-27, 30-31, 34-42, 53, 89-91, 94-95,
Smith v. Doe, *538 U.S. 84 123 S.Ct. 1140 (2003),* 104 105, 166
Social disorganization, 98, 101-102
Social learning theory, 25, 28-29
Social skills training, 72, 74-75
SONAR, 51, 61, 64, 66-67
SORAG, 51, 62, 64, 66-67
Specialist, 52-54
Static-99, 51, 62, 64-65, 67, 97
Sterilization, 21, 68-69
Strain theory, 101-102
Stranger danger, 10, 15

T

Testosterone, 24-25, 33, 68-71
Treatment, 67-78

U

Unlawful surveillance, 1, 3-4, 186-187

V

Video voyeurism, 3
Vindictive rapist, 39-41
Voyeurism, 3, 23, 80
VRAG, 61-64, 66

Sexual murderer, 12-14, 16
Sexual psychopath, 12-13, 16-17,
    22, 55, 57, 82
Shriner, Earl K., 83